HOW MUCH DOES YOUR HEAD WEIGH?

THE BIG BOOK OF FACTS

Marg Meikle

Illustrated by Tina Holdcroft

Scholastic Canada Ltd.
Toronto New York London Auckland Sydney
Mexico City New Delhi Hong Kong Buenos Aires

Scholastic Canada Ltd.
604 King Street West, Toronto, Ontario M5V 1E1, Canada

Scholastic Inc.
557 Broadway, New York, NY 10012, USA

Scholastic Australia Pty Limited
PO Box 579, Gosford, NSW 2250, Australia

Scholastic New Zealand Limited
Private Bag 94407, Botany, Manukau 2163, New Zealand

Scholastic Children's Books
Euston House, 24 Eversholt Street, London NW1 1DB, UK

Library and Archives Canada Cataloguing in Publication

Title: How much does your head weigh? : the big book of facts / Marg
Meikle ; illustrated by Tina
    Holdcroft.
Names: Meikle, Marg, author. | Holdcroft, Tina, illustrator. | Meikle, Marg.
Funny you should ask.
    | Meikle, Marg. You asked for it. | Meikle, Marg. Ask me anything.
Description: "Formerly published as Funny you should ask, You asked for
it, and Ask me anything".
Identifiers: Canadiana 20190204249 | ISBN 9781443182454 (softcover)
Subjects: LCSH: Questions and answers.
Classification: LCC AG195 .M454 2020 | DDC j031.02—dc23

6 5 4 3 2 1   Printed in Canada   114   20 21 22 23 24

MIX
Paper from
responsible sources
FSC
www.fsc.org   FSC® C016245

*To Noel and Mac, my two boys, and to
their dominant Saskatchewan chatting gene.*

*And to school librarians everywhere:
Keep on getting kids to ask questions and
to question their sources.*

— M.M.

How do flies land on the ceiling?

and Other Amazing Answers About ANIMALS

1.

If dogs are colour-blind, how do guide dogs know when to stop or go at a traffic light?

Guide dogs for the blind are working dogs. So are other assistance dogs, like hearing-ear dogs, and those who assist people in wheelchairs. They are highly trained dogs, but just dogs nonetheless.

Working dogs like to play. Many of them are keen on romping in the snow or chasing a tennis ball, but for these dogs their job comes first. They guide their owners day in and day out, from landmark to landmark, stopping at stairs, curbs and intersections. This guiding is safe, much faster than walking with a cane, and inspires a lot more confidence.

Part of a guide dog's job is dealing with traffic. Traffic lights come in three colours, of course, but dogs can't tell green from red, or green and red from amber. So how do these colour-blind dogs deal with traffic lights? It turns out they don't watch traffic lights at all. Guide dogs are trained to stop at all intersections. They have to listen to the owners, who might want to turn right or left, so the dog waits for a command. If the person says "Forward," the dog starts up, unless there is any traffic coming. If so, the dog won't move.

What if the light is red? If there is no traffic coming and the light is red the dog has no idea, and just goes. When there is a traffic box

Dogs aren't the only animals who are colour-blind. Most animals see just shades of grey. Birds and some fish see some colours, but the only animals that have the same range of colour vision as humans are apes and some of the higher monkeys.

that clicks, the dog can hear the clicking of the changing lights and know when to go. The beeping crossings are great. There is one sound for north-south and a different sound for east-west, so the handler knows when it's safe to go.

2.

How do flies land on the ceiling?

It helps to know that flies are a lot more like helicopters than planes. Flies can't fly parallel to the ceiling too well because their wings might touch it, but they can fly straight up or down as well as horizontally. Flies are very versatile aircraft.

A fly does something of a half loop to land on the ceiling. It is moving upward at a little over 30 cm per second. As it approaches the ceiling it puts all six of its legs out, with the front two sticking upward a bit. It extends those two legs above its head and they touch the ceiling first. When those legs make contact, the fly grabs on (insect legs are particularly good at this sort of thing on almost any surface). Then it rolls bellyward in a half loop and the other four legs contact and adhere. The fly actually ends up facing the opposite direction from the way it was flying. To get off, it just drops down.

Flies are very light. It takes 10,000 of them to make 1 kilogram.

A fly is far more tolerant of gravity than humans. Humans can only withstand a gravitational (or G) force of 10; we would black out if we zipped up to the ceiling any quicker. A fly reaches a G force of about 200, and a jumping flea also reaches close to 200.

3

3.

Is it true that one "person year" is the same as seven "dog years"? How was this figured out, and does it work for other animals?

That 1:7 ratio of so-called human to dog years is an odd one, because how can we use "human years" on a dog? What we are doing is comparing the animal world to the human world, and it doesn't really work. (It doesn't stop us from trying though.)

Scientists originally came up with the 1:7 ratio by looking at the physical, sexual and social maturity of dogs, as well as information on their behaviour. What scientists figured out was that in the first year, a dog goes from birth to about the same stage as a fifteen-year-old person — physically, sexually and socially. Then in the second year it goes up to about twenty-four in human years. After that, the answer is: it depends. The ratio was averaged out to 1:7 because humans often live to around seventy and dogs to around ten.

So the 1:7 thing doesn't really work. It is more of a sliding scale. Most basic dog owner's manuals have a chart that averages the breeds and compares dog ages. Generally, dog people don't even like those ratios. Dogs are living much longer now than they used to because of excellent nutrition and better medical care. What works best is to just generalize about stages of life. By six months a dog is like a six-year-old child — ready to begin school. By one year a dog hits puberty and could reproduce, but isn't really ready. Two years is like young adulthood — dogs are physically mature but have lots of room for more mental maturity.

What about cats? Comparing with human ages just isn't done. Mostly cat people just talk about life stages. An eight-year-old cat is in an early geriatric (old age) stage and a fourteen-year-old cat is definitely geriatric.

Zookeepers don't compare animal ages to human ages either. Part of the reason is that they look after animals with such different lifespans. Elephants live to sixty years or so, and a lot of the small animals live only three or four years. If the animal came from the wild, the zoo doesn't know how old it was to begin with. Zookeepers look at the teeth for wear, but that comparison is only a guess because in the zoo the nutrition is often better and the animals lead an easier life than in the wild. So zoo staff mostly just figure out whether an animal is young, middle-aged or old.

The ratio for the years also depends on the size of the dog. Big dogs like Great Danes and St. Bernards don't live as long, maybe eight to ten years. But smaller dogs, like all of the toy breeds, Miniature Poodles and Westies, have longer life expectancies of fourteen to sixteen years, so their age ratio would be different.

Why do dogs' and cats' eyes go a funny colour in photographs?

If you shoot all your pictures outside you won't have a problem. But use a flash and you've got the glowing-eye thing happening. If you don't have a pet, you probably thought that photography disasters were confined to the red eyes of humans. With humans this happens because you use a flash in a low-light setting, when the pupil of your eye is dilated (opened wider to let in more light so you can see even when it's dark). When the flash hits the eye, it bounces off the back of the retina and back out through the pupil of the eye. That red you notice is blood. You see a so-called "red reflex," which is really the red colour of the back of the eye, or the fundus, with all its blood vessels.

The new cameras have "red-eye reduction" which gives two flashes in a row. The first flash illuminates the fundus. By the time the second flash goes off, your pupil is still constricted from the first flash, so you don't get red in your photo.

This is similar to what happens with dogs and cats, but with dogs and cats you see a green glow. Their retinas are more complex. They have an area of reflective cells called *tapetum lucidum* on the topmost layer of the retina, which gives them the ability to see better in the dark than humans. So a flash photo or bright light reflects off the *tapetum*, which can be green or yellow or blue, producing that same greenish glow as when car headlights shine into an animal's eyes.

5.

Do slugs have any purpose whatsoever, or do they just lie around looking slimy?

Slugs are one of a gardener's worst enemies. These pests chew up young plants and vegetables and eat holes in leaves. Controlling them is tedious and difficult. But these slimy creatures do have a greater purpose, and their own place in the food chain or ecosystem. Slugs are the original recyclers. They eat decaying vegetation, dead leaves, fungi, some animal feces, carrion and even other slugs. Slugs are then eaten by ground beetles or small mammals like voles and moles, or snakes, birds or beetles. So the circle of the natural world continues . . . in its own slimy way.

6.

Why is a lion the "king of the jungle"? Lions don't even live in the jungle.

It's true, lions don't live in the jungle. Lions like grassy plains and open savannah. They live mostly in Africa, south of the Sahara Desert. There are also a few hundred lions living in the Gir Forest National Park in India.

Way back — from 1,500,000 years ago right up to 10,000 years ago — lions lived all over the world: in the Balkans, the Middle East and even all over North America. Some may even have lived in what is now your city! Slowly they disappeared from everywhere except Africa and India, and even there, lions are really surviving well only in the national parks.

The lion is probably regarded as the king of the animals because of its legendary ferocity, but why do people continue to think the lion is the king of the *jungle?*

It's a big mix-up from history. Jungle means "overgrown land." And back before TV and air travel, when people learned about the world from a few travel writings, the word got out that all of Africa was a wild jungle. Certainly parts of Africa are a jungle, but the English figured it *all* was.

Tarzan (or Edgar Rice Burroughs, who wrote the Tarzan books) was a big part of the problem. Tarzan, or King of the Apes and Lord of the Jungle, lived in Africa — at least, that's where the books are set. In the very first book, Tarzan kills a tiger. OOPS! Tigers live in India. The Tarzan books also show the lion as a jungle beast who lives alone. They ought to show the lion as an animal in charge of a pride (a group of female lions and their cubs) that lives on the grassy plains. However, the fact that this information was wrong didn't seem to hurt book and movie sales.

There are no lions in *The Jungle Book* by Rudyard Kipling, or in the movie by Disney. Good thing, since the story takes place in a tropical jungle in India. The Disney movie *The Lion King* got it right too. The movie begins with the lions roaming the savannah, but the action shifts to the jungle when Simba runs away from the evil Uncle Scar. Simba is amazed with the jungle and feels very out of place there. He knows, as you do now, that lions belong on the plains.

7.

Do chickens have lips?

Not really. Chickens have nothing soft like our lips, just a hard beak. Since there is no such thing as chicken lips, it's simply a weird expression that means "something imaginary." It's kind of like saying "horsefeathers" to mean nonsense. If somebody serves you a dish called chicken lips, they're just having fun.

8.

Why do zebras have black and white stripes?

Camouflage is the obvious answer, but where is there a black and white forest or jungle? Tigers blend in with their stripes in tall grasses, but zebras really stand out. What was the point of Mother Nature painting these elegant creatures in black and white?

The animals that prey on zebras are busiest during the cool hours of sunrise and sunset. It turns out that the black and white stripes show up as grey from a distance, which helps the zebras blend in with the low light.

And the other reason, which is very cool, is that if a zebra herd gets attacked, the wildly moving jagged stripes of the whole herd of zebras confuse the predator.

So there you go. Colour isn't everything when it comes to camouflage.

Seagulls' colouring works so they can be seen. Seagulls are white so that other seagulls can see when one gull is eating . . . and realize that there's good fishing. That's why gulls usually attract other gulls.

9.

Do dogs and cats have belly buttons?

Indeed they do. If you look — which can be tricky with all of that hair — it looks more like a scar, but it is a belly button. All mammals have a navel or belly button. It's the connection point for the umbilical cord that carries nutrients and oxygen from the mother to the developing baby. Once the mammal is born, that cord isn't needed anymore because the baby gets its own oxygen and food. With humans, the cord is cut off and the short stump that remains dries up and falls off. The mother cat or dog chews off the umbilical cord and the stump will then also dry up and fall off.

When a mammal is hatched from an egg, the way a platypus is, it also has a belly button/scar, but it is even harder to see. The scar is from where the developing animal was attached to the yolk sac inside the egg.

Why "innies" or "outies"? When the stump of the cord withers and falls off it usually leaves an "innie," or concave scar. But sometimes, because of how a baby develops and how the cord heals, it turns into a convex "outie." If it makes you crazy to have an "outie" you can get a plastic surgeon to change it when you are fully grown. But it's far easier just to count yourself special, since "outies" are far more rare than "innies."

10.

Why are flies attracted to manure?

Because manure is a favourite place for flies to breed. Flies like any decaying organic matter, such as decomposing grass, but manure has it all. It's nice and moist and warm — it's even edible! Manure is, basically, fly heaven.

Manure is a problem in horse barns, because stable flies also suck a horse's blood. This painful and annoying experience can drive horses into a frenzy, or even a stampede. Any horse subjected to this constant agony — even if it's only the hint of flies flitting around — can hurt itself by stamping its feet over and over again, damaging its hooves and joints, losing weight and getting sick.

Talk to anyone who works with horses and they will tell you that keeping the flies away is an ongoing battle. When you know that a 500-kilogram horse produces over 20 kilos of waste a day — that's over 7000 kilos a year — you can understand the importance of fly management.

The life cycle of a stable fly is around three weeks, from egg to adult. In her three-week life a female fly can lay 20 batches of eggs, with 40 to 80 eggs in each batch. Do the math. Each fly could lay 800 to 1600 eggs in less than

Just in case you need to know: Horse people tend to call the fresh stuff "droppings," which becomes "manure" when it gets stomped into straw and shavings in the stall, or put into piles behind the barn.

one month. Think how many flies there are. If just half are females, each laying 800 to 1600 eggs during its life . . . It can quickly add up to millions, which explains why fly prevention rules.

So, what do horse people do? Get rid of the fly's breeding grounds and protect the horses from any flies that are around. For starters, keep the manure out of the stalls by cleaning it up daily. Usually the stalls get a big cleaning every morning and piles of droppings are picked up every two or three hours — something horse people call skepping. You have to shovel droppings out in the pasture too. Then what do you do with it? Let it dry by spreading it out, or compost it so the flies won't want to hang around. Gardeners will love it!

Or, you could fight flies with fashion. There are fly masks made of mesh that let horses see and hear, but don't let the flies bite their faces. Mesh or fleece blankets or sheets and leg wraps are good, too, even a fringe that attaches to the bridle and swings as the horse moves, shooing away the flies.

11.

How did duckbilled platypuses get to look the way they do?

At first glance, the platypus doesn't look or act like any other animal. It is a monotreme — a mammal that lays eggs — which is rare to start with. There are only two other monotremes; both are species of anteater found in Australia, Tasmania and New Guinea. Monotreme means "one-holed" because — unlike most mammals — the platypus uses the same body opening to reproduce and to eliminate body wastes. In Australia, the platypus is called Mallangong, Tambreet or Boonaburra in Indigenous languages. Rock paintings of the platypus are estimated to be at least eight thousand years old.

The scientific name for a platypus is *Ornithorhynchus anatinus*, which means "bird snout," for its rubbery duck-like bill. Its common name, platypus, means "flat-footed." Add the tail like a beaver's, the poisonous spurs, the fur coat, and the fact that it spends most of its time in water, and you see just how unusual platypuses are.

They are great swimmers, and although they're awkward on land, they live in underground burrows that can be up to 20 m long. They can "roll up" the webbing between their toes to expose their claws for digging in a mole-like fashion. All of these features are combined in a package that is usually around half a metre long and weighs just over 2 kilos — smaller than a domestic cat. So go figure on this beast.

Nevertheless, scientists have been trying to "go figure" for years. The first sighting of a platypus by Europeans was in 1797, near what is now Sydney, Australia. They thought it was a combination of reptile, bird, fish and mammal, so they sent specimens to England to be studied. People there thought it was a hoax, and one zoologist even tried to separate the platypus bill from its pelt. This specimen is in the British Museum of Natural History in London — you can still see the marks from the zoologist's scissors.

The platypus went against everything people knew about mammals. Mammals, as vertebrates, have backbones; so does a platypus. But the platypus lays eggs. It feeds its young milk like other mammals do, but it has no teats. Instead it has slits in its skin where the milk seeps out. The babies suck on the mother's fur to get their milk.

There have been only a few platypus fossils found. In 1971 two newly discovered platypus tooth fossils were estimated to be 25 million years old. After that, other fossils were found — a piece of jawbone, a hip bone and a skull. Then in 1984 a platypus jaw with three teeth was found in New South Wales. It is at least 110 million years old. This specimen is from the ancestor of today's platypus, *Steropodon galmani*. In 1985 an almost complete skull of a fossil platypus was found. Then in 1991, two fossil teeth found in southern Argentina were estimated at 61 to 63 million years old. This is the only evidence we have that platypus-like creatures may have existed outside of Australia. (Scientists believe that at one time Australia was connected to Antarctica, and that was connected to South America.) Some scientists say that the platypus is "the end of the line" for some of the very

One "platypus" jaw fossil is at least 110 million years old.

earliest mammals — mammals that had many
of the characteristics we associate with reptiles.

The platypus is often thought to be
primitive, but it's actually pretty "high tech."
Its rubbery bill is covered with hundreds of
thousands of sensors that are sensitive to touch
and to the electric currents that are created
by the movement of small prey like shrimp,
insects, worms, shellfish, frogs and fish eggs.
The bill is so sensitive that a platypus can even
detect prey that is buried under mud or rocks.

12.

How can chickens run around with their heads cut off?

Freshly decapitated chickens will flop around
a lot. They will even run around with their heads
cut off for a few seconds, flapping their wings
wildly.

How does this happen? The adrenalin in the
muscle tissue gives the bird convulsions, making
it look like it is still alive. Chickens flap and flop
for about thirty seconds before they are totally
dead. That movement can carry the headless
chicken along a few metres. The chicken isn't
really running, but it looks like it is.

"Running around like a chicken with its head
cut off" has become an expression we use about
someone who is frenzied. We also call this going ape,
having kittens, flipping your lid or blowing your stack.

13.

What colour is the axolotl?

If you think I'm making this up, think again. This is a legitimate question, but first let's tackle this question: what the heck *is* an axolotl?

It's a salamander that never changes into an adult, sort of like a tadpole that never becomes a frog. And it's big. Axolotls have blunt snouts and large mouths. They are not to be confused with mud puppies, although both creatures live in water and have feathery external gills. You can tell the difference because mud puppies have four fingers and four toes, but axolotls have four fingers and five toes. An adult can grow to 30 cm from its toes to the tip of its tail.

Axolotls stay at the larval stage for their whole lives, and they can even reproduce without having reached the adult stage. Scientists have found that they can make the axolotl metamorphose — change — into an adult salamander by injecting it with a hormone called thyroxin.

Axolotls come from Mexico, mostly in Lake Xochimilco, the lake that Mexico City was built on. The name comes from the Aztec god of games, Xolotl. It was believed he could transform himself into an axolotl to get away from his enemies. The ancient Aztecs used to honour axolotls, and eat them too.

What's their colour? Axolotls are darkish grey, mottled with green or occasionally with silverish patches. Their eyes are yellow with iridescent irises. Some axolotls, especially those raised in labs, have mutant genes that make them albino. These axolotls are all white, with red eyes. They are even creepier looking than regular axolotls.

14.

Can animals be allergic to people?

There haven't been any significant studies done on this topic, but there is anecdotal evidence that animals might have allergies to people. A veterinary diagnostic laboratory in the U.S. tests dog and cat blood for antibodies to a variety of antigens. (An antigen is something that is foreign to your body.) One of the antigens they test for is human dander. Dr. Hugh Chisholm of the Atlantic Cat Hospital in Halifax, Nova Scotia, had a patient who tested "high positive" for antibodies to human dander. He said, "High antibody levels are interpreted by some clinicians to represent an allergic state. It may be possible that this cat is allergic to his owners!"

15.

Why are people allergic to animal fur, but not human hair (considering humans are animals too)?

Allergies result from the way your body responds to the presence of foreign proteins, so the reason people aren't allergic to human hair is because it's not foreign. In fact, it turns out that people aren't actually allergic to any animal's fur, or even its feathers, but to the proteins that are present in its skin secretions, saliva and urine. Animals shed small flakes of skin called dander, and microscopic particles of protein are in the dander. The particles are so small they float in the air, and can stick to furniture, walls, clothes, carpets and so on. It's very hard to get rid of them. Then there are those other substances that people may be allergic to — pollen, dust and mould — which can cling to an animal's fur, especially if the animal spends time outdoors.

Some people think that dogs that shed less are safe for people with allergies. But allergists say there's no such thing as a non-allergenic cat or dog, since all dogs and cats have skin, saliva and urine. However, some breeds of cats and dogs may secrete less protein than other breeds, or a protein that a person is less sensitive to. The best pets for an allergic person are those that don't have hair or fur — like fish, lizards, turtles, salamanders and ants.

One-third of U.S. and slightly more than half of Canadian households have one or more cats. More people are allergic to cats than to dogs — around one-third of all patients with allergies in North America are allergic to cats — and cat allergies tend to be more severe too. Cats have a special protein called "Fel d 1" that is often responsible for these allergies. This protein is transferred to the hair as cats lick themselves — something they do for so much of their day you could think of a cat as a walking spitball. Since the hair they shed is covered in dried saliva, people with allergies can get reactions even when they don't handle the cat.

Female cats produce less than two-thirds of the Fel d 1 of male cats, and neutering a male cat decreases the level of Fel d 1 it produces. Unfortunately, for allergy sufferers, Fel d 1 can last for a long time — months or even years after the cat is gone from a home.

Dr. Stanley Coren, a professor of psychology at the University of British Columbia, did a study of people with allergies to their cats or dogs. Doctors had advised all 341 of the people he studied to remove the pets from their living areas. But only one in five of the study subjects followed doctor's orders.

What's the *strangest* thing people are allergic to? Would you believe water? There are only about thirty-two of these cases in the medical literature. A recent case is that of a man living in California. Since age ten, whenever he lets any kind of water (tap or sea water) touch his skin, he develops severe itching and white welts on his skin within five minutes, rapidly leading to a headache and severe respiratory distress.

Water is an essential part of the body, so it's almost impossible to avoid water touching your skin during the day. In fact, many people like sports involving water, such as swimming or surfing. But the young man in California quickly learned how to wash and dry himself very rapidly indeed. In his case, scientists have absolutely no idea what's going on. The man has no change in his blood histamine levels — a strong marker of an allergic reaction — and when scientists try treating him with various antihistamines, the drugs make absolutely no difference at all.

16.

Can an animal catch an illness from a human?

Animals often get the rap for giving diseases to humans, but according to Dr. Hugh Chisholm at the Atlantic Cat Hospital in Halifax, Nova Scotia, it can also work the other way. Zoonoses, or zoonotic diseases, are those that can be transmitted between people and animals. The most common things transmitted from human to animal are parasitic, fungal and bacterial diseases, but in theory it's also possible to transmit viral diseases such as rabies. Common parasites that your pet could catch from you are *Giardiasis* (cysts in food, water, feces or soil), tapeworm (a flat worm that can grow up to 6 m long), roundworm and scabies. Scabies is an infection caused by tiny mites that burrow under the skin and cause severe itching, scabs and hair loss. In animals it's called mange.

Then there is *Salmonellosis*, an intestinal bacteria that can cause severe diarrhea and fever (in humans we call it food poisoning), and ringworm — which is not actually caused by a worm, but by a fungus. It can easily be passed from human to animal. All in all, your pet shouldn't feel too confident about its health around you.

17.

If snow is so cold, why do bears and other animals hibernate in it? Wouldn't they get hypothermia?

Hibernation is a way of surviving. When there's not much food and it's really cold out, sleeping through the winter makes lots of sense. Part of an animal's method of coping is to slow down its heart rate and lower its body temperature. Chances are that if you saw a hibernating animal you would have trouble telling if it was dead or alive.

Dr. Larry Wang, once a zoologist at the University of Alberta in Edmonton (where it gets seriously cold in the winter), is one of the top international researchers in mammalian hibernation. He says "mammals don't usually hibernate in the snow. They have burrows underground, nests in hollow trees, or dens in caves or rock piles." He adds that the temperature in the immediate area around a hibernating animal is usually warmer than the surface air temperature, and that the surface snow acts as an insulator. "When the air temperature is -20° to -30°C in Alberta, the underground burrow temperature of the Richardson's ground squirrel is about 0°C." The animals need that snow insulation, because without it the burrow temperature could be even colder, causing the animal to either stop hibernating, or freeze to death while hibernating.

Hypothermia occurs when a warm-blooded animal's body temperature is "below the normal level or range [it] typically exhibit[s]," says Dr. Wang. So hibernating animals actually *are* hypothermic because their body temperatures are much lower than normal, around 0° to 5°C instead of their normal temperatures. (A steady body temperature is a feature all mammals share, but not all mammals have the same body temperature. Ferrets, for example, can range from 37.8° to 39°C, pigs are around 39.2°C, and cows can range from 37.8° to 40°C.) However, hibernating mammals can spontaneously re-warm themselves to normal body temperatures because they have internal heat-producing mechanisms, like shivering, that can operate even when their body temperatures are very low. We humans shiver when we are cold, too, but when we get to 32°C our bodies stop shivering and emergency treatment is needed.

Humans study animal hibernation because we can apply the information to medical treatments on humans. In brain and heart surgery, organs are now pre-cooled. Researchers have also figured out that the amount of blood reaching a hibernating ground squirrel's brain goes down by 90% or more from the amount circulating when they are awake and running around. Scientists are studying these animals to see how they handle reduced blood flow to the brain. What they learn may inspire ideas for new treatments for people who have suffered strokes, which usually involve an interruption of the flow of blood to the brain. Unlike human brains that have undergone a stroke, the brains of hibernating animals are not damaged by the reduced flow of blood.

18.

Why don't birds' feet freeze in the winter?

Birds who don't take off to warmer climates in the winter have ways of dealing with the weather. Some grow more feathers, which they can fluff up for extra insulation when they need it. Like humans, some birds use shivering as a way to warm up — that movement increases heat energy enormously. And water birds paddle like mad to keep their feet from freezing into the ice. Almost all birds tend to stand on one leg a lot, holding the other up in their belly feathers to warm it. Where it is really cold, many birds go into a state of near hibernation overnight, which reduces their body temperature so they don't lose as much heat to the cold air.

The primary "bird trick" that makes the winter bearable is in the vein and artery system of the legs. The blood vessels going *out* to the legs run alongside the blood vessels coming *back*. This lets the cold blood of the limbs that are exposed to the cold "exchange temperature" with the warmer interior blood of the body, in a system that is more advanced than in humans. In this way there can be circulation of blood that is an even temperature, allowing the bird to keep moving — that's what keeps the brain and other vital organs going.

Why do birds fly south for the winter? Because it is too far to walk!

What would seem to be the most obvious example of really big cold feet is Antarctic penguins. They use the heat-exchange system, as well as a clever way of varying the diameter of their blood vessels, to control the rate of blood going to the feet.

19.

Why are they called "border" collies?

Have you ever watched a border collie in action? Go, go, go. Work, work, work. Border collies need a job. That's because shepherds on the border of England and Scotland bred them to work herding sheep.

There have been sheep dogs for centuries, but the exact blend of characteristics that typify border collies was finally arrived at in 1894, in attempts to breed dogs that were super-smart and very athletic. Now these dogs are herding livestock all over the world. Border collies love to take part in obedience and agility trials and Frisbee competitions, and they make great and loyal pets — as long as they are kept busy.

The name of a dog's breed often tells us a lot about it. For example, the German shepherd was bred in Germany in the 1880s to herd sheep — like the border collie. But as the country became more industrialized there were fewer pastures to keep watch over. However, the breed's intelligence and other fine qualities convinced the police and military to use these dogs in their work. In fact, the motto of Captain Max von Stephanitz, the first breeder of the German shepherd, was "utility and intelligence." German shepherds have also been used as guide dogs for the blind since the 1920s.

Fido is a common dog's name. It means "faithful" in Latin.

During World War I, because of the negative association with anything German, the breed lost popularity. In the U.S. the name was changed to shepherd, and in England and Canada to Alsatian. But the soldiers returning from Europe were so full of admiration for the breed that even with the same anti-German sentiment during World War II, these strong and clever dogs were put to work as guards, mine detectors and messengers. The Americans formed an association called "Dogs for Defense," which provided thousands of German shepherds for service in the army.

20.

How can birds stand on a telephone wire and not get electrocuted?

To get a complete electric circuit, you need to touch two wires at the same time. If you look at the wires between utility poles, you see either two separate wires, or two together that are insulated. Either way, the bird isn't completing the circuit, so current can't flow. Some large birds, like condors or eagles, or even big fruit bats, can touch two wires with their two huge wings, and they *do* get electrocuted. It's estimated that in the U.S., about a million birds a year are killed this way.

Why is a giraffe's tongue purple?

Purple or blue-black, the giraffe's tongue is enormous and muscular. It can be up to 54 cm long, and is designed especially to scoop up the acacia leaves giraffes love so much. That tongue needs to be strong, since the giraffe will often eat for 16 to 20 hours a day. A giraffe can maintain itself on less than 7 kilos of leaves, but it often will eat up to 29 kilos of the feathery-looking foliage a day. But why is its tongue that colour?

> When do giraffes have eight legs?
> When there are two of them.

It turns out that the tongue is probably purple for no good reason at all. Dr. Pat Carter, an evolutionary biologist at Washington State University, figures there was no evolutionary reason for the giraffe to have a purple tongue. The purple colour does not give the giraffe any better chance of surviving, so it really doesn't matter what colour it is. The tongue colour may be genetically linked to another trait that is uniquely giraffe-like, such as its spots or neck length. The gene for a purple tongue might simply "come with" this other characteristic. This notion reminds us that not all traits have a "purpose." Dr. Carter says that there are some traits that seem to be random, and make no difference to how the animal survives — maybe the tongue colour of the giraffe is one of them.

However, Brian Keating at the Calgary Zoo thinks the dark tongue colour might be a form of sun protection. Because the giraffe's tongue is outside of the mouth so much (eating all those acacia leaves) this theory makes sense, though so far there is no way of knowing for sure.

Other animals with purple or blue tongues are the Shar-Pei dog, the Blue-tongued skink (found in Australia, Tasmania and New Guinea), and the Chow Chow dog. A fable about how the Chow Chow got its blue-black tongue goes like this: When God was painting the sky blue, He spilled a few drops of paint as He worked. The Chow followed after, licking up the paint — and from that day on the Chow Chow had a blue tongue!

Why didn't they invite the giraffe to the party? He was a pain in the neck.

Why are giraffes so slow to apologize? It takes them a long time to swallow their pride.

Giraffe Facts

◎ Giraffes are mostly quiet beasts, but when they do make mouth noises, they can moan, moo or snort, as well as grunt, bellow or bray.

◎ Every giraffe has a different set of markings.

◎ Giraffes have seven vertebrae in their huge necks, the same number as humans.

◎ The average male giraffe is 5.3 m high – about three times the height of the average man.

◎ Giraffes aren't keen on lying down: they even give birth standing up.

22.

If the dinosaurs died out because of the asteroid that hit Earth, why did the mammals survive?

Scientists have been debating how the dinosaurs became extinct for decades, and the debate will probably continue as paleontologists continue to make new and startling discoveries.

From the fossils that have been found, scientists believe that dinosaurs appeared at the beginning of the Mesozoic Era (245-208 million years ago), and were the most common form of animal life for the next 160 million years. Then about 65 million years ago, the dinosaurs disappeared. But why?

According to Russell Jacobson, a paleontologist/geologist at the Illinois State Geological Survey, there are two main theories about how the dinosaurs died out. Some scientists believe that it happened gradually over a long period of time, and that dinosaur populations were on the verge of extinction before any catastrophe happened. Other scientists believe that dinosaurs disappeared suddenly when the Earth collided with a comet or an asteroid about 65 million years ago. The explosion caused a period of darkness and acid rain from the soot and dust in the atmosphere, which in turn caused climate changes and affected the dinosaurs' food supply.

Scientists believe that there have been at least five mass extinctions, where about 60% of all known plant and animal species disappeared in a short time. But even though we call it extinction, dinosaurs didn't completely disappear. Some of them evolved into a group of animals that are now present in almost every environment — birds.

So, recognizing that some groups of dinosaurs did survive, it's easier to understand that other species could also adapt and survive. Some of these animals might have burrowed underground — maybe to enter a sort of hibernation period — and many of them were scavengers who could live off the carcasses of dinosaurs or other animals.

Other scientists believe that the major groups of mammals were around long before the dinosaurs disappeared. There were small marsupials (animals that raise their young in a pouch, like opossums) and insectivores that were similar to shrews and hedgehogs. But it was only after the dinosaurs disappeared that the mammals became the dominant land animals. Within 10 million years of the dinosaurs' disappearance, mammals of every kind were living on the land, in the seas and in the air.

◉ The word dinosaur, meaning "fearfully great lizard," was first used in 1842 by Sir Richard Owen.

◉ The person who discovers a new dinosaur usually gets to name it. The name might describe how paleontologists think it behaved (**Tyrannosaurus** means tyrant lizard), or the place where the fossil remains were found (**Albertosaurus** was found in Alberta), or how it looks.

◉ One of the most unusual names is **Irritator** — because the people who found the fossil made it look different by adding plaster to the bones. That really irritated the paleontologists.

◉ Dinosaurs ruled the Earth for about 160 million years. Modern humans have been around for less than 300,000 years.

23.

Why is it that the female lion does the hunting and not the male lion?

It is purely a matter of body dynamics. The females are slimmer and they can move faster. They are truly great hunters, and without that huge mane, they can hide more easily. (Just imagine a male lion hiding behind a tree! His mane would give him away.) Besides, the male is busy guarding the hunting area for his family.

24.

How do worms see in the dark underground?

They don't, because worms have no eyes. They simply move slowly and feel their way around. Despite their lack of eyes, they do sense the light, because they have light-sensitive organs on their heads and tails. Why do they care about light if they can't see? Sunlight would dry out their skin and eventually kill them, so that's why they live underground.

And what do worms eat down there? Raw dirt and ground-up minerals. According to agricultural researcher Mary Fauci, worms living near the soil surface eat organic matter like fallen leaves and dead grass. They also eat small organisms like bacteria or fungi that live on plants. As well as eating, they excrete (or "cast," as the gardening industry puts it when it is trying to sell worm castings). These castings are very nutritious for plants. That's why you want worms in your soil and in your compost.

25.

Why do dogs chase cats, and why do cats and dogs fight?

Dogs don't chase cats simply because they are cats. A squirrel would do nicely. We simply associate dogs and cats since they are both pets. We even have a phrase for it — "fighting like cats and dogs."

Dogs instinctively chase small animals. It's part of their programmed need to hunt, called "prey drive." Dogs are predators, and movement triggers their instinct to hunt even though we feed them good food and they don't actually need to hunt at all to survive. Certain breeds of dogs were developed for particular hunting qualities. Terriers were bred to kill rats, for example, and retrievers were bred to be assistants to their masters in hunting. They will gently pick up the prey and bring it back to their master.

You can train your dog not to chase cats, but without such training dogs will always go after them. Most trainers think it's a good idea to teach your dog that cats are off limits at all times. Teach your dog "No" or "Leave it," and say it whenever it chases a cat. A water gun also comes in handy — just squirt the dog when it chases after a cat, to distract it.

If dogs and cats are raised together they will usually get along well. They will play, sleep together — even share the same water bowl. But introducing a dog into a cat's household, or a cat into a dog's household, might lead to problems. And even if a dog gets along with its own feline housemate, it might chase other cats when it encounters them outdoors.

26.

Can dogs watch television?

Dogs seem to be able to watch television. Or are they just listening? Observations from a student's science fair project showed that younger, smaller dogs respond more consistently to television than older, larger dogs.

Until they learn to talk, we'll never really know what dogs can actually see, but we're fairly certain it isn't as much as we can. Humans and dogs see things differently, and the television tube was developed for our eyes. Televisions are actually flickering (updating and lighting up the screen) many, many times in a second. This is fine for us because we can't detect the flicker, but dogs have a higher ability to detect flickering, so the screen must come across to them as annoying flashing images. Also, humans have eyes that face forward and decent binocular (two-eyed) vision and depth perception. Dogs have eyes facing the sides, and their depth perception is much lower.

We know for sure that dogs can hear the television — TV doorbells set off my border collie. If dogs' most acute sense — smell — could somehow get in on the act, they would be glued to the television day day and night.

27.

How much wood would a woodchuck chuck if a woodchuck could chuck wood?

According to Cornell University, a woodchuck would chuck about 315 kilos (if it could). They say that compared to beavers, groundhogs/woodchucks are not adept at moving timber, although some will chew wood. A wildlife biologist once measured the inside volume of a typical woodchuck burrow and estimated that — if wood filled the hole instead of dirt — the industrious animal would have chucked about 315 kilos worth.

28.

Are bats really blind, and can they fly in the rain?

Bats are not blind — their sight is just dandy. The reason we erroneously think they might be blind is that bats use a unique system called echolocation to manoeuvre in the dark. It is like a sonar system — bats send out short high-frequency sounds, many of which we can barely pick up. The sound waves bounce and echo off objects and reflect back to the bat. The reflected frequencies are slightly different and the bats can determine from this change in frequency where to locate the objects. But this system only works for up to 40 m, so bats rely on their sight too.

Bats have been given a bad rap — just

think of rabies fears, even of Dracula! They are sometimes called flying mice, but the truth is that they are closer to primates or humans than to mice. Check out their arms and fingers! Because bats seem like flying rodents, they tend to creep people out, but many bats are really important in keeping the night-flying insect population down.

There are around a thousand species of bats, which make up a quarter of the mammal population on Earth. We still have to work hard to preserve bats, though, because they are so important in the food chain, and because they reproduce more slowly than any mammals their size on Earth — most have only one young a year!

Bats are the only mammals that fly, and, according to Bat Conservation International, bats *will* fly in the rain. However, the high humidity that comes with rain can affect the movement of sounds through air, so bats might have more of a problem flying then.

Some wildlife centres house bats in their refrigerators to keep the bats in hibernation until they can be safely released back outdoors.

29.

How much water can a camel hold in its back?

The idea that a camel might be able to hold *any* water in its back is pretty amazing. Amazing, but not true.

The hump is a very good example of adaptation. Camels need some way to survive the desert's extreme climate, since camels are huge, and the desert is hot and dry, with little food to be found. Camels get water from food and from whatever actual water they can find. But the amazing thing is that the camel can go a long time without a drink of water — a week in really hot weather and up to a couple of months when it is cool. If we humans lose more than 12% of our weight in fluids, we die, but camels can hold on even if they lose 40%.

This is partly because they have some built-in water conservation systems — what water they take in they use very carefully. Camels don't sweat much, and if they do their fur holds onto the sweat and uses it to help cool them down. Their very stinky urine is hugely concentrated, which means that they don't pass much water through that way either. And they have particularly small and clever blood cells, which continue to work and circulate even when dehydration causes a camel's blood to get really thick.

So is the camel's hump the key? Not for water storage — that is a myth. The truth is that the hairy, floppy "canteen" on the back of the camel holds fat, not water — up to 45.5 kilos. It's there to live off when there is no food around. When it is really difficult to find a meal, the camel's hump shrinks, gets flabbier and flops over to the side. That would take about two weeks. Amazingly, camels can regain their weight in mere minutes by drinking a huge amount (up to 100 L) of water.

Camel Facts

◎ Think goat: a camel will also eat almost anything, just as a goat will.

◎ Can you close your nostrils? Camels can. They need this trick to keep sand from blowing up their noses.

◎ A racing camel has to be able to maintain a speed of 35-40 kph for 10 km.

30.

Do fish ever sleep?

For sure fish don't yawn, because you would need lungs and a diaphragm to do that. But sleep? That depends. If you believe that sleep means you have to have your eyes closed, then fish don't sleep, because they have no eyelids. But they can restore energy and save energy by resting. Scientists measure sleep by looking at brain waves. They know fish sleep because they can see the fishes' brain waves getting slower, and the frequencies getting lower, as they fall asleep.

Some fish hang around logs or on rocks so they even look like they are sleeping. Some sharks have to keep moving even when they're resting, because their method of breathing requires them to push water through their gills.

Dolphin Facts

◉ A dolphin – which of course is a mammal, not a fish – can turn off half its brain and rest it, but keep the other half agile enough to watch out for predators. This kind of resting is called unihemispheric deep sleep. It isn't deep by our standards, though some species of dolphin manage to cobble together 7 hours of sleep a day, with the longest "nap" with half a brain taking all of 60 seconds!

◉ Dolphins don't just "wake" to watch out for predators. They have to stay alert enough to surface every once in a while to breathe. Young dolphins surface every 2 minutes or so; mature dolphins can hold out for up to 10 minutes.

31.

Why do dogs drink out of the toilet?

Wouldn't you if you were a dog? Fresh, cold water right at your height — none of this bending over and lapping out of a bowl nonsense. In fact, if you were a dog, wouldn't you wonder why humans want you to bend over so much . . . and why they pee into such a great water bowl?

But your dog should not be drinking out of the toilet bowl. You know what goes in there, and you don't want your dog catching a salmonella bacterial infection, which spreads through human feces. If that thought isn't gross enough — one lick on your face from your precious pet after he's been toilet lapping and there's a good chance you'll get it too. Plus, the cleansers used to clean toilets could also make your dog really sick, or even kill him.

If all of this hasn't convinced you to keep the toilet lid down, here's one more reason. When your pet drinks from the toilet, it's impossible to keep track of how much water he's drinking. Why should you care about that? Because if your dog is sick, knowing if he's drinking too much or not enough water can help the veterinarian figure out what's wrong. So keep a bowl of fresh cold water around. (And if you are feeling generous, raise it up to toilet height. You can buy little tables with holes cut out to hold the bowls for just that purpose.)

32.

Do birds have a sense of smell?

They most certainly do, but unlike other animals, birds don't rely primarily on their sense of smell to find their mother or their dinner. Because of the superb qualities of the bird eye, birds use their eyes and their ears first, and then their noses. Birds' eyes are far larger in proportion to their heads than humans' eyes — up to fifteen times the proportional weight. They can have up to six to eight times better distance vision than we do. Birds' eyes are flatter, giving them a larger focus area, and they can have as many as five times the light receptors as we do. The result? They can see far better in a wider area and in much lower light than we can.

There is always an exception to the sight-over-scent rule, though, and it is the kiwi, the only bird with external nostrils way down at the end of its bill, so it can actually sniff around and find a meal. The kiwi can find worms by smell alone. That's a good thing — its eyesight is really poor. Other than the kiwi, most birds have a very small part of the brain devoted to smell perception. It's called the olfactory lobe.

Birds with really big beaks are often really great smellers. Some scientists with a sense of adventure tried pouring bacon fat on the ocean surface. It brought black-footed albatrosses (with really big super-charged seagull-type noses) from almost 29 km away.

And what about the old idea that a mother bird will reject a nestling that has been handled by a human because of the human's scent? There is no hard scientific evidence to support it, and now you know why there could be some doubt: smell just isn't such a big deal for most birds.

33.

Where did the goatsucker bird get its name?

Put goatsucker right up at the top of your list of unfortunate names you have encountered. (If you don't have such a list, this would be a great place to start.) This is not the name of just one bird, but the name of a whole order, *Caprimulgiformes*, which is related to the Greek word for "goat milker." (An order consists of a group of similar birds.) These birds have drab-coloured plumage, are primarily night fliers, and range in size from raven to sparrow. Within this order are various species including the nightjar, the nighthawk and birds with another odd name: owlet frogmouth.

But why is it called a goatsucker? Because these birds (who have been known since ancient times) happen to eat insects that hang around goats at night. Perhaps because of their odd, overly large mouths, the goatsuckers were wrongly accused of actually milking the unsuspecting goats by drinking directly from their udders. The term goatsucker is slowly being replaced by a more accurate and apt name, nightjar. That's because the bird's strange, hollow, monotonous sound is jarring to hear at night.

34.

What is the longest recorded flight of a chicken?

Believe it or not, thousands of folks gather every year in Wayne, Nebraska, to attend the annual Chicken Flying Contest and to see how far chickens can fly when scooted out of a launch pad (a mailbox) with a toilet plunger. (The record is thirteen seconds of air time.) But many other folks don't think this practice is particularly good for the chickens, so let's just look at the facts.

The chicken's ancestor, the wild red jungle fowl, could and would fly if it had to. Aerodynamically speaking though, there is a reason chickens today don't fly. All of the poultry family is designed for a life on the ground. The shape of their feet, and their small wings, don't lead to a life of flying about. Also, because of selective breeding, chickens have bigger pectoral muscles (or chicken breasts), which make flying more difficult. Some smaller and lighter breeds can fly enough to get them over a fence to raid a garden, but most just stay on the ground. If you need to, some farmers clip one of the chickens' wings to "ground" them.

35.

Are there any other crossbred animals like the mule?

There are lots of other *hybrid* offspring — that's where the two parents are genetically different. The best-known example is likely the mule, a cross between a male donkey (or jackass) and a female horse (or mare).

The mule was bred around three thousand years ago as an ideal pack animal. The horse contributes the size and strength, and the donkey kicks in the amazing sure-footedness and the really long lifespan. The resulting animal, the mule, has the additional attributes of putting up with heat better than a horse can, and needing less food and water. It's a win-win situation.

If you cross a female donkey (jenny) and a male horse (stallion), you also get a mule, which is known as a hinny or hinney, an animal smaller than the donkey/mare cross. Like the mule, it cannot produce offspring.

This is because crossbreeding works best with animals from the same species, with each having the same number of chromosomes. A

horse has sixty-four chromosomes and a
jackass has sixty-two, so they are able
to produce a new animal, but one
that can't reproduce.

> **What
is black and
white, white and
black, black and white?
A zebra caught in a
revolving door!**

The male parent of the
crossbred animal goes first in the
name. All zebra hybrids (which
are also bred as pack animals) fall
under the generic term "Zebroid,"
and are usually called Golden Zebras.
Technically, they are actually Zorse (zebra
x horse), Ze-Donk, Zonkey or Zebrass (zebra x
donkey), and Zony or Zeony (zebra x pony).

36.

Why and how do cats purr? And why do they hate water?

There are theories galore, but no one has
really nailed it. Here are a few of the better
ideas:

Why?

- Purring is a good way for mother cats to
  communicate with their young. Newborn
  kittens can't see, but they can feel the
  vibrations of mom purring.

- It's a sign of contentment. A mother's purring
  tells her kittens that things are fine, and a
  kitten nursing can purr to the mother to say
  the same thing.

- Sometimes cats purr to calm themselves
  down when they are stressed, like while they
  are giving birth, or while injured, dying or
  just frightened.

- Sometimes cats just want to purr — it isn't
  a reflex, it is a voluntary act.

How?

- ◉ By drawing the vocal cords (or bands) together and apart twenty-five times a second.
- ◉ By vibrating the membranes, called "false vocal cords," which are the fleshy folds that are behind the cat's real vocal cords.

Cats can vocalize more than a hundred sounds, but dogs can only come up with ten.

Now to the second part of the question: Why do cats hate water? Not all cats hate water, but most do. There's a breed called the Fishing Cat, that's found from northern India to southeast Asia. It's such a good swimmer that it will dive into the water and go after fish. It will even get low enough in the water to grab a duck from underneath! Then there's the Turkish Van, which loves to takes baths — and will jump into your tub or a lake to do so. This very large domestic cat seems to have a virtually waterproof cashmere-like fur, mostly white with rust or blue/black around the ears and on the tail.

Cougars will swim across small lakes and cross streams — they just look for a shallow spot. Some of the big cats that live in hot climates, like tigers, lions, jaguars, ocelots and jaguarundi, seem to love water.

But that's just two very rare breeds and some really big cats. Does the average domestic cat hate water? Catherine Ulibarri, a veterinary professor at Washington State University, has a theory that because fur is animals' protection against the cold, they try not to get it wet if it could cause a problem that would threaten their survival. So domestic cats and big cats that live in cold climates, like lynx and bobcats, will avoid water.

Not all domestic cats actually hate water. Dr. Janice Crook, a veterinarian in North Vancouver, was treating a big tabby cat named Johnny, who'd torn a ligament in his hind leg. When asked how it happened, his human said that Johnny had slipped while getting into the shower — he and Johnny shower together every morning!

Where do cats like to swim?
In the puss-ific.

What do you call a cat that swims in the ocean?
An octo-puss.

How much does your head weigh?

and Other Bizarre Bits About YOUR BODY

37.

How much does your head weigh?

The average human head weighs about 7.5% of a person's body weight. So if you weigh about 40 kilos, your head weighs around 3 kilos. If you are a 90-kilogram person, your head weighs about 6.75 kilos.

There's a lot in there to make up that mass. Your head has twenty-two bones — the cranium, which protects the brain, has eight bones; and the face, fourteen. So when you get tired of holding your head up high, you know why. It's heavy!

38.

If people never cut their hair, how long would it be when they're fifteen?

Each hair grows from its own follicle. As new cells are produced in the follicles, they push the older cells upward. This is what makes the hair grow. The hair itself is not alive, just the cells in the follicles. New cells are produced for a certain amount of time, depending on where on the body the follicle is located. Then the follicle goes through a rest phase. During this phase the existing hair falls out. When the follicle returns to its active state, a new hair starts to grow in its place. So the maximum length that your hair can grow depends on how long the growth phase is. For most people, scalp hair can keep growing anywhere from two to six years. At any moment, 85% of your head of hair is growing while 15% is resting.

Most hair grows about 1.3 cm per month, or 15.6 cm a year. (This can vary, depending on your age, your genetics and the state of your hormones.) The longest hair you could expect to grow would be about 94 cm (6 years x 15.6 cm/year = 93.6 cm).

Hair follicles on different parts of your body are programmed with different growth phases and different rates of growth. Eyelash hairs grow more slowly than scalp hairs, and they grow for only about four months before new hairs replace them.

Some Hairy Facts

◎ The palms of your hands, the soles of your feet and your lips are the only places on your body surface where hair doesn't grow.

◎ There is an average of 100,000 hair follicles on your scalp. Most brunettes have 155,000, blondes 140,000 and redheads only 85,000. You lose up to 125 hairs from your scalp each day.

◎ You have about 5 million hairs on your body.

◎ Curly hair grows from flat follicles, wavy from oval follicles, and straight from round follicles.

◎ The longest recorded hair was that of Swami Pandarasannadhi, head of India's Thiruvadu Thurai monastery. In 1949 his hair was reported to be 7.8 m in length.

◎ Mata Jagdamba of Ujjain, India, had hair that measured 4.16 m in 1994. It was the longest on record at the time. In 1998 that record was broken by two brothers from northern Thailand. Hu Saelo had hair 5.24 m long. His brother, Mr. Yi, who had turned 87 in 1997, had hair 4.85 m long. Then in 2004, Xic Qiuping of China recorded hair measuring 5.627 m. He had not cut it since 1973.

39.

Why does hair change colour as a person gets older?

This process is encoded in your genes — you come from your parents programmed for certain things, like which pigment and how much pigment you have in your hair, and when you will go grey. Children's hair colour changes with age. Most "tow headed" white-blond children turn into brunettes because the cells producing that inherited pigment grow and the hair darkens. And the reason your hair goes grey eventually is that cells at the root of the hair, which produce pigment, gradually die off as you age.

And why does our hair get lighter in the summer? When pigments are exposed to sunlight they lose some colour — the way dark-coloured things fade if you leave them in the sun. This mostly happens in the summer when there are so many hours of sunlight. In the winter, indoor lights don't contain the same light energy as sunlight, and won't fade things as fast.

40.

Why do we have fingernails?

Your fingernails protect the tips of your fingers and your toenails protect the tips of your toes. Fingernails also help you to pick things up (unless you're a nail-biter, that is). Most animals have some kind of nails, but they're not always as flat as human nails. Some animals have sharp, curved nails called claws, and others have thicker, rounded nails that we call hooves. Your nails are made of a protein called keratin. That's the same stuff that human hair, bird feathers, horse hooves and bear claws are made of.

The hard part of your nail is dead, and that's why it doesn't hurt to cut your nails or your hair. But the root or flesh part where the nail grows from — your cuticle — is alive. That's why a hangnail hurts so much.

Your fingernails can tell a lot about your health. In order to build protein, you have to have a healthy body. The colour, shape and growth of your nails help doctors diagnose some illnesses. A really severe illness, like a heart attack or pneumonia, will interrupt growth at the nail root, and doctors will see an indentation across your nail. Other oddities can show lung disease, kidney failure, arsenic poisoning, iron deficiency and even psoriasis. A white tip and whiteness near the root are actually signs of healthy nails.

◉ Dr. William Bennett Bean studied how his nails grew – for 35 years. He found that it takes six months or so for fingernails to grow from the roots to the tip. That's about 3.6 cm a year. The longest finger grows nails the fastest, while toenails take up to four times as long. Nails also grow fastest during the day, but grow more slowly as you get older. Nails grow faster on pregnant women, and faster in men than in women.

◉ Sridhar Chillal of India hadn't cut the nails on his left hand since 1952. In 2014 he had a total of 9 m of nails. That included a 1.978-m thumbnail and 1.645-m index fingernail. He cut his nails in 2018.

41.

Why do you close your eyes when you sneeze?

It's a reflex. Your eyes snap shut when you sneeze, and it's pretty much impossible to keep them open. The nerves serving the eyes and the nose are very closely connected. If you stimulate one nerve, like in your nose when you sneeze, often it will trigger some response in the other. It's like having your eyes water when you yawn.

There's a kids' rumour or an old wives' tale that if you keep your eyes open when you sneeze, your eyes will pop out. But it's just a tale. Even if you *could* keep your eyes open, they wouldn't pop out.

Sneezing is just an extreme form of breathing. When you sneeze, air is exhaled violently through your nasal passages. So why do we sneeze? To keep foreign material out of the body. If you inhale particles like dust, the tiny particles will excite your nose and trigger a sneeze. You'll sneeze if you have a cold too, or if you have allergies.

Some people sneeze when they go out into the bright sunlight. That's called the photic sneeze reflex. It happens to 16% to 25% of the population. It is also genetic — you have a 64% chance of inheriting it if one of your parents is a photic sneezer.

The most chronic fit of sneezing was by Donna Griffiths of Pershore, England. She caught a cold and started sneezing on January 13, 1981... and stopped 978 days later. She likely sneezed about a million times in the first year.

We sneeze for other reasons too. Pepper and strong-smelling things like ammonia, or strong-tasting things like hot chilies, don't trigger our smell or taste senses. The receptors that respond are pain receptors, and the response is a reflex to protect us from inhaling something dangerous.

The particles ejected in a forceful sneeze have been clocked at 166 km per hour.

42.

Do you really get only one set of eyelashes? And why do lashes stay one length when other hair keeps growing?

No, eyelashes keep getting replaced. They grow as long as they need to be to do their job. What's their job? Eyelashes are a bit like nose hair. Eyelashes are there to keep dust and sweat and dirt and bugs and airborne particles out of your eyes. They are also designed to protect your eyes from the glare of the sun.

The eyelid protects the eyeball, and the eyelashes are responsible for screening matter out of the eye. If anything comes toward the eye and the very sensitive eyelashes, or if anything moves suddenly, the lids blink hard by reflex, to protect the eyeball. When you blink by reflex, the eyeball is quickly washed with a coat of tears and mucus to clean it off. That keeps it healthy and moving properly. We blink every two to ten seconds, and all of this happens without us even noticing.

43.

Where do you go to the bathroom in an igloo?

First of all, you have to let go of the idea that you need a flush toilet to be able to go to the bathroom. It takes running water to make a toilet flush, but in the far North when igloos were used as homes, there was no running water. The people who used igloos had a different idea that worked just as well.

Igloos or dome-shaped snow houses come in two styles: large winter residential dwellings and small, hastily constructed hunters' huts for single-night stays. The big winter house was actually a series of snow domes connected by passageways. Fifteen to twenty people lived inside, reclining on skins spread on the floor, and on low platforms. The temperature was always around freezing.

No one has really lived in these winter homes since the 1950s, although hunting huts are still used. Both structures are built in spirals from within, using blocks of snow, which makes great insulation.

We know about bathrooms in igloos because of a Danish explorer, Therkel Mathiassen. He was a member of the Fifth Thule Expedition (1921–1924) and wrote about igloos in *Material Culture of the Iglulik Eskimos*. "The largest single snow house I have seen was lined with skin and measured 18 feet [5.5 m] in diameter, and 8 feet [2.5 m] high. There was a central store room, from which were doors to the house, to two smaller side rooms for clothing and meat, and a wooden door to the dogs' room, in one side of which was a small opening into a separate little snow house which acted as a latrine."

At the time, urine was collected in large urine tubs for use in preparing animal skins. The ammonia in urine cuts grease, so the Inuit also used it to wash hair and clothes.

The single-night hunting igloos are another story. Usually about four hunters travel together and make an igloo 2 m in diameter. That's close quarters. The floors are covered with caribou skins. Men can pull back the caribou skin and urinate onto the floor of snow. The warm urine burns a hole into the snow and freezes. It's a little trickier for women, who lean against the wall, peel back the skins from the floor and urinate. It's all very clean.

How come your tongue heals faster than the rest of your body?

Gash your lip or bite your tongue and you'll find that indeed mouth wounds heal faster than anywhere else on your body. Your *oral mucosa*, or the lining of your mouth, heals faster than other skin. But why? Because your mouth happens to have the right combination of factors to make it an ideal site for letting wounds heal and growing new tissue. It has an excellent blood supply, and that blood carries the oxygen, nutrients and proteins you need. There are also growth factors, clotting factors and antibodies in the mouth, which, combined with the warm temperature, make the mouth a perfect site for speedy healing.

45.

What causes albinism?

People and animals born with no colouring at all in their hair, eyes or skin have albinism. Animals, plants, and people from any racial group can have albinism — they lack the pigment or colouring matter that most of us have. Pigments come in lots of shades: for example blue, brown or green eyes; the wild feathers of a parrot or the stripes of a zebra or a tabby cat. Skin gets colour from a dark pigment called melanin. Caucasians, or white people, have less melanin than Black people do. People with albinism have no melanin at all. Their skin tends to look quite pink, because their blood vessels are showing through. Their hair is snow white. Albino people need to wear sunglasses in the sun because their eyes have no pigment for protection from very strong light. (For this same reason you will find that people with blue eyes want to put on sunglasses sooner than people with brown eyes, because they have less pigment in their eyes.)

Colouring is passed on from your parents through your genes. Albino people also inherit their lack of colour. Some albino parents might have children who do not have albinism, but those same children might later go on to pass on albinism. Or it might not happen again for many generations.

There are also albino plants. They lack chlorophyll, the green food material. With no food, albino plants quickly die.

Freckles are just little round spots — concentrations of the skin pigment called melanin. Some people get them when they go out in the sun, others live freckle-free. And kids get freckles far more than adults.

46.

Why do old people shrink?

Shrink sounds like a strong term, but it is true. Old people lose height and muscle and fat, so they get smaller. Their spines begin to degenerate and compress, making them shorter. That's partially gravity taking hold. We all get shorter in the course of a day because water gets squeezed out of the discs of the spine. However, it is permanent in older people because there is less water in the discs. Younger people have more water to begin with, and spring back to height at night.

Add to this the fact that the vertebrae can crush as you get older because of a condition called osteoporosis. People with osteoporosis have bones that aren't dense enough to hold their weight. Some older people also can't stand up straight — they stoop because of the crushed vertebrae.

Almost everything to do with shrinkage relates to diet and exercise. So get lots of exercise, fresh air and good food with plenty of calcium. That way you will have done your part to stay as big and strong as possible. The total amount you will shrink depends on how much you stay in shape. Generally, a man might lose 3 cm, and a woman 5 cm, between ages thirty to seventy.

47.

Why do we forget?

Actually, there is no evidence that we ever forget anything. It is all in your brain somewhere. But remembering is like trying to find something in your room when it is a big mess. The key to retrieving information from your brain, just like finding your shoes in your messy room, is in how we organize our thoughts (or our stuff!). And with memory, the trick is to teach ourselves how to remember things. So when people say their memory is going, what is really happening is that their retrieval system isn't working well.

Everyone has different methods of learning. Some people need to hear someone explain something, others need to draw themselves a diagram or read it for themselves.

If you want to remember something, you first have to learn and understand it, and consciously think of a cue to use when you want to remember it. How you do this depends on your learning style and the method of retrieval that works best for you.

There are loads of books and courses on improving your memory. Some of the basic ideas include coming up with a trick or a mnemonic to help you remember something. You have to tell yourself how to remember this person or this thing. Maybe you will connect a name to a physical feature, like deciding that the man you met called Chuck Brown has a round head like Charlie Brown, and Chuck is a short form for Charlie.

Maybe a corny verse would help:

I before E
Except after C,
Or in rhyming with A,
As in neighbour and weigh.

You might need to say something out loud twice, or write it down so you can see the word. Or maybe you have to sing it to yourself. These are all cues you are setting up. Everything is in your brain somewhere, it just takes the right cue to get it out. So if you really want to remember something, figure out what will work for you when you store it.

To remember the notes of the treble-clef lines of music:

Every Good Boy Deserves Fudge (E, G, B, D, F)

The notes of the bass-clef lines are:
Girls Buy Dolls For Amusement (G, B, D, F, A)

To remember the Great Lakes, say HOMES:

Huron, Ontario, Michigan, Erie and Superior

To remember how to set clocks when daylight saving time starts and finishes:

Spring forward, fall back.

48.

What happens to all the chewing gum we swallow? Does it stick up our insides?

Chewing gum usually makes its way out, just like everything else you put in your mouth and swallow. But if you swallow a *lot* of gum, it can actually clog up your digestive tract. Best advice — just chew your gum, don't swallow it.

49.

Why were people smaller in the old days?

Why? Nutrition. In the old days (not even a hundred years ago) most people ate what they could grow and put away, so their nutrition would depend on where they were farming or what they could buy or barter. We've got better food now, but more than that, we have methods of preserving our foods by refrigeration and other techniques. We can eat anything all year long, because we can now transport food around the world. This improved nutrition, including more protein, often makes for bigger babies and children.

Here's something else to think about. Folks "back then" were considered normal-sized for their time. It is just that the next generations have gotten bigger and bigger!

50.

Can you really drink your urine?

The answer is yes, you can, and some people do. But the question is, would you really want to?

People drink their urine for a variety of reasons. It is an ancient practice, and the people who do it claim that it helps their health by boosting their immune system. There are many stories about drinking one's own urine bringing miraculous cures from awful diseases. Urine therapy is particularly popular in India and in Germany. It is called the Water of Life or Life Elixir.

This is why people drink urine: They think that when the kidney makes urine it takes excess vital parts out of your blood along with the water that needs to pass through. They think that urine is not simply waste, but is full of nutrients, hormones, enzymes and antibodies that are filtered out of the blood. It is also believed that morning urine is the richest and the best for you.

If this really grosses you out, there is one time when you had better get over it. Say you are stranded in the middle of the ocean on a life raft, or in the middle of the desert in extreme heat. No water means dehydration, even death. So go for it. This is survival, and drinking your urine can save your life.

51.

Do conjoined twins have the same DNA?

Understanding how twins are born should clear this up. Conjoined twins are always identical and have the same DNA. Identical twins occur when one fertilized egg splits in two, so there was only one set of DNA for starters. The egg splits to make twin embryos and, *voilà*; two sets of DNA exactly the same. Identical twins share 100% of their DNA and are always the same sex.

Now pay attention, because this may be about you. Fraternal twins (the kinds that don't look the same) happen when the mother releases two eggs which *both* become fertilized. They can be the same sex or different sexes, just like any other siblings.

With conjoined twins, the separation of the one egg into two embryos wasn't complete. This is probably because the separation started too late in their development. They are still physically joined at some part of their body, like the back of the head or the side of the trunk. Some share vital organs like the liver or heart. In some cases one twin doesn't develop fully and can seem like just a tumour on the healthier twin. One in 85,000 to 100,000 births results in conjoined twins — so it is a rare occurrence.

Conjoined twins were once called Siamese twins because of Chang and Eng Bunker, the most famous conjoined twins, who were born in Siam (now Thailand) on May 11, 1811. They travelled with circus sideshows until they settled in the United States and married two sisters. They lived to be sixty-three years old and had twenty-two children between them — Chang had twelve and Eng had ten. They were very good marksmen and keen runners — clearly they figured out how to work together.

In order for doctors to surgically separate conjoined twins, the twins have to have separate sets of organs. Since 1950, hundreds of operations have been performed, with varying success for one or both twins' survival.

52.

Why is it called a funny bone?

It's not even a teeny bit funny when you hit yourself hard on what people call the funny bone. And it's not a bone, either. It's called the ulnar nerve and it runs through a groove in your ulna, which is one of the two bones in your forearm. The place of extreme pain is in your elbow, where the nerve and the bones are really close to the surface. Since they stick out extra far, it is even easier to whack yourself on the funny bone. Believe it, whacking a nerve is far worse than whacking a bone. It's like a gigantic crazy session of pins and needles and pain all jumbled up, so much so that you might cry and laugh at the same time. That's one of the theories of why it's called the funny bone. (Some people think it's called the funny bone because the other bone that the ulnar nerve runs through is your humerus bone. Get it — humorous!)

Yeow!

If people are always shedding skin cells, why don't tattoos come off?

Wait a minute; if tattoos could come off, wouldn't your freckles flake off too? Something isn't right here, so first we need to figure out how your skin works. It's a bit like an onion with layers. The top several layers of skin cells make up the epidermis. The dead skin you see is from cells constantly dividing from the base layers of the epidermis and moving up to the surface to flake off.

Right below the epidermis is the much thicker dermis. Tattoos are applied by sticking a needle a couple of millimetres into your skin, which gets the ink all the way into the dermis. So even after all the superficial epidermal cells have sloughed off, tattoo ink remains in the dermis, which stays put.

Tattooing goes on in most parts of the world and has been happening since the time of the ancient Egyptians. Lasers have come along in the past few decades to remove tattoos, but they are terribly expensive, don't always work and might cause scarring. So that snake tattoo you thought you'd love forever? How about a nice temporary version? They are cheap and will wear off in a matter of days, but still pack enough of a punch to shock your mother.

54.

How do you go to the bathroom in space?

This is the question most often asked of NASA. That's no surprise. There is no gravity at all up there, but people still have a biological need to expel fluid. The possibilities for disaster are endless. Astronauts go to the bathroom like we do, because every Space Shuttle has one toilet for both men and women. It is sort of like ours. But in outer space, air is used instead of flowing water to remove waste. And you have to sit really firmly on the seat to make sure that nothing floats up.

Then the astronauts compress the solid wastes and store them onboard until they can be removed after landing. Because of how liquids react in zero gravity, the moisture in the solids sort of boils away quickly. The air is filtered to get rid of the odour and bacteria, and then returned to the cabin.

A space toilet is not simple, and it's not cheap. In 2007 NASA paid $19 million for a Russian-built space toilet to install in the International Space Station. By the way, astronauts brush their teeth just like we do on Earth. And there is no shower on the Shuttle, so astronauts must make do with sponge baths until they return home.

55.

Why do my fingers and toes get wrinkly in the bath (and why doesn't the rest of me)?

We humans are pretty much covered with hair everywhere but the palms of our hands and the soles of our feet. In many places your hair is so fine you wouldn't dream of calling yourself hairy. (A magnifying glass will help to spot the hairs on "non-hairy" spots like noses or fingers.) We have glands at the base of each strand of hair that make something called sebum. It is an oily coating that keeps our skin from taking in too much water, sort of like a light wetsuit over our body. Skin absorbs lots of water when you sit in the bath, but here is a clue related to your question: the skin on the hands and feet has the thickest epidermis (the outer layer of skin) on the body, but neither the palms of the hands nor the soles of the feet have any sebum.

When the skin on our hands and feet takes in water (or, to use a technical term, when there is capillary action), the outer skin swells up but the inner skin layers don't. That means that there's an excess of the outer layer of the epidermis, called the *stratum corneum*, relative to the inner layers. The result — the "excess" outer skin wrinkles.

Something that results in a similar look happens in the dog world. Some dog breeds, like the Shar-Pei, have a lot more skin on their face than other breeds with the same size head. To fit closely on the head and not droop like a curtain, the skin forms wrinkles. Imagine that wrinkly skin as the outer layer of skin on your finger, and the Shar-Pei's skull as the inner layer of skin on your finger — the outer skin has "gathers" that the underlying skin doesn't.

Why don't the hands and feet produce any sebum? You wouldn't want to try grabbing things or walking with "greasy" hands and feet!

Want to try an experiment? Try coating one hand with oil soon after you get in the bath and see if the other gets more wrinkles.

56.

Why do we have nose hair?

Your nose hair is simply a filter to clean up the air you breathe. It is there so that any small bits of dirt and dust trapped in the mucus coating the nose hair won't make it into your lungs. Nose hairs are called *vibrissae*. If you ever go to a very polluted city, you will find that when you blow your nose the tissue looks like a filter from a dryer or pool — full of dirt! The nose hair has to work extra hard to keep you healthy.

The scary part is how older men sometimes have extra-long nose hair sticking out from their noses. This has spawned an industry of some pretty weird appliances, like electric nose-hair clippers.

57.

What are you really doing when you crack your knuckles?

You are creeping people out, for starters. Very few things drive folks as crazy as hearing someone cracking their knuckles and popping their joints — except maybe running their fingernails down a blackboard. About one-quarter of the population has this extremely annoying habit.

What you are actually doing is pulling apart the two bones of your finger joint and letting a lubricating fluid, called synovial fluid, zip into the gap between them. Because you're increasing the space between your bones, the pressure on the fluid (which contains carbon dioxide) goes down, and little gas bubbles form. The pressure keeps dropping until the gas that was dissolved in the synovial fluid is able to escape as gas bubbles. It is the same principle as when you open a can of soda and the bubbles of carbon dioxide pop and crackle to the surface.

It takes fifteen minutes for the fluid to build up enough pressure so you could crack your knuckles again. If you happen to be "a cracker," you will constantly be told that you will end up with arthritis. That's not true, but you are in fact pulling your joint beyond its regular range of motion, stressing out the ligaments and tendons in the process. Do it enough and it may not return to its normal function. You don't want to end up with a weaker grip — or lose friends and relatives by being so annoying — so stop cracking your knuckles!

58.

What are goosebumps?

Goosebumps are formed when the tiny muscles in your body's hair follicles contract when you are cold, making those hairs stand on end. This doesn't look like much on a blond child, but when our much furrier ancestors got cold, it would have been pretty impressive, because humans used to have denser, longer hair all over their bodies. The goosebumps fluffed up the hair, which trapped air and made an insulating coat around the body. With evolution we have lost this denser hair that we don't need any more, but our "piloerector" muscles still produce goosebumps.

There are a lot of emotional rushes that can trigger your autonomic nervous system's feedback process and give you goosebumps, too. A rush of adrenaline, the natural hormone surge we get when faced with stress, was useful for our ancestors' "fight or flight" response. If someone were threatening to attack you, your "fight" response would be to fluff up your hair to look bigger and scarier. Think of lions or bears — or your cat! They still do the same thing. The expression "Don't get your hackles up" really means "Don't let your piloerector muscles give you goosebumps."

Other automatic responses to emotions are blushing, gagging and getting butterflies in your stomach.

59.

How come we have wrinkles?

Wrinkles are part of the deal — if you are going to grow old you are going to get wrinkles. You could think of them as being like rings on a tree trunk, sort of a badge of honour for the years you do service. You will earn your wrinkles. Some people inherit sensitivity to sunlight and therefore the tendency to wrinkle.

You can avoid having more than your fair share of wrinkles by drinking plenty of water, by staying out of direct sunlight and wearing sunscreen and a hat, and by not smoking. That's because smoking affects the blood supply to your skin's top layer, and it becomes damaged. Smoking can trigger the release of an enzyme which breaks down the elasticity in your skin. Losing weight or muscle tone also makes you wrinkle.

You can't avoid the major wrinkle factor: time. Gravity affects the skin over your muscles and it will eventually sag into little folds. Your skin cells start to replace themselves more slowly and the inner layer of your skin begins to thin. At the same time, the fat cells under that layer start getting smaller.

And holding all of the fat and skin cells together is a network of collagen and elastin fibres, which begins to loosen and unravel. With all of this conspiring against you, you don't have a hope to avoid frown lines. So don't get stressed about wrinkles — laugh about them, and you'll get laugh lines, the most pleasant wrinkles of all.

60.

What makes bruises?

Ecchymosis: that's the medical term for bruises. And if you have ever fallen off your skateboard or whacked your head on something, you know just how *ecchy* it feels. The purplish-brownish mess, which can also be raised and really yucky, is from where blood vessels have broken and blood has leaked into the bruise area.

To get even more graphic, a bruise is reddish or purplish-looking on the first day you acquire it — the true colour of blood inside your skin. Then over the next couple of days your body chemically breaks down the pooled blood cells and your bruise becomes more blue and purple. Around day six, things go green, and after that, yellowy-brown. For the most part, it takes about two or three weeks to get your skin back to normal.

You can speed healing along a bit by applying ice or, even better, frozen peas. Put the bag of peas in a towel and hold it on your injury to reduce the blood flow to the area and possibly reduce the size of the bruise.

61.

How come when you put someone's hand in warm water when they're sleeping, they pee?

Been to summer camp lately? This is a classic practical joke. It works mostly because feeling or hearing any kind of water can make you think or dream about more water, and that tends to make you pee. It works in the same way as running water when you are *trying* to urinate — it often helps to get you going. Nurses in hospitals sometimes do this for patients recovering from surgeries where the lower regions have been traumatized.

Why does it work? No one knows for certain — this isn't the kind of topic that scientists have worked on much. But it seems to be a reflex. Warm water may trigger the parasympathetic part of your nervous system, which can relax your sphincter muscles. Ever put your hands in warm water to wash dishes, only to suddenly feel the urge to head for the bathroom?

The hand-in-the-bowl-of-water stunt doesn't always work, but if your victim is in the right frame of mind he or she will be changing the sheets.

62.

Why does poison ivy itch so much?

The oil in the sap of poison ivy, urushiol, puts the "poison" in the poison ivy. And get this: you only need a billionth of a gram (a nanogram) to get a rash and itch like mad. Five hundred people could itch from the amount covering the head of a pin. Just over 7 g of urushiol could give every person on Earth a rash.

Not absolutely everyone reacts to poison ivy, but most people do. It's a very common allergy. Even touching your shoes or pants that have rubbed onto the plants can give you allergic contact dermatitis. In other words, a nasty rash.

The old saying is "leaves of three, leave it be." So if you see this plant with its set of three distinct leaves, leave it alone!

What can you do if you do come into contact with poison ivy? First, don't touch or scratch your skin, at least until you can wash it. Wash your hands, the affected area, then your hands again. Cold water closes your pores to the urushiol oil. If you can avoid touching or scratching the area, you have a better chance of avoiding a rash.

A plant called jewel weed — which often grows alongside poison ivy — is a good remedy. Juice from the crushed leaves and stems, rubbed all over where you were exposed to the poison ivy, should slow down the itching and spreading. (Jewel weed has oval leaves with round-toothed edges. Its yellow-orange, trumpet-like flowers have dark red spots. You can also buy jewel weed soap and sprays.)

Even after using jewel weed, you still have to stop from scratching. A thick paste of baking soda and water, plastered on the rash, can help with the itching.

63.

Why do you blush when you have a crush on someone, or when you get embarrassed?

Blushing is like holding a flag over your head that says, "Look at me, I am really uncomfortable here!" Your nervous system reacts to stress in a number of ways, including blushing. Like goosebumps, blushing is an automatic and involuntary reaction to attention that you don't want. When you have an emotional power surge — when you get scared, nervous, embarrassed, shy, flirty (like when you have a crush on someone), or when you tell a lie, get angry or get upset — you can get stressed and become very hot. You're blushing! What is happening with your body is this: your blood vessels are widening slightly to allow more blood to get to your skin. Your face has the most blood vessels, so that's where the blushing is most obvious.

Four out of five people blush, and if you are a blusher, there's not much you can do about it — it is part of your wiring. It's also part of being human. One of the things that separates us from animals is the ability to blush. (Others are using our thumbs the way we do, and talking.)

Not everyone blushes. Women blush more than men; small children hardly blush. If your parents are blushers, you likely will be

too. It's not much consolation, but know that
studies have proven that if you blush when you
are embarrassed, you seem more likeable.

For some blushers, sipping cold water when
they know they are about to get into a dicey
situation helps head off a red face by fooling
the part of the brain that controls blushes into
thinking "I'm a cool cat." If you are a blusher,
what do you have to lose?

64.

Can you die from constipation?

Everyone is different, but if you go three or
four days without bowel movements you are
likely constipated. That's when it hurts to go,
and when you produce hard and dry stools.
This is a very common problem and you likely
won't die from it, but you can get yourself into
trouble if your bowels don't move regularly.
Medical people used to advise eating your
bran or cornflakes to stay regular. Now they
are realizing that a simple leftover like cold
potatoes helps keep you regular. So instead of
carrying a doughnut to school for your lunch or
snack, consider a spud.

You can get stopped up from sitting at a
computer for too long or from generally being
inactive. Also from not drinking enough fluids
or not eating properly. As hard as it is to hear
this, know that junk food and rich food are not
your friends if you are constipated. Get your
act together and your digestive system will
thank you. Continue to have problems, and you
could have them for the rest of your life. Have
a glass of water, an apple or a couple of prunes!
And relax; it will all come out nicely.

65.

Why do I get an ice cream headache when I eat ice cream too fast?

Some people call an ice cream headache a "brain freeze." Whatever you call it, about a third of the population gets this annoying blast of pain in the brain. It is what is called a referred pain, where you *feel* the pain somewhere apart from where you are *receiving* the pain. Why this happens isn't conclusive, but when affected people eat really cold food or drink extremely cold drinks, the nerves that travel to the brain seem to be stimulated by the cold touching the top of the mouth. Then the blood vessels in the front of your head do a quick expansion/contraction dance to give you a sharp headache. (It's not really your brain, but *brain freeze* sounds better.) The way it happens feels a bit like a migraine headache, but luckily an ice cream headache goes away just as fast as it comes on. And here is a fascinating tidbit: about 90% of people who get migraines also get ice cream headaches.

A brain freeze isn't anything to be concerned about, but is a weird feeling nonetheless. Don't like it? Slow down when you are eating or drinking anything really cold, or keep the food or drink far from the back of your palate, and you should avoid the whole phenomenon.

Did men really wear high heels?

and Other Strange Facts About CLOTHES

66.

Why is it impolite for boys and men to wear a hat indoors, but not for a woman?

It's all about history. These days, some students may wear hats to school — it is up to the individual school district. But wearing hats indoors has been mostly limited to women.

A lot of the hats we wear are functional — to keep our ears warm, or to keep the sun off. Sometimes hats are simply a fashion statement: "I am conventional," or "I am flamboyant." Then there are the hats that are symbols of something else. Think about it — anyone with power tends to wear a head covering, and any ceremony usually involves hats. Queens and kings wear hats. The military, ministers and rabbis, brides and graduates wear symbolic head coverings (although throughout history it was more common than now). Hats were also symbols of class and status. Up until the eighteenth century most of the posing to do with hats was a male game. Think of Napoleon Bonaparte. He had a hat that said, "Look at me, I have an important position!"

Since men wore hats for symbolic reasons, they have also had most of the rules about manners pointed at them. The rules have traditionally said that men must always take off their hats when they come indoors unless it is a place of worship where you must have your head covered.

Why? Part of this is also about men and their tendency, historically, to fight. If you uncovered your head, it showed respect. A knight would doff his helmet to show he relied on the protection of his host as long as he remained under his host's roof. A king expected knights to show respect for the throne by uncovering their heads when he arrived. It showed the chain of power — only the king didn't doff. Women have always had more leeway because women have been more peaceable.

The biggest rule for either male or female: Don't wear your hat in a theatre and block the view of others!

67.

Why are wedding rings worn on the third finger of the left hand?

Marriage is a downright prehistoric tradition. Wedding rings date from ancient Egypt. It was thought that there was a vein of blood running from the third finger of the left hand directly to the heart, called *vena amoris* or the vein of love. So the wedding ring should be worn on that love finger.

Why wear rings at all? The ring is a never-ending circle, a simple, unbroken band that is meant to signify the continuity of your love, even after death. The Egyptians wore rings made of bone, ivory, reeds or leather. Nowadays most of us wear rings of gold or silver, and diamonds or other gems are often inset into women's engagement or wedding bands.

68.

Is it true that men were the first to wear high heels?

Yes, it is true. You wouldn't believe what men used to wear on their feet. Men's shoes today are truly boring. Back in the twelfth century, in Europe, men wore shoes called *crackows* or *poulaines,* with long pointed toes. Sometimes the wealthy wore these shoes up to 60 cm long, although the average citizen only wore 15-cm points. These shoes were made of soft leather, so wooden clogs called pattens were worn below the shoes to protect them.

Then about four hundred years later shoe styles for both men and women went to low-cut, square-toed slippers. People got crazy with the toes, rolling them back and even slashing the leather to show the coloured lining. The toes got so wide that a law came out to limit the size.

High heels came in during the late sixteenth century. It was Louis XIV of France who really popularized them. He was a short monarch who wanted to be taller. (Even today a curved heel is called a French, or Louis, heel.) These were floppy shoes with square toes and long tongues, fastened with buckles or big bows. Men also wore wide-topped boots that were soft leather, and often shoes with really loose lacy hose. If you can picture the cat in *Puss in Boots,* that's the kind of boots we're talking about.

Shoemakers moved on to using stiffer leather in the eighteenth century so they could make higher boots, and high-heeled buckled shoes with pointed toes. The middle of the nineteenth century saw shoes beginning to be mass-manufactured, making them affordable to the general public. Mass manufacturing also meant shoes weren't as specialized anymore, and men's shoes today are certainly not as fancy as they once were.

69.

Why are my jeans more comfortable than anything else I wear?

Blue jeans started out back in the 1870s as clothing for miners and cowboys in the United States. Here's how it happened. Levi Strauss followed the miners to California during the big gold rush, thinking he would sell them tent canvas. He quickly found out there was a much greater need for sturdy work pants, so he used the heavy fabric for what he called "waist overalls" or "great pants." These pants were good for work wear because they were strong and long lasting. Levi Strauss also figured out how to rivet the corners of pockets so that they couldn't rip.

Eventually the fabric for the pants changed to blue denim. Some say it's called denim because it is the serge or strong twill fabric from Nîmes, France, or in French: *de Nîmes. De Nîmes* became *denim*. Eventually Strauss dyed the denim blue, and the name "great pants" or *genes* became *jeans*. But jeans were still practical, not cool. Cool came along in the 1950s as movie actors James Dean, Marlon Brando and others wore blue jeans.

So the cool, the young and the rebels began
to wear jeans, and now everyone does. Why?
The sturdiness means that once you have a pair
broken in, you know that these pants aren't
going to wear out right away. Unlike other
clothes that get washed out and limp as they get
older, denim gets softer and more comfortable
the more you wash and wear it, because of the
flexible properties of the twill weave. The colour
gets nicer as it fades, too. No wonder jeans are
everyone's favourite clothes.

70.

Why did women wear white gloves for formal occasions?

Gloves have been around for a long time.
It makes sense. Your hands get cold, or need
protection from heavy work, so you cover them.
Gloves have been found in an Egyptian tomb
from around 1350 B.C.

By the Middle Ages (the fifth to fifteenth
centuries) gloves went from purely functional
to highly decorative, and were worn by royalty,
the rich, the powerful and church officials.
More functional armoured gloves were worn for
hunting or fighting. In the thirteenth century
women began wearing ornamental elbow-length
gloves.

A whole language of symbolism started
to develop around gloves. If you threw down
a glove, it challenged someone to battle. If a
knight or soldier picked it up, the challenge was
accepted. If you gave someone a folded glove, it
meant you would carry out a contract in good
faith. A lady often gave a glove as a love token.

Since gloves were most often given as gifts, they were high-status objects and often, in the Elizabethan era, they were held, not worn.

Then the white glove thing got started. By the nineteenth century wearing white gloves was considered proper for ladies, in order that their hands would not touch others', particularly those of men, when shaking hands, dancing and so on. White gloves were part of formal wear. Because white gloves are hard to keep clean, they indicated a woman of superior social class, a woman who probably didn't do her own cleaning — she was above that, and could go around wearing white gloves.

Although gloves used to be worn for all formal occasions, you rarely see them anymore as part of a dressed-up outfit.

71.

How did it come about that men wore pants and women wore skirts? Didn't "cave people" all dress alike?

It's about function, purely and simply. Long past the cave men's times, men and women both wore a form of skirt. Egyptian men wore a form of loin skirt. Romans wore tunics and togas. These are all variations on a basic wrapped cloth. Men continued wearing various forms of "skirts" or robes, short or long, well into the fifteenth century.

Of course there are exceptions, which are mostly about work and labour divisions. Since Roman times, men figured out that although robes and skirts were comfortable and simple, they weren't very practical. The custom of men wearing pants had to do with their work roles as soldiers, nomads, farmers, riders and hunters. (An exception to this involves Scottish men wearing kilts — heavy wool skirts — for everything.)

In some societies there was also a keen interest in keeping women unable to work or fight. Women's wearing of trousers is a fairly recent innovation in most cultures — less than sixty years in most places.

Why didn't women get trousers? There is a practical answer to this question. A skirt or "dress" is easy to make — two flat pieces of fabric with two simple seams. Even easier, a sarong or toga is just a woven piece of fabric that's then wrapped around the body. Trousers are much more difficult to sew than dresses, so they were only made when needed for men's work. In fact, a lot of men today who sit at desks or who do jobs that aren't physically strenuous might be quite happy to wear a robe or skirt if that fashion ever came back!

Why do women's blouses open on the opposite side from men's shirts?

Women's button right over left, men's left over right. But why? There are loads of theories, but no absolute answer. Of course these theories all favour right-handed people or at least acknowledge that more people are right- than left-handed.

Originally all clothes hooked or clasped or

buttoned right over left (the women's way). Then something happened to make men's closures go the other way. Buttoning left over right is supposed to be easier for right-handed people. History says that a man could adjust his shirt (or pants) with the left hand while keeping the right hand warm in his pocket. That left his right hand free to grab the sword that he wore on his left side. It's all about self-defence — and it has carried on. Women's clothing stayed with the original right-over-left method.

There is also a theory that had something to do with women and their dressers. No, not the dressers that you put clothes in, but the personal maid who would help you dress. If you are standing in front of someone and buttoning them up, it is easier to button from right to left, so according to this theory, that is why women's clothes button the way they do.

Another theory is that women would carry children in their left arm and use their right hand to unbutton their blouses for breast-feeding. But since women nurse their babies from both breasts, this theory doesn't hold up.

Can humans spontaneously combust?

and Other Weird But COOL STUFF

Can humans really spontaneously combust?

First things first. What exactly is spontaneous human combustion? It's when someone literally burns up for no obvious reason. You've probably seen something like it on TV shows.

But does it really happen? Over the last four hundred years, there have been more than two hundred cases reported. Charles Dickens even wrote about spontaneous human combustion in 1853 in his book *Bleak House.*

Most of the reported cases seem to involve old people living in England — the sort who sit around in armchairs a lot. Reports usually describe the bodies as being very badly destroyed. In some cases there may be a limb or two left intact — a hand or maybe a foot. Sometimes there might even be a slipper still on the foot. Apparently, spontaneous combustion leaves behind a greasy-smelling sooty mess, but causes no damage to items right near the body. If someone were sitting in a chair in front of the television, the person would be a pile of soot. However, the television and the chair would be fine except for the burn mark on the seat of the chair. Go figure.

It's pretty gross and pretty unbelievable, but reports keep coming in. What people can't figure out is whether a fire has somehow been set outside the body. Scientists figure that there must be a cigarette or a fireplace accident that sets people on fire. True believers say otherwise. However, you should know that people rarely actually see spontaneous human combustion happen — just what's left behind.

74.

Do eelskin wallets really demagnetize credit cards?

I hate to be the bearer of bad news, but this is an urban myth (something everyone regards as true, but really isn't). It is widespread, but a myth nonetheless. Eelskin does come from eels, but the skin doesn't have anything to do with electricity. Muscles make eels "electric," and when the eel dies, the electricity dies too.

There are two magnetic forces present in many wallets. A bank or credit card has a magnetic strip, a fine layer of oxide with tiny tracks on it like a computer disc. Information such as a person's name and account number is digitally encoded in that strip. The other magnet is on the magnetic clasp on the wallet. Eelskin leather is so delicate that manufacturers almost always use magnets rather than snaps for the wallet clasps. When a credit card magnet runs across the strong magnet in the clasp, that reaction wipes out the information on it. Banks hear about this a lot. The bank will tell you to get a plastic sleeve to store your cards in so that the magnetic areas don't touch, or to get a new wallet.

Sometimes though, you will hear about cards being demagnetized in wallets with no magnetic clasp. It could be just wear and tear on the cards, but there is a new theory. Korea has over-fished the eels whose skins are used for wallets. The eels used to be 10 by 60 cm, but now they are pencil-sized. It costs the same to tan the small skins as the large ones, so now tanners also use the huge hagfish, or slime eel. (It is called that because it has big pores that ooze slime and oil.) The theory is that hagfish, even after tanning, secrete slime. Maybe that slime demagnetizes cards. This is one theory. Another is that metallic residue left over from the tanning process could be causing the reaction.

75.

What's the story on the yo-yo?

Yo-yos were invented in China around 1000 B.C. A yo-yo was a simple spinning toy made of two ivory disks and a silk cord. Yo-yos were also around in ancient Greece. A Greek vase that dates to 500 B.C., in the Berlin Museum, shows a painting of a boy playing with a yo-yo. There are workable yo-yos in the National Museum in Athens that are made from joined ceramic discs.

That's not all. In the Philippines, yo-yos were used as weapons as far back as prehistoric days. The yo-yo was made of heavy hunks of flint attached to long leather thongs. The hunter would wait in a tree for his prey to pass by. He either knocked it out with the yo-yo, or tangled the thong around the animal's neck like a bola. If he missed he could try again because the yo-yo came back.

Yo-yos were also popular in the 1790s in Europe. There are paintings of monarchs like England's young King George yo-yoing, for example. Adults loved yo-yos, and there were clubs that staged contests. Back then yo-yos were called *emigrette* or *joujou*. The English called them *incroyable, bandolore*, quiz or Prince of Wales's toy. *Joujou* might be where yo-yo comes from, although it is also the word for "come back" in Tagalog, the language of the Philippines.

Yo-yos came to North America in 1866, but it wasn't until Donald F. Duncan saw them in 1928 that the yo-yo craze took off. Duncan hired incredible champions who went to schoolyards and neighbourhoods to demonstrate the yo-yo and its charms. There were competitions and prizes, championship arm patches and tin pins. The heyday of yo-yoing was the Depression. Because the toys were inexpensive, it was the perfect pastime. Even now there are freelance yo-yo pros around the world. Get practising!

16.

How does a lava lamp work?

You mean how do you get those big globs of goo slowly moving around inside glass globes filled with coloured liquid? A lava lamp works in mysterious ways.

Craven Walker invented lava lamps or lights in England in 1963. First he called it an animated motion mood lamp. Then he showed it at a trade fair in 1965 as the Astrolight. Adolph Wertheimer, a clever entrepreneur, bought the American manufacturing rights and started to manufacture them as TV lights — sort of an adult night light. The ads said: "A motion for every emotion." It sounds corny now, but in 1965 the Age of Aquarius folks were very keen for things psychedelic.

So what is that floating goop? It's a wax mixture. The lamp works like this: A 40 watt bulb heats the liquid and the waxy glob expands until it becomes less dense than the liquid surrounding it. (Less dense means the wax will float and rise.) When the globs get to the top of the globe, farther from the heat source, the wax cools again, contracts, gets heavy and starts to sink. The cycle repeats as the wax gets light and rises, gets heavy and sinks. Because of the nature of the waxy substance, as well as floating and sinking it also changes shape at the same time.

Of course it isn't as simple as just wax and water. There are apparently eleven secret ingredients mixed in vats in the Chicago manufacturing plant. They are carefully matched so that the wax doesn't break up into tiny bits and stay that way. You could say that the "glob factor" is the key to a great lava lamp.

What is Prince William's favourite colour?

Here are some facts about, Prince William you may not know.

⊚ He was born June 21, 1982, at 9:03 p.m. at St. Mary's Hospital in Paddington, London, which makes his birth sign Cancer. Weight at birth: 3.43 kg.

⊚ His royal title is His Royal Highness the Duke of Cambridge. When he was born it took a few days for his parents to name him, so he was referred to as the Prince of Wails.

⊚ He is sometimes called the Earl of Strathearn while in Scotland, and Baron Carrickfergus while in Northern Ireland.

⊚ His full name is William Arthur Philip Louis Mountbatten Windsor. His actual last name should be Schleswig-Holstein-Sonderburg-Glucksburg-Saxe-Coburg-Gotha. However, the Queen decreed that royal descendants would take the name Windsor.

⊚ Childhood nicknames: Wills, Willy Wombat, His Naughtiness, William the Terrible, Billy the Basher. Other nicknames have been Billy the Fish (after a comic book character), Dreamboat Willy and His Royal Sighness.

⊚ He is second in line to the throne of England, after his father, Prince Charles.

⊚ He has an English cocker spaniel called Lupo.

⊚ At 15, Prince William ranked No. 1 on the men's list in the annual International Best-Dressed Poll.

⊚ And, last but not least, blue and dark green are his fave colours.

His Royal Sighness

Billy the Basher

18.

What if someone was born on February 29. Would they be a year old in four years, or do they celebrate their birthday on March 1?

It seems that if you are a "leap day" baby, things could go a few different ways for you. Likely, your pals and brothers and sisters will tease you about not having a birthday three out of four years. But it can work in your favour, since leap day babies still tend to celebrate their birthdays, but on either February 28 or on March 1. When there is a leap year they have a major blowout on February 29.

But why do we have a leap year at all? It's about leftovers — leftover time, to be exact. It takes a day for the Earth to spin once on its axis. And it takes a year to go around the sun. Actually, 365 days, 5 hours, 48 minutes and 45 seconds. Julius Caesar decided that a correction was needed, so every four years we add one day to our year to use up these extra minutes — that's where the leap day comes in.

Knowing this, you can figure out that you have a 1 in 1461 (365 + 365 + 365 + 366) chance of being a leap day baby. And if you are, here's how to figure out if this is your year: You get a birthday if the year is divisible by 4, and not divisible by 100 unless it is also divisible by 400. So 2000 was a leap year, but 2100 won't be.

But February 29 has special significance even if you weren't born that day. It's also known as Sadie Hawkins' Day, the day when women can propose marriage to men. In former times, it was always the man who proposed to the woman, or to her parents.

For at least four hundred years, apparently, European folk custom has said that a woman may propose marriage in a leap year. If the man should refuse the offer, he has to give a consolation prize of a silk gown.

Where did that idea come from? There are a few theories. The best one is the legend that St. Patrick originated the custom back in the fifth century, when both priests and nuns were allowed to marry. On behalf of her fellow nuns, the powerful abbess St. Bridget complained to St. Patrick that the nuns could not pop the question to their admirers. The two saints arrived at a compromise, whereby every fourth year the sisters would have the chance to propose. (Patrick refused the offer, but gave Bridget the gown.)

So that's the notion for this turnaround in the male-female roles, but that doesn't explain about Sadie Hawkins or about February 29 specifically.

Sadie Hawkins was a cartoon character in a strip called "L'il Abner" by Al Capp. She was the daughter of Dogpatch mayor Hekzebiah Hawkins. Sadie was unmarried, so to find her a husband, her father gathered a group of bachelors together, then got them to start running. Moments later, Sadie set out after them, caught a man, and married him. The other unmarried Dogpatch women thought it was such a great plan that Sadie Hawkins' Day became an annual event. College and high-schools students in the U.S. picked up the idea after the strip ran in 1937, and started having Sadie Hawkins' dances (and dressing up as hillbillies), around the first Saturday after November 11, the day appointed by Mayor Hawkins.

Eventually, St. Patrick's fifth-century custom got mixed in with Al Capp's cartoon spinoff, and February 29 — the day women could propose to men — ended up as Sadie Hawkins' Day, even though it probably *ought* to be called St. Bridget's Day.

And about your age if you're a leap year baby? There's no law, so you can say whatever you want, that you're turning three or twelve.

79.

What is the typical amount of water it takes to put out a house fire?

It turns out that this is a question that highly skilled practitioners and engineers in the fire industry have spent years trying to figure out. There is no typical amount of water, because there is no typical fire. According to John Vokes, former Director of the Fire and Safety Division of the Justice Institute of B.C., fires vary depending on a number of factors:

- what the house is made of, and its design
- how long the fire was burning — and how hot it got — before someone tried to put it out
- how much oxygen (needed for the burning process) is getting to the fire
- the flammability of material on walls, floor and ceiling
- whether there are sprinklers at work
- the presence and flammability of fuel and other materials near the fire
- the method of and type of equipment used to apply water to the fire

To put it another way, it may take under 10 L of water to extinguish a small fire in a 108-square-metre house if the firefighters catch it after only two minutes of burning. But it might take close to 10,000 L to extinguish the fire if it is allowed to burn in the same house for twenty minutes.

Of course the question of how much water is needed to extinguish a fire is particularly important to rural communities with volunteer fire departments, where the response time can be longer.

80.

What is the world's circumference?

The first person to figure out the circumference of the Earth was Eratosthenes (276–195 B.C.). He was a Greek mathematician and scholar who ran the Great Library at Alexandria. Today he is known as the "father of geography."

Here is the amazing way he figured out the calculation. Eratosthenes read about a deep well in Cyrene (now called Aswan) in southern Egypt, a well that was entirely lit up by the sun at noon, just once a year. He knew that this would only happen when the sun was directly overhead. He also knew that on the day when this happened in Cyrene, the sun was not directly overhead at the same time in Alexandria, because at that exact time in Alexandria, vertical objects cast a shadow. So at the time that the well in Cyrene was completely lit, Eratosthenes measured the shadow cast by a pole in Alexandria. Using his knowledge of geometry, and knowing the distance between Alexandria and Cyrene, he determined that the circumference of the Earth was 250,000 *stadia*. (A *stadion* was the commonly used measure of length in the ancient world. Professional pacers were hired to walk from one place to another while counting their steps.) Eratosthenes's calculation translates to about 40,000 km — a figure that's remarkably close to the Earth's actual circumference at the equator, which we now know is 39,842 km.

81.

Why did people bind their feet?

The Chinese custom of binding feet —
where the mother, sister or nurse of a girl aged
three to five would wrap her feet tightly so
they wouldn't grow naturally — was around
for about a thousand years. A 3-metre-long
bandage was used to wrap the foot tightly,
bending the toes over and breaking the bones,
eventually forcing the ball of the foot closer to
the heel. Over time the toes were permanently
bent in toward the foot. In the era of foot
binding, it was desirable to have feet that were
shorter than 10 cm when full-grown. These tiny
feet were called "golden lotus" or "lily feet."

Binding made a girl more "valuable" as a
wife because such tiny feet were thought to be
dainty, elegant and a sign of good breeding —
much the same way that the wearing of tight,
confining corsets by Western women from the
1500s to the 1900s was thought to be elegant
and attractive. Many poor people did not bind
their daughters' feet because they could not
afford to have women who could not walk and
do work.

There are a couple of stories about how this
custom started in China. One is that it began
in the eleventh century when the emperor's
daughter was born with deformed feet. To be
sure that the girl would not be embarrassed,
the emperor decreed that only women with
small feet were desirable. As a result, women
began to bind their feet to make them as small
as possible. The other story is that it started in
the tenth century when girls wanted to imitate
the emperor's concubine (his second wife), who

was required to dance with her feet bound.

Either way, having bound feet meant that the girl would have a lot of trouble walking. She would have to take very tiny steps, and often needed to have a servant or a cane to help her keep her balance. The gait of girls with bound feet was called the "willow walk." Often women with bound feet were confined to their homes, since walking was so painful.

Special shoes called "lotus slippers" had soft soles and a soft padded upper that covered the whole foot. Women spent hours embroidering the slippers, and they were kept spotlessly clean and were often perfumed — partly because bound feet stank under all those wrappings. You can see these slippers in many museum collections.

The practice of foot binding was officially banned in 1911, but it carried on for a number of years after that. There are still a few very elderly women living who have bound feet.

82.

Why are the keys on the keyboard not in alphabetical order?

You've probably only ever used a computer or cellphone keyboard/keypad, so this will take some imagination. The first keyboards were on typewriters. They were designed so that each letter was on the end of a separate bar of metal. As you hit the key, the metal bar swung forward and hit the sheet of paper, placing the inked letter where you wanted it.

The first keyboards were arranged in a logical way — alphabetically. However, we use some letters more than others. Often-used letters close to each other would jam each time their swinging bars collided. No one could pick up any speed, making typing a very frustrating process.

Christopher Sholes patented what is close to the current typewriter in 1868. (The first recorded patent for a typewriter was granted to Henry Mill, a British engineer, in 1714, but it was nowhere near as practical as Sholes' design.) In 1872 Sholes went back to the drawing board. He figured out which letters were used the most, and rearranged the sequence on the keyboard, so that when you typed *ing* or *th* or any of the other common combinations of letters, the keys would be spread out in such a way that the metal bars would never jam. What he came up with is called the QWERTY keyboard, after the six letters in the top row, starting at the left.

It took a while for typists to catch on to the QWERTY keyboard, but it is the standard even today. There has been one significant attempt to replace the QWERTY keyboard. The Dvorak, named after August Dvorak, who taught education at the University of Washington, was invented in 1936. Dvorak decided that the middle row should contain the vowels for the left hand (*a, e, i, o, u*) and the most frequently used consonants for the right hand (*d, h, t, n, s*). He thought his set-up let typists go faster, but people complained that it was too much trouble to learn something new.

The QWERTY keyboard is pretty much the only part of a typewriter that is also part of a computer. We've come a long way since 1872.

◎ Mark Twain (who wrote *Tom Sawyer*) bought one of the earliest typewriters. He was the first American author to deliver a typewritten manuscript to a publisher: *Life on the Mississippi.*

◎ Using only the top row of the keyboard, you can type the word TYPEWRITER. Here are some more top row words: PROPRIETOR, REPERTOIRE, REPETITORY and PERPETUITY.

◎ The longest word which can be typed using only the fingers of the left hand is: AFTERCATARACTS. Slightly shorter words are: STEWARDESSES and REVERBERATED.

◎ The longest words which can be typed using only the fingers of the right hand are: JOHNNY-JUMP-UP, LOLLIPOP, POLYPHONY, NIMINY-PIMINY and HYPOPHYLLIUM.

◎ The longest word which can be typed using only the middle row is ALFALFAS.

◎ The following sentence uses every letter of the alphabet: "The quick brown fox jumps over the lazy dog."

◎ The letters used most often, in order, are: *e, t, o* and *s.*

◎ The letters used least often are: *h, j, x, z* and *q.*

83.

Why do bulls like red?

They don't, but they certainly fooled you.
It isn't the red at all. Bulls charge because the
matador is swinging the cape around, and bulls
have been trained to charge the cape. It's the
motion that gets them going, not the colour.

But let's go back a bit. What's with
bullfighting anyway? The first fight was in
Spain in 1133, honouring the coronation of King
Alfonso VIII. For about five hundred years this
wild spectacle was reserved for commemorating
big events or entertaining important guests.
Then it became more widespread and popular
with the common folk.

Slaying bulls has always been a
controversial practice. In the mid-1500s
Pope Pius V tried to stop bullfighting,
but he was ignored. It is still
popular in Mexico, which
is home to the largest
bullfighting ring in the
world.

One thing is clear.
You can't fight a bull
— it's going to win.
What the matadors
are trying to do
is avoid the beast
by using their wits,
grace and dexterity.
Which brings us back
to the red cape. In fact,
matadors often start
with a larger magenta
(pinkish-purple) and yellow

cape called a *capote*, and then go to a smaller red cape, the *muleta*. The cape is a moving target, which helps keep the bull (who has poor eyesight to start with) focussed. Of course, he is focussed on the cape that keeps moving, so the matador can manipulate the bull all over the place — specifically, away from his own body.

Why red? For the benefit of the fans. It stands out in contrast to the plainer colours of the ring, making it easy for the spectators to see the bullfighter. And the colour red excites people, so they enjoy the bullfight more if the matador swings a red cape.

84.

Why do most TV and radio stations start their names with a W or K?

In the U.S., "call letters" usually begin with W or K. In Canada they usually start with C. Why? There is an international treaty monitored by the International Telecommunications Union in Geneva, Switzerland, that specifies the first call letters for commercial broadcast stations in different countries: Mexico is X, for example, and Canada is C. This is how operators keep radio, TV, ship-to-shore and aircraft telecommunications straight. The U.S. uses K and W, although since they are so large geographically and have so many radio stations, they actually use A and N too. You would likely only run into call letters starting with N and A if you were involved with the navy and coast guard or amateur radio.

In 1934 the U.S. Communications Act

stated that broadcasters west of the Mississippi River use K call signs, and those east of the Mississippi use W. There are a few exceptions to this rule, as some radio stations were in business before 1934, like KYW in Philadelphia, KDKA and KDQ in Pittsburgh, and WHO in Des Moines.

Before 1912, radio stations could use any call sign they wanted. A few of the surviving three-letter call signals were from the days before the call-sign legislation, when stations came up with their own names. In Chicago, WGN was first owned by the *Chicago Tribune* Newspaper and stands for "World's Greatest newspaper." WLS, for "World's Largest Store," was owned by Sears Roebuck.

Armed with this knowledge, you can usually figure out airplane and boat registration too, since they use the same first letters as the broadcasters.

85.

Why are barns red?

Because other barns are red. That's a dopey answer, but it is partially true. The truth is that the first barns weren't painted at all. Most farmers couldn't afford paint, and besides, they thought it was showy and just not done. But in the late nineteenth century, farmers started painting their barns a dark red. No one knows exactly why, but likely the best theory is that red oxide is quite inexpensive, and could be mixed with milk or linseed oil to make red paint. The red oxide pigments came from Binney & Smith (the Crayola people), who have always been in the colour business. Of course, paint helps preserve wood — that would appeal to the thrifty farmers. And the red looks so good with the green fields. Once red was established as the barn colour, paint manufacturers took off with it.

Not all barns are red, actually. Sometimes they are white, green, blue or grey. The colour tends to depend on the area, as folks do what their neighbours do, or what their ethnic tradition suggests. In some parts of central Kentucky, barns and fences and other farm buildings are black. That came from using lampblack and diesel fuel. (It's a really cheap wood preservative, but imagine the smell — and don't light a match!)

86.

Why does the water in the toilet flush the opposite way in Australia? What would happen if you flushed it right on the equator?

Time out. Toilets, sinks and bathtubs don't necessarily drain the opposite way south of the equator. It's a widespread myth that they do, because of the Earth's rotation. (An episode of *The Simpsons* was even devoted to the topic.) But it is a myth. Check out sinks and toilets and bathtubs around you. They all drain slightly differently, because of several reasons — the way they were manufactured, how the water squirts into the bowl, and the way the drain is shaped — *not* because of the rotation of the Earth. This is true in both hemispheres and on the equator.

Okay, why would we think they drain

differently in the first place? Because of what is called the Coriolis force. The rotation direction of hurricanes, for example, depends on the Coriolis force, among other natural forces. These forces make very large things like cyclones, hurricanes, tornadoes and even ocean currents spin counter-clockwise in the Northern Hemisphere and clockwise in the Southern Hemisphere. The Coriolis Force doesn't affect the drainage in your tub, sink or toilet, though, because the drainage action lasts such a short time.

The word "john" for toilet may date back as far as fifteenth-century England. Instead of outhouse they called it Jack's house or Jake's house. It could also be called Cousin John's, then just john.

87.

How does the non-stick surface stick to the pan?

When you paint a smooth surface you have to rough it up a bit with sandpaper to get the paint to stick. It's a similar principle with pans. The first non-stick pans were made either by blasting the pan with grit to make little pits in the aluminum, or by spraying it with some kind of a lumpy coating. This gave the non-stick stuff something to cling to.

But it was still hard to get the non-stick stuff to stick, and it was very easy to damage the pan's surface with a fork or other metal tool. Also, after a while the non-stick stuff would start to peel off. So the manufacturers tried adding a sticky molecule to the non-sticky molecule and applying this to the pitted pan first, as a primer. Then a coat of non-sticky stuff was put over that, and finally another layer of non-stick with some kind of "toughener" was put on the top to protect the non-stick layer. Lots of non-stick pans are still made this way.

Teflon was DuPont's original brand name for the non-stick coating. Roy J. Plunkett, a chemist, discovered this tetrafluoroethylene resin accidentally in 1938. It was very heat-tolerant, and so slippery that virtually nothing would stick *to* it or be absorbed *by* it. DuPont registered the name Teflon in 1945. Today there are Plunkett Awards given for "innovation with Teflon."

DuPont later came up with a new way — called "smooth technology" — to get the Teflon to stick to the pan. The pan is not pitted first. Instead, a new kind of sticky molecule is used that can "lock" itself to the smooth pan. This lets the next layers fuse together better, so that the pan is more durable. However, metal tools and high heat (which softens the non-stick molecules) are still the enemies of non-stick pans.

Some authorities claim that parakeets and other small birds can be harmed by exposure to fumes from heated non-stick pans, so don't hang your budgie cage near the stove — for more than one reason.

Teflon is one of the few substances the human body doesn't reject, so it is used in making heart pacemakers, artificial eyes, substitute bones and replacement hip and knee joints. It has also been used in outer space on electrical wires, nose cones, fuel tanks, and the outer skins of spacesuits to shield them against the heat of the sun.

88.

What is that swirly thing at the barber's shop, the one with red and blue and white stripes that twirl?

The short answer is that it's called a barber pole, but how it came to be is the interesting part. When you go to get your hair cut, how would you feel about having a tooth pulled out at the same time? For six centuries in Europe, that is exactly what could happen, because barbers could practise surgery too. They were

called barber surgeons, and by 1361 they had their own religious guild (like a professional association), which became a trade guild by 1462. The barbers' and surgeons' guilds didn't separate until 1745. Barber surgeons did a lot of bloodletting in those days.

And what exactly is bloodletting? It used to be prescribed for lots of diseases, even for fevers or hemorrhaging (internal bleeding). Be glad you live in our times. Barbers got into the bloodletting business in 1163 when the Pope decided that the monks had to stop doing it.

And here's where the barber pole comes in. It symbolizes that bloodletting business. The patients would get a strong grip on a staff or pole, to make their veins stick out, then (among other methods) the barber would attach leeches to the person, and catch the blood in a basin. Then they'd bandage up the patient with strips of linen.

Believe it or not, those bloody bandages would often be hung outside on the staff to advertise the barber surgeon's practice. They would twirl in the wind, inspiring the spiral pattern of red and white that was eventually painted on poles to advertise the barber business. The first poles even had a leech basin on top, which eventually became the ball. Blue was sometimes added to red and white on the poles, perhaps representing the blue veins along with the red blood and white bandages.

89.

What is the highest number?

The very biggest number that actually has a name is googolplex. One googol is 1 followed by 100 zeros, or 10 to the 100th power or 10^{100}.
If you write it out it looks like this:
10,000,000,000,000,000,000,000,000,000,000,
000,000,000,000,000,000,000,000,000,000,000,
000,000,000,000,000,000,000,000,000.
Edward Kasner, an American mathematician, popularized the term googol in 1938. His eight-year-old nephew came up with the name googol when his uncle asked him to make up what he thought a huge number would be called.

Kasner came up with googolplex too. It is 10 to the googol in power, or 10 followed by a googol zeros: $10^{10^{100}}$. Printing that out would take up the rest of this book, so we won't.

Useful Facts
The number 1,000,000,000,000,000 is called different names in different countries. Here's how it works in North America.
1,000 is one thousand.
1,000,000 is one million.
1,000,000,000 is one billion.
1,000,000,000,000 is one trillion.
1,000,000,000,000,000 is one quadrillion.
1,000,000,000,000,000,000 is one quintillion.

But that's the largest *named* number. The truth is, there is no largest number, because whatever number you can get up to (say a septillion) you can always add 1 . . . then 1 more . . . then 1 more . . .

The British officially adopted the "American" system, known as Short Scale, in 1974. Formerly, one billion in Britain was one million millions, which today is called one trillion. Some parts of the world still use the "old British" system, kown as Long Scale.

There's no such thing as a "zillion." It's just slang for a really big number. Now you can use more precise names!

Name That Number

- **sextillion:**
1,000,000,000,000,000,000,000
- **septillion:**
1,000,000,000,000,000,000,000,000
- **octillion:**
1,000,000,000,000,000,000,000,000,000
- **nontillion:**
1,000,000,000,000,000,000,000,000,000,000
- **decillion:**
1,000,000,000,000,000,000,000,000,000,000,000

90.

Why is it called WD-40?

WD-40 is slippery stuff that solves a lot of problems — spray a little on your bike chain, or on a squeaky door hinge. It was called that because the folks at Rocket Chemical, a small company of only three employees that developed WD-40, got it right on the 40th try. WD stands for water displacement.

Why do people wear underwear?

and Other Crazy Facts About CUSTOMS

91.

Why do people wear underwear?

Basically, to cut down on laundry. It's just a layer between your skin and your clothes that helps keep your clothes clean. And it's not even a new idea. Loincloths are underwear, and they were popular in Crete 4000 years ago. It's hot there, so decorated loincloths were often the total outfit. There are also records of the Egyptians wearing material tied around the body, under their clothes, as far back as 3000 B.C. As time went on, women took to wearing short skirts as underwear, and around 200 A.D., the forerunner of the brassiere showed up, a sort of breast band, called a *strophium* or *mamillare*.

People didn't really call it underwear until 1879. In late 1849, Amelia Bloomer started *The Lily*, a newspaper designed to inform women about their rights. She supported the idea of wearing an outfit comprised of a skirt below the knee, with long, full, ankle-length pants or pantalettes underneath. Her aim was to free women from having to wear restrictive clothing. Eventually such pants were called "bloomers" despite the fact that the fashion was a failure at the time. Today some people call any baggy undies "bloomers." The garment that we now call women's underpants didn't really come along until the early 1900s.

Longjohns is a word that comes from the world of boxing. In 1889 John L. Sullivan, a boxer who always wore long underwear pants (or should we call them undershorts that were long?) became the last Bare-Knuckled Champion of the World. (Why bare-knuckled? His

75-round knockout of Jake Kilrain at Richburg, Mississippi, on July 8, 1889, was the last heavyweight title bout under the London Prize Ring — or bare-knuckle — rules.) Since John L. Sullivan was so famous, his underwear became known as John L's or Long John's, until they eventually lost the capitalization and became just longjohns.

Undershirts and tank tops were a big step for women's freedom from fashions like corsets — a tight-fitting support undergarment that included metal or whalebone "stays" (supports) that were laced up tight to narrow women's waists and "improve their figures." Such clothing wouldn't let women move or breathe freely or play sports easily. Less restrictive undergarments like undershirts came along in the mid 1800s — but for sports only. By 1900 there were fancier silk and lace versions for women, and plain shirts for men. By the 1930s the bra won out for women, and by the 1940s and 1950s it was mostly men who wore undershirts.

Nowadays there are boxer short styles for women, a fashion that dates back to times when women's undies were looser, not fitted as they are today.

Underpants are also called: skivvies, unmentionables, panties, bloomers, undies, knickers, drawers, gaunchies, step-ins, scanties, unwhisperables, small clothes, inside clothes and underpinnings.

92.

Why do they call T-shirts T-shirts?

Here's the answer: because they are shaped like a T. Today in the U.S. the T-shirt industry sells over $7 billion a year in printed T-shirts. They started out as underwear, but in the summer heat of World War I, American soldiers in Europe were allowed to wear lightweight undershirts as shirts. Compared to their hot wool uniforms, this seemed like a dream come true. By the time World War II came along, the T-shirt was the norm for the troops.

It took the movies to get the public involved. When John Wayne and Marlon Brando wore T-shirts in the movies in the early 1950s, the public was shocked. But in the 1955 movie *Rebel Without a Cause*, when James Dean — the coolest guy ever — wore a T-shirt under an open shirt, the world took notice and the fashion took off. Hippies in the 1960s took to tie-dyeing T-shirts, and as silk-screen processing became more advanced, printed shirts took off too. Nowadays T-shirts are everywhere, and everyone has a drawerful.

What kind of shirts do golfers wear? TEE shirts.

Here's an idea for saving your favourite-ever T-shirt: turn it inside out, and sew up the arm holes and the bottom. Then turn it right side out again, stuff it with polyester fibrefill and hand-stitch the neck closed. Now you've got a great pillow that carries your own memories, and is cozy to boot.

93.

Why do people clink glasses before they drink?

This custom comes from the days when folks — in particular, Greeks and Romans — didn't trust each other too much. In fact, toasting today is a custom that survives an ancient "mutual trust" ceremony. Poisoning was fairly common in those days. (Want to get ahead in the world? Knock off your opponent.) So here's how people made sure they would come out alive from a social event: pour a little of your wine into your fellow drinker's glass, and vice versa, to seal the deal. Since you'd each have part of the other's wine, there's no way you would poison *him* or he would poison *you*. This became such a custom that even friends would do it. And of course, when the wine exchanged glasses, they would clink a bit.

The early Christians made a custom of glass clinking. If you are giving someone good wishes and you both have a glass in your hand, you might as well *do* something with that glass. Besides, the Christians thought the clinking of the glasses sounded like church bells. Also, being superstitious, they felt the sound could

scare away the devil. So the clink "boosted" the good wishes. Along with your toast — "Cheers," "Here's mud in your eye," *"Skål,"* or whatever — you would clink your glasses together. The Christians called this "the kissing of glasses."

Why do guests clink glasses at a wedding reception to get the bride and groom to kiss? It's like a toast (a term that comes from when the Romans would flavour their drinks with spiced toast) but it's a shortened version. You can read about clinking/kissing in *The History of the Kings of Britain,* written by Geoffrey of Monmouth in 1137. Geoffrey writes about a banquet in 450 A.D. where it might have all started, but in a reverse sort of way. At that banquet King Vortigern kissed someone he was interested in marrying after he made a toast, and married her that evening. Now you have to wait for the reception to do the clinking/ kissing.

Here's "Here's to you!" or "To your health" in other languages:

British: *Cheers!*

Chinese: *Wen Lie!*

French: *A votre santé!*

German: *Prost!*

Greek: *Yasas!*

Hebrew: *L'Chayim!*

Hungarian: *Ege'sze'ge're!*

Gaelic: *Sláinte!*

Italian: *Alla Salute!*

Japanese: *Kanpai!*

Polish: *Na Zdrowie!*

Russian: *Za vashe zdorovye!*

Spanish: *Salud!*

Swedish: *Skål!*

94.

Why do people go all out for the sixteenth birthday and not the fifteenth or fourteenth? Shouldn't you celebrate the eighteenth birthday, for becoming an adult?

Throughout history, every culture has had its own way of marking the different stages in the life cycle. Sociologists and anthropologists call these rites of passage. The transition from childhood to adulthood is certainly a stage worthy of acknowledging and celebrating, but *when* to do it has varied greatly.

One example comes from the Jewish tradition. For Jewish boys, thirteen is the most important birthday. A Bar Mitzvah is held on the Sabbath nearest the day a boy turns thirteen. At this age, the boy is considered to be responsible for himself and his actions before God and his fellow man. Jewish girls have a similar ceremony, a Bat Mitzvah, on their twelfth birthday.

In England up to a few generations ago, and in France, nobles presented their daughters to the reigning monarch when they were about sixteen, to show they were old enough to become socially active — that is, marriageable.

In 1748 in the U.S., a similar ritual of presenting young women "to society" began with fifty-nine colonial Philadelphia families holding a "Dancing Assembly," which eventually became known as the "Debutante Ball." The "Deb" Ball was a chance for young women to be introduced into society — and to eligible young men from "good families." These balls were usually very elaborate, and extravagant gifts were showered on the young ladies.

The expression "Sweet sixteen and never been kissed" was tossed around with lots of giggles and blushing. But it was a serious thing. By the 1920s some families gave an extra present if the young woman could answer affirmatively. In some parts of the U.S. — even in a few places in Canada, such as military bases — debutante balls can still be an important part of a girl's life.

In Latin America girls look forward to their *fifteenth* birthdays. A girl's entrance into womanhood and her eligibility for marriage is celebrated at her *Quinceañera* (also known as the *Quince*, or *Quince Años*). In the beginning the *Quinceañera* symbolized a girl's time of renewed devotion to the church, but more recently it has been celebrated as the age at which she is old enough to begin dating. The event can be as elaborate as a wedding. Attendees wear gowns and rent formal wear, and there are limousines, photo sessions, catered dinners, dance parties and arranged flowers. This is a serious rite of passage to mark a special day in a girl's life.

As for when you become an adult, you can drive in most places at age sixteen. You can vote at age eighteen in many countries, although it is still age twenty in Japan. In Russia, people are issued an internal passport at age sixteen, to recognize that they are now considered adults. Still, it is more commonly believed that you have to be twenty-one to have reached maturity.

Why? Tradition. In Britain a person "comes of age" at twenty-one, and this has been the case since the Norman invasion in 1066. It is thought that this was because the thirteen- and fourteen-year-olds who had been going into battle were far too young. They didn't have the strength to wear armour or to carry a huge lance. Age nineteen was used next, but it was upped to twenty-one for reasons which seem really wacky today. In the days when a nineteen-year-old inherited property, it could take a couple of years to deal with the paperwork, so — according to one source — the age of maturity was bumped to twenty-one to make the legalities easier.

Birthday Facts

⊚ In ancient times a birthday was considered to be the only time a person could be helped by good spirits or harmed by evil ones. Relatives and friends would bring the birthday boy or girl good wishes, thoughts and gifts to ward off the evil spirits.

⊚ Birthday parties or *kinder feste* were invented in Germany. For that day the child was the centre of attention and got gifts from family and friends.

⊚ Ancient Greeks celebrated the birthday of Artemis, Goddess of the Moon, and likely invented the birthday cake by their custom of bringing cakes to her temple. The cakes were round, in the shape of the full moon, and were decorated with candles representing the moon's glow. We probably got the idea of making a wish and blowing out the candles from the time when people thought that the smoke from a fire could carry their prayers up to the heavens.

⊚ Driving away evil spirits was an ongoing theme. That's what birthday smacks, pinches, spanks or bumps are for. In Belgium this goes even further – the families of birthday children will sneak into their bedrooms in the morning and prick them with a needle. But the birthday kids better brave it out. Some believe that if they cry then, they will cry all year.

95.

Why were left-handed people considered "evil" and forced to become right-handed?

Weird, huh? Even the Latin word for left, *sinister*, now has an association with the words bad or evil. At one time everything left was considered bad. That is because it wasn't "right" — people thought it just wasn't natural. So it is very important to put your right foot forward when entering a house, going on stage, or starting to walk. Considering anything to do with the left hand as both unlucky and evil is one of those nasty blanket superstitions that's especially hard on the 10% of men and 8% of women who are left-handed.

Left-handers have an advantage when fighting, which might be why right-handers have been so suspicious of them. This goes way back to medieval times. The spiral staircases in castles back then would coil clockwise (going downstairs). The story goes that the direction was set so the knights defending the castle could easily swing their swords about when coming *down* the stairs, while the attackers would have a problem swinging their swords coming *up* the stairs. But wait . . . this worked only if both the attacker and the defender were right-handed. So if a lefty was attacking, he might win over a righty defending.

This lefty advantage carries on in sports today. Lefties do very well in sports where you confront your opponent face to face, as in fencing, tennis, boxing, cricket, ping-pong or baseball. Since so many people are right-handed, facing a lefty can throw them off their game.

96.

How come people who are in love always give chocolates, and why is chocolate associated with Valentine's Day?

Nobody ate chocolates until the nineteenth century, when a British chocolate maker figured out how to make chocolate smooth and velvety. As a drink though, it was hot stuff in Mexico and Spain. In 1519 when Cortés showed up in Mexico, he found the Aztec Empire run by Emperor Montezuma, who was probably the original chocoholic. Montezuma drank litres of it every day out of golden goblets. It was thicker than our hot chocolate, dyed red, and had a chili-pepper flavour.

Cortés conquered the Aztecs, but hated the chocolate drink until he took cacao beans back to Spain and figured out how to add sugar and spices instead of chili peppers.

So what's the connection with love? Montezuma believed that chocolate made him very appealing to his harem of wives, which likely started the rumour of chocolate's connection with love . . . and eventually associated it with the day that celebrates lovers, Valentine's Day.

It's actually a chemistry thing. Just like coffee and tea, chocolate can fool with your brain. The theobromine (giving a mild caffeine-like buzz) and the magnesium (which comes in some tranquilizers and calms you down) give the chocolate eater a pleasant sensation. Chocolate isn't proven to make you more ready for love, but it tastes great and makes you feel good. What more could anyone ask for?

97.

Why do people salute by putting their hands to their foreheads?

It is not entirely clear why, but there are some good theories. Back in ancient Europe it was common for people to carry arms or weapons. The custom was that men coming toward each other must lift their right hand to show that they had no intention of using their sword. That is likely how a number of friendly gestures got started, like tipping a hat, saluting, waving, or shaking the right hands. All of these gestures say: "This is peace, we're not going to fight you."

By the time of the Roman Empire, salutes were part of the whole formality of the military. The salute at that time involved putting your right hand up to shoulder height with the palm out. The head wasn't touched yet — it was just a sort of tight-elbowed wave.

When knights who were wearing steel armour would ride up to each other, if they recognized the other knight or just wanted to display friendship, they would raise their visors to expose their faces. The knights held the reins in their left hand and did the visor lift with their right hand.

One form of salute we still use is doffing your hat to a superior. The hand moves up to the vicinity of the hat, but the hat isn't actually removed.

In the military, a subordinate salutes an officer and the officer must then return the salute. It is all about respect and discipline. In the military, a salute is absolutely compulsory, unlike the common but non-compulsory custom of shaking hands among the general public.

A wave is a kind of salute, as is the thumbs-up gesture ("All is well" or "It's okay"). Doffing your hat, kissing a person's hand, kissing both cheeks, shaking a hand or curtsying are all forms of greetings or salutes. None of these have the stand-up-straight quality of the military salute though, which is most impressive to watch.

The military and scouts aren't the only ones who salute or make a salute-like greeting as a sign of respect. Martial artists commonly salute with a bow when greeting each other, as a mutual show of respect for each other's skills and abilities. That salute had a practical application too. Martial artists were very cautious in the old days, and a handshake or a raising of the hand was considered either too threatening or an invitation for attack. So the bow works.

98.

Why are there crescent moons on outhouse doors?

That's a good question. Why not full moons or stars or even square windows? The window is to let air and light in, obviously, and also for decoration. But why a crescent moon?

At one time the doors to women's rooms were marked with moons. This custom came from the Roman Goddess of the Moon, Diana, who wore a crescent moon in her hair. Men's rooms were marked with suns. So why not suns on outhouse doors? Maybe it's just that crescent moons are a whole lot easier to cut out than suns.

Maybe a better question is this: why are people so crazy about outhouses? Do we think outhouses are funny because we're glad we don't have to use them much? In most of North America you've usually got to go camping to find a real outhouse these days. In many other parts of the world indoor plumbing is not so common. If you ever travel to somewhere without flush toilet facilities, you might just have to try out the bare hole in a seat or bench. Remember, if someone directs you to the biffy, the backhouse, the johnny or the latrine, they're probably sending you to an outhouse.

There once was a fellow
named Hyde.
Who fell down a privy and died.
His unfortunate brother
Then fell down another
And now they reside side by side.

99.

What does the nursery rhyme Ring Around the Rosie mean?

Ring-a-ring o' roses
A pocket full of posies,
A-tishoo! A-tishoo!
We all fall down.

We've all heard this rhyme. It's sung to accompany one of the most popular nursery games — join hands, dance in a circle chanting this ditty, and you all fall down at the end. But what's it really all about?

The story goes that the "ring around the rosie" is about a rosy rash, a symptom of the Great Plague of London, which devastated the population of London, England, around 1665. Posies were the herbs that people carried to protect them from the Plague, and sneezing was the last symptom before they fell down dead.

Well, sorry to disappoint, but the rumour spreaders are reading a little more into it than is meant to be there. There are dozens of variations on this rhyme, all as full of nonsense as this one, so to say that it has deep meaning probably isn't so. It's just a game for circling and falling down, that's all.

Interview some kids and adults, and see how many of them "always believed" that that rhyme was about the Plague. Probably most of them will have bought into that particular tale.

100.

How did jumping rope originate?

It's an old game, perhaps even thousands of years old. There are drawings of rope makers in Egyptian tombs. They used the hemp plant, an herb with a stringy and tough stem, and twisted and twisted it to make it stronger. When people figured out how to make rope, they soon figured out that twirling a rope around and jumping over it was possible. Jumping rope was likely an adult's game at first. There is an ancient Greek statue of a maiden "skipping" with a vine rope. Then, when boys started to work at rope factories, they became the rope jumpers.

Double Dutch came along pretty early too. It just took two ropes being turned in two different directions. It is called different things in different places, including Double French, Double Irish, Double Orange and Double Rope.

The weird thing, from today's perspective, is that only in the last hundred years or so have girls been allowed to jump rope. It was solely a boy's game until then. Boys didn't sing while skipping, but did pepper, Double Dutch, and so on. Likely a big factor in letting girls play was the newer clothing designs that made moving around a lot easier. When girls started jumping rope, the boys stopped.

It was girls, though, who added all the songs. Many of them were originally clapping songs. Some books contain these songs, but mostly jump-rope rhymes get passed on orally over the years. This is partly because little girls really get into it before they can read much, so verses are memorized and passed on by word of mouth. Ask your mother for her favourites.

101.

Why do some people have a wake after a funeral?

Some wakes are wild, even drunken, parties that usually happen after a funeral. This kind of gathering is called a "wake" because that is another form of "watch." That is what many people did when someone died — the mourners would keep watch through the night. This custom has been around for hundreds of years.

Some people think that this kind of wake is in bad taste, and disrespectful to the person who has died. Others feel that when you are sad it is good to get together with others and mourn together. You can talk about the person who died, and party to celebrate his or her life. Wakes are particularly popular in Ireland, so people often call them an "Irish Wake."

The wake may come from a medieval custom called "rousing the ghost" that had mourners partying to test if the corpse was really dead. If that sounds bizarre, it was because sometimes, in the old days, keeping "watch" was to make sure the body didn't get buried unless it actually *was* dead. Remember, there weren't scientific instruments then to test whether a person was really dead. So the party was a send-off . . . unless it happened to "wake" up the dead if they were still alive!

102.

Why are boats and ships given female names?

Nowadays boats and ships aren't always given girls' names, but a boat or ship is mostly referred to as feminine. You always call it a "she," not a "he." That mostly dates back to ancient times. It has to do with the fact that the word for "ship" is a feminine word in most languages, like French or Latin. English nouns don't have this gender connection, but somehow Englishmen picked it up and it stuck. (Those female figureheads often seen on the prow of a ship were to frighten away evil spirits, by the way. They weren't connected to the name or gender issue.)

Naming boats has always been a bit tricky. In ancient times people believed that a name was an integral part of a ship, and if you changed that name, all sorts of nasty things might happen. The ship would be cursed. There are lots of stories about ships being lost or smashed after a name was changed. Since most ships were originally named after gods, changing the name would insult and anger that god as well as the sea gods. It is still considered to be unlucky, unless the ship's name changes when the boat gets a new owner.

The best names are easy to remember, easy to spell, easy to pronounce and mean something significant to the owners. Thirteen-letter names are unlucky, but if you can come up with a seven-letter name, you will have luck. Names with three *a*'s are considered good, especially ones like *Niagara* or *Arcadia,* since they have seven letters and three *a*'s.

Some of the most popular pleasure-boat names in the U.S. are *Odyssey, Serenity* and *Obsession*. Up there in the top ten are also *Escape, Therapy* and *Solitude*. These top names are all pretty serious. There are lots that are much sillier and more in the spirit of fun and boating. *Mama's Mink, Second Mistake, Branch Office, Fuelish Pleasure, Run Aground Sue, Slippery When Wet, Tooth Ferry, Aliens Ate My Buick, This Side Down* and *Never, Never Land* are but a few.

When you are naming your boat, keep in mind that some time you might have to call for help on the radio. So if your boat is called **None of Your Business, Scatterbrain** or **Hasty Banana**, you are going to sound like an idiot.

103.

Why do some women change their last names when they marry?

In our society, names have often been the property of men because it is usually fathers who give their surnames to their children. Traditionally, boys are supposed to bring honour to that name when they become men, as girls will exchange their names for their husbands'.

This ties in to women's position historically. Through much of history, women owned nothing, and were regarded as the property of their fathers — and after they married, of their husbands. But women have often preferred to be known by their own names. Many found that being called by their husband's name and "Mrs." made them feel invisible. Other women didn't mind at all.

Sometimes though, the man or society made the choice. If a woman called Mary Smith married John Brown she became Mrs. John Brown. There's not much of her left in that name. Mrs. Mary Brown was an improvement, but there were times when Mrs. John Brown was the only accepted form. Some women even "took on" their husband's profession, as with Mrs. Doctor John Brown.

Early feminists paved the way for the fairly common practice today of women choosing to keep their own names. The most famous was Lucy Stone, who retained her name when she married in 1855. Feminists were working on all kinds of other issues too — education, the vote, property rights, and the right to divorce. The Lucy Stone League was founded in 1921 in North America to encourage more women to follow her example. Prominent Lucy Stoners in the 1920s included Margaret Mead, Amelia Earhart and Edna St. Vincent Millay. There were some people doing this in the 1940s, but it has only been in the past forty years or so that the practice has become fairly common. The etiquette books reflect this too. *Emily Post* in 1922 says, "a wife always bears the name of her husband." The 1981 *The New Bride's Book of Etiquette* talks about how to keep using your own name for bank accounts and so on, if that is your choice.

The term "maiden name" is out of favour. "Birth name" or "woman's own name" is more proper. Today many women keep their names because their careers are under their own name, and it's easier for their professional lives. It used to be just movie stars who did that.

Many women have a deep emotional attachment to their names, so they don't want to take someone else's. This is totally a woman's choice, but that doesn't mean that people around her are always happy about it. Her in-laws, parents, friends and husband might have an opinion. Legally, in North America a woman has the right to change her name, and she has the right to not change her name.

Some modern women believe that even by keeping their own names they are identified with their fathers. They choose some new name of their own, usually one associated with their mothers, or some personally meaningful name.

Here's the big question: if women keep their own names, what do you name the children? Most give the father's name and more and more often the middle name is the mother's last name. Some double-barrel the two parents' names, like Jingleheimer-Schmidt. In the next generation or two it will be interesting to see what happens with children's surnames. Will names simply be added and added? How about McGillicuddy-Glockenspiel-Jingleheimer-Schmidt?

104.

Why are valentines heart-shaped and red, and why do they symbolize love?

That heart shape? It's questionable. That shape usually seen on valentines is similar to a real heart with the twin lobes of the atria — similar but not terribly close. Some artist has definitely played with that real heart, probably in the 1400s where it shows up as one of the suits on a deck of playing cards. Desmond Morris, the famous anthropologist, thinks it looks like stylized human buttocks, which apparently have romantic connections. Some think the top of the heart looks like women's breasts and that the narrow part at the bottom could be a tiny waist.

The redness of the valentine is likely associated with the colour of blood pumping through your heart. People who believe the theory that the heart is like a woman's breasts figure the red colour would have to be connected to a woman's lip colour.

A heart as the symbol for love has been around since at least the twelfth century. St. Valentine's Day has been a celebration of love since Roman times. Back then young people would gather together and each young man would get to draw a young lady's name. This couple were "valentines" for the year, and exchanged love tokens. This custom eventually transformed into love notes and cards passed around on February 14 to mark the day. The simple illustration of a heart would be an obvious adornment for such cards and letters.

Valentine cards were available for sale as early as 1800.

135

105.

Why do people get on a horse from the left side only?

They don't all the time, but most people mount from the horse's left side most of the time.

Many Western horses are trained to let you mount or dismount from either side. That's because there might be situations where you need to do that. Say you sprain your left ankle, or you are on a trail or a ridge where there is no room to mount on the left but there is room to mount on the right. It is smart to know how to mount from both sides.

Why this left/right thing? It is definitely geared toward the majority of the population who are right-handed, and it has historical roots in the military. Right-handed people are more comfortable using the right leg to swing over the horse. (Right-leggedness is the most common too.)

Another reason people mount horses from the left is because soldiers carrying swords could not mount from the right. Right-handed people wear the sword on the left side of the body. If you tried to mount the horse from the right side, your sword would be in your way.

We know much about horsemanship from the peoples of the East, such as Persia in the seventh century B.C. They started the custom of the approach (by grooms) and the mount and dismount (by cavalrymen) from the left side. Mounting was done by springing onto the bare back of the horse, unless a groom or companion would give you a foot up. Another way would be to plant the butt of a javelin held in the left hand, and use the leverage on it to vault astride the horse, swinging your right leg over. Some Greek vase paintings, illustrating what appear to be riding-school lessons, demonstrate this type of mount.

A very early book on equestrian matters, written by Xenophon in the fourth century B.C., is called *On Horsemanship*. It shows clear mounting instructions, including a rider being able to mount and dismount from both sides.

Since horses get used to the one-sided mount, they tend to look upon any attempts to mount on the "wrong" side in an unfavourable manner — they buck.

106.

Why do ladies and girls have to shave their legs and armpits?

No one *has* to shave. In many places in the world it's just fine to have hair on your legs or in your armpits. But in North America, those who want to get rid of it rip the stuff out with painful devices like wax, or submit to electrolysis (tiny needles zapping the hair follicles), or shave and shave and shave and pluck and pluck and pluck. Keeping gals smooth and hairless is a big business.

When we started to shave our legs isn't so hard to answer, but *why* is tricky. That's because there hasn't been much information, historically, about how women dealt with hygiene. In order to put together a picture of the history of body-hair elimination, you have to look at diaries, statues and paintings. Greek statues of women showed no body hair, and those women were considered full of beauty and grace. Their legs only showed if they were engaged in military or hunting activity. And you never see armpit or leg hair in old paintings — artists throughout history have ignored reality. Only in the past hundred years have nudes been painted that looked like real women.

Showing a real woman, hair and all, came along with the invention of the camera in the late nineteenth century. A 1913 movie likely started the armpit shaving business. *Mabel's New Hero* (also called *Fatty and the Bathing Beauties*) was filled with gals sporting the new sleeveless fashions . . . and clean armpits.

Razor ads began running in 1915 in *Harper's* magazine, shortly after an ad ran for one of the new sleeveless dresses, picturing a model with her arms over her head, showing off her hairless underarms. The caption read, *Summer Dress and Modern Dancing combine to make necessary the removal of objectionable hair.* Whether it was objectionable to some advertising folks, or whether women genuinely didn't like showing their hair — they certainly started buying razors.

Why do we shave our legs? Throughout history, women's legs had mostly been covered, so when women's legs began to show (as hemlines started going up in the twentieth century), a movement began to get rid of leg hair too. By 1925 dress hems were at the knee, and bingo! — even though women wore stockings, they wanted to remove their leg hair because they didn't like the feeling or the look of it sticking out of nylon stockings.

107.

Why do grooms carry their brides over the threshold?

This is a weird one, as it falls into the category of a tradition, although it doesn't mean the same thing today as it did years ago. Way back when, grooms carried their brides over the threshold (through the doorway) to ward off bad luck, because new brides were considered to be powerful and doorways were thought to be full of power too. If the bride happened to step over the threshold starting with her left foot, or tripped going through the door, that would be very bad luck. But the taboo has no effect if she is *lifted* into the room — sort of like sneaking past the spirits that guard the place.

Admittedly, a custom like this is hard to swallow in the twenty-first century. So is the notion that brides were often captured, rather than being willing partners in a marriage. Carrying the bride over the threshold was sometimes the only way to get her through the door.

108.

What is the origin of rolling out the red carpet?

Red is a powerful colour — the colour of blood and danger and fire and roses. Red symbolizes life but is also thought of as the colour of aggression, vitality and strength. It is a colour steeped in superstition and myth. But why?

Think: dye. Red textiles have always been highly sought after, but before chemicals for dyeing came about at the end of the nineteenth century, it was incredibly difficult to get a great red colour that was both light fast — didn't fade — and washable. Three thousand years ago the Phoenicians figured out how to extract dye from molluscs (a snail called the *Murex trunculus*) to get reds and the deep violet called Tyrian purple. The catch was that you had to gather an enormous number of molluscs, which made the resulting colour so expensive that it was primarily reserved for royalty. This is why the Roman Emperors wore a toga with purple stripes to show their high rank.

Mexican cochineal beetles were crushed to get red dye, and Spanish explorers brought it back to Europe in the early 1500s. Red was the distinctive royal colour throughout the Middle Ages. It is still the royal colour of Great Britain, and the primary flag colour of the United States and Canada.

Red has come to be associated with royalty, pomp, circumstance and ceremony. When there is a ceremonial event there is usually a red carpet, although the expressions "roll out the red carpet" or "the red-carpet treatment" were first heard in 1934. As these things tend to go, the term has been adopted by the advertising industry, so stores looking for customers promise them "the red-carpet treatment." Good thing they don't have to go hunting for molluscs to do it.

109.

Who thought up "thumbs-up"?

Thumbs-up is a gesture, and like head-shaking or rubbing one's tummy, hand gestures are a sort of sign language — a non-verbal cue. Some gestures can be taught to very, very young children (under one year). Some gestures are extremely handy when you travel, like sticking out your thumb to hitch a ride . . . unless you happen to do it in a country where it is considered a very *rude* symbol (sort of like telling someone to "stuff it"). This could get you into big trouble. However it came about, thumbs-up is a hugely popular gesture.

Although it is grammatically incorrect (it ought to be "thumb-up"), "thumbs-up" has been generally accepted as a gesture of approval for at least four hundred years, and likely longer. It seems there isn't much more to it than the fact that "up" means good and "down" means not so great. And it might have had something to do with the phrase, "Here's my thumb on it," an old English saying that was used to finalize a contract or seal a deal. The two parties did a sort of "high-five" with wetted thumbs.

The thumbs-up sign might even be connected to the ancient Romans' gladiator fight. The audience would *cover* their thumbs if they wanted to spare the life of a defeated gladiator who had fought bravely. That's what Desmond Morris, in his fascinating book called *Body Talk*, says. Through "mistranslation or ignorance," as he puts it, "this opposing pair of gestures eventually changed from 'thumb cover up' to 'thumb up.'"

Another hand signal that is used in the

same way is what Morris and his colleagues, who wrote the entertaining book *Gestures,* call "the ring." That's where you put your thumb and forefinger together to form an *O*, which is understood in many cultures as "okay."

While we're at it, here's another gesture that is oddly popular around the world. "Thumbing your nose" is when the tip of your thumb touches the tip of your nose and your fingers are spread out and pointing up (and sometimes waggling). Most schoolchildren will recognize this gesture as a tease, an insult, a way to mock someone or something. Sort of "Nyah, Nyah" with the hand. This one is often called "the five-finger salute."

110.

What's the story behind lighting the candles on the birthday cake?

We have Artemis, the Greek goddess of the moon, to thank for the birthday cake. She got moon-shaped honey cakes to celebrate her birthday (Get it — moon goddess gets moon cake?) and the rest of us followed suit with round cakes to celebrate our birthdays. The idea of lighting one candle on your birthday cake for each year you have been around comes from the Greeks too. The superstition says that if you can blow out every candle with one breath after you make your wish, it will come true . . . as long as you tell no one what you wished.

There is also a belief that when you eat the words on a cake they will come true — so a bite of "Happy Birthday" will bring you happiness.

Another tradition says that the way your birthday goes will set the pattern for the coming year — so try not to cry on that day, or you will for the next 364 days too.

What did one candle say to the other? Don't birthdays burn you up?

Why do we put candles on top of a birthday cake? Because it's too hard to put them on the bottom.

Why do we eat popcorn at movies?

and Other Fascinating Facts About FOOD

111.

Why do we eat popcorn at the movies?

Mostly because popcorn is cheap and easy to get. (Plus it's crunchy and tastes great too.) Popcorn has been around for at least 5600 years. The story goes that the chief of a New England nation handed the Pilgrims a bag of popcorn on America's first Thanksgiving Day in 1621. Of course the popcorn wasn't in the red-striped paper bag we see today; it was presented in a deerskin bag. The Pilgrims ate it the next morning for breakfast with sugar and cream — the first puffed cereal. It didn't catch on as breakfast cereal, but it has been a favourite snack food for a long time.

What's popcorn's connection to the movies? People had been eating popcorn in their homes and buying it from street vendors since Jolly Time brand popcorn showed up around 1914. When movies were first shown in the 1910s, they were usually in fancy theatres where food was not allowed. (There was no sound to the movies then, so all that crunching would be really distracting.) After the stock market crashed in 1929 these expensive theatres closed. Smaller and cheaper places opened. The theatre owners soon realized that their customers were bringing in popcorn they had bought from street vendors, so they started to sell popcorn in order to make that money themselves. Even in tough times, people usually had a nickel for a bag of popcorn. And with the coming of "talkies" — movies with sound — all the crunching was masked.

The great thing about popcorn is that it

costs very little to produce and there is a high profit because there is no middleman — just buy the corn from the producer, then make and sell the final product yourself.

Nowadays theatres make most of their profit from the concession stand. This is especially true if the theatre is showing expensive first-run films. So, as well as being a treat for moviegoers, popcorn helps keep the theatres in business.

Popcorn Facts

◎ 98% of the kernels should pop. If not, the popcorn is likely stale or low quality.

◎ The unpopped kernels are known by lots of different names (other than "maddening" and "hard on your teeth") such as duds, spinsters, UPKs (unpopped kernels), or old maids.

◎ Don't keep popcorn in the fridge because it dries out.

◎ Not all corn pops — popcorn is a special corn whose nuggets explode when the water in them is heated and expands to steam.

◎ Before corn poppers were invented, popcorn was often made in a shallow cooking pot placed on the fire. Coarse sand was placed in the bottom of the pot, and the corn was mixed in. As the corn popped, it rose to the surface, leaving the sand behind.

◎ Popcorn is popular in theatres all over North America, but if you went to the movies in Israel you might eat sunflower seeds. In Egypt you'd get cheese on pita bread and falafels, and in Nigeria theatres sell little fried cakes with peanuts and hot pepper. No matter where you travel, you will always find Coke!

◎ Many theatres don't use paper bags anymore. Cardboard containers are quieter, especially for the romantic scenes. Theatres also wanted to stop kids from blowing up the paper bags and popping them!

112.

Did Sir Isaac Newton really get hit on the head by an apple . . . and if so, what kind was it?

This is a question of utmost gravity. And it is ripe with opportunity for bad jokes. But we will get to the core of the matter.

Apples have been around for a long time. Archaeologists have found evidence of apples from 6500 B.C. and we know that the Egyptians grew apples in the thirteenth century B.C.

Over all these years, a lot of apple lore has come along. Fruit in the Garden of Eden tempted Eve, and it is assumed that the fruit was an apple. William Tell shot an apple off his son's head. Newton came up with the law of gravitation by seeing an apple fall from a tree in England in 1666. But what kind of apple?

Was it a Gravenstein (Get it: gravity)? No. Gravensteins are from Italy and came later. Was it a Newton? No. Newtons are from New Town, Long Island, in the U.S., and came along in 1759.

The apple was from a tree called the Flower of Kent, a variety from around 1629. That particular tree was so famous that it was well looked after until it died in 1814. Then the wood was used for chairs.

While this famous tree was still alive, more trees were made from it by grafting parts of it onto new roots. That's called propagation. So babies of the famous Newton Flower of Kent apple tree have been planted in front of Physics labs all over the world. Those trees remind scientists that sometimes the best discoveries come from the simplest places.

113.

Why do so many kids hate liver and Brussels sprouts?

There are four basic reasons why these two foods are different from ones that kids will eat. Liver and Brussels sprouts taste bitter, have unusual textures, and smell odd. Add to that their colour — or lack of colour, since Brussels sprouts get to be a rather pale green when cooked, and liver goes sort of grey. Yuck. Probably the strongest reason of the four is the taste. Children's taste buds are just developing, and haven't matured enough to enjoy these two goodies. Liver actually tastes more bitter to a child's taste buds than to an adult's.

114.

How about freezing water — what's faster, hot or cold?

Not surprisingly, cold water beats hot water from the tap at the freezing race. But not by more than fifteen minutes (at least for a tray of ice cubes), so it is hardly worth worrying about. However, if two buckets were set outside on a freezing day — one with very hot water at 95°C, and the other at 50°C, the hot water would freeze first!

What gives? Well, there are a number of factors at play. If the water is hot enough, evaporation will take away some of the mass of the water, so there is less to freeze. And hot water will likely "supercool," which means that rather than a thin layer of ice starting on top and freezing down from what becomes an insulated covering, the ice starts to form from within and freezes fast. The other factors include convection, dissolved gases and conduction — but basically, with much hotter water, the hot beats the cold.

115.

Why do you cry when you cut an onion?

It's actually a very long story, but basically people cry because cutting the onion releases enzymes that mix with other molecules, converting the sulphur compounds in the onion to molecules that produce strong smells.

The body reacts by producing tears to keep the nasty chemicals away from the eyes. The conversion takes about thirty seconds from the time the onion is first cut, and the whole thing is over in about five minutes (unless another onion is cut!).

There are a few things people can do to make sure not as many of the stinky burning molecules make it as far as their eyes. The chemicals are soluble in water, which means that if the onion is cut while it's being held under water, most of the chemicals go down the drain. That way, not as much gets into the air to drive people's eyes crazy. Other good ideas are to heat or freeze the onion to slow down the reaction between the sulphur compound and the enzyme, to chop them in a breeze, or use a fan to disperse the chemicals.

Different kinds of onions contain a different amount and type of sulphur. Some are harsher and some are milder, so people can pick their onion according to their tolerance level. It's worth the tears, since onions taste great, have lots of nutrients (including vitamins B, C and G), and have many other great characteristics such as anti-inflammatory, anti-allergic and anti-asthmatic properties.

116.

What is the record for the heaviest watermelon? And how big was the biggest pizza? Who decides? And how do you prove it?

If you think you have accomplished something extraordinary, you might want to talk to the folks at Guinness World Records. Biggest, smallest, tallest, heaviest, weirdest . . . Then there's the collection of the largest, the youngest, the oldest . . . You name the superlative, Guinness is interested. Read the latest *Guinness Book of World Records* to get the idea. It comes out every year. Break a record and you can get in the book and receive a certificate.

But you have to prove you've broken a record. You can do that by sending in a digital recording of your feat, or a link to your YouTube video (if it is a timed event, make sure the clock shows). You should send in good colour photos too. If a local newspaper covers your event, send in the clippings. Then you have to document your claim. (You need at least two independent witness statements by a person of community standing — such as a doctor, a lawyer, a police officer or a professional sports official.) You can't be related to the witness. This all helps the committees at Guinness decide if you really have achieved what you say you have.

Most of the hundreds of categories have guidelines, so it is best to get in touch with the folks at Guinness to get specific information from them. They will also tell you if your proposal for a new category is acceptable. Good luck.

Now, about those food records:

- ◎ The biggest watermelon grown weighed in at 159 kg, in 2013.

- ◎ Matthew Willenijns of Ludwigsburg, Germany, had the biggest pumpkin grown — a walloping 1,190 kg — in 2016.

- ◎ The biggest pineapple was the 13-kg monster grown in 1978 in Tarauaca, Brazil.

- ◎ The largest circular pizza ever baked was 40.09 m in diameter. It was made in 2012 in Rome, Italy.

- ◎ The largest hamburger ever made was 1,164.2 kg, made in 2017 at Pilsting, Germany.

- ◎ Palm Dairies Ltd. in Edmonton, Alberta, made the world's largest ice cream sundae in 1988. It weighed 24,908.8 kg and contained: 20,270.7 kg of ice cream, 4394.4 kg of syrup and 243.7 kg of topping.

- ◎ The largest ice cream soda float was made by Coca-Cola Co., beating its *own* record, in 2007.

117.

Why is there fizz in our sodas? What is pop made out of?

More than two thousand years ago, Hippocrates, who has been called the "Father of Medicine," believed that the fizzy mineral waters from natural mineral springs were beneficial to health. So the early Greeks and Romans began to use them for bathing. Later on, during the Middle Ages, people started drinking the waters, and claimed that they were healthy tonics.

English chemist Joseph Priestley is famous for his work with gases and for discovering oxygen. But Priestley also invented soft drinks. He got interested in science after he met inventor Benjamin Franklin, who was visiting London in 1766. Priestley started doing experiments that involved dissolving different gases in water.

The story goes that Priestley lived beside a brewery, and became aware of a gas that was produced by the fermenting grain used to make ale. He figured out how to produce the gas, carbon dioxide, and discovered that it tasted tangy and was fizzy when it was mixed with water. That was the beginning of carbonated water or seltzer water. By 1772, Priestley had built a machine to produce carbonated water. The navy used these machines to improve the quality of drinking water aboard ship on long voyages. Priestley then wrote a book about his findings: *Directions for Impregnating Water with Fixed Air, In Order To Communicate To It The Peculiar Spirit And Virtues Of Pyrmont Water, And Other*

Mineral Waters Of A Similar Nature. (Whew!)

A few years later Torbern Bergman, a Swedish chemist, figured out how to make large quantities of carbonated water, using chalk to produce the carbonic gas. Simons and Rundell of South Carolina got the first U.S. patent for mass manufacture of "imitation mineral waters" in 1810, but carbonated drinks didn't, become popular until after 1830. At first the drinks were unflavoured and were sold mostly by pharmacists. Eventually fruit syrups and herbs were added. Lemon-flavoured soft drinks came first; ginger ale and root beer became popular later.

One of the big problems was trying to keep the carbon dioxide bubbles from escaping from the beverages. In 1892 a machine shop operator in Baltimore, William Painter, came up with the "Crown Cork Bottle Seal" that kept the beverages from going "flat." By 1920 more than five thousand bottlers existed across the U.S.

Originally the drinks were called seltzers, after a famous German mineral spring. Eventually they were all called "soft drinks," to distinguish them from "hard" or alcoholic drinks. They were recommended as a substitute for liquor. The nickname has always been "soda" because of the bicarbonate of soda that was used to produce carbon dioxide. We also call soda "pop" because the first bottles were stoppered with corks that popped when they were opened.

Industry statistics show that soft drink consumption in Canada is declining. In 2018 the average Canadian consumed 65 L a year, compared to 109.7 L in 2006

118.

Why do refrigerators turn bananas black? And why do bananas get bruised as they age?

These two questions have related answers. Bananas go black as they age, but those aren't bruises. Even bananas that have never been touched will go black. That's because ethylene, a natural hormone, ripens the fruit . . . but doesn't know when to quit. There's no way of stopping the production of ethylene, although you can slow it down by finding a place that isn't as cold as a refrigerator but is cooler than your kitchen counter. When you put the banana in the refrigerator, it produces another compound called polyphenols, which also turn them black. Cold temperatures, which are foreign to bananas' natural tropical environment, kill the surface cells on the banana peel, and that's what produces the polyphenols.

Check it out though. Black or not, if the banana hasn't over-ripened it will be fine under its covering. You can even freeze bananas. If you coat peeled bananas in chocolate first you have a fabulous frozen treat.

Some authorities say that chimpanzees and other primates go for the whole banana, peel and all. Others say primates do peel bananas before eating them and that they peel their bananas from the opposite end that we use. Next time you're at a zoo, see for yourself how they eat their bananas.

119.

When you want to boil water, is it faster to start with hot or cold?

It's faster to start with hot water. If someone took two identical pots, filled one with hot water and the other with the same amount of cold water, then put them on two identical stove burners at identical settings, it would be obvious which would boil first.

Recipe books tend to suggest starting with cold water, but that's so you don't assume they mean for you to use boiling water when that's not what they want. Cold tap water is also likely to be safer for human consumption, because hot water can contain more dissolved minerals.

120.

How big a bubble can you blow with gum?

Susan Montgomery of Fresno, California, blew the biggest bubble from bubble gum in 1994 — a 58.4-cm bubble. She once burst a bubble with such a loud pop someone thought it was the sound of gunfire!

What about the world's largest soap bubble? In 1996, Alan McKay of New Zealand used a bubble wand, dish detergent, glycerin and water to make a bubble 32 m long.

121.

How much Kraft Macaroni and Cheese Dinner does the average kid eat?

Kraft Dinner, or Kraft Macaroni and Cheese as it is known in the U.S., is the ultimate comfort food. It's called Kraft Dinner in Canada, where the population eats more "KD" or "Vitamin K" per capita than anywhere else in the world. (This was long before the band, the Barenaked Ladies, made Kraft Dinner so famous in their song, "If I Had a Million Dollars.")

But before we get onto why kids love this unusual orange delicacy so much, let's just pause to praise pasta for a moment. Spaghetti came to North America mostly in the 1920s with the wave of immigration from southern Italy. The story goes that Prohibition (a period when the production and sale of liquor was illegal in the U.S.) helped the popularity of pasta because you could find a glass of wine at some Italian restaurants, where spaghetti was the main dish sold. People started trying pasta . . . and liking it. Pasta caught on fast. It is cheap, quick and easy for even the least experienced cook to prepare. Boil water. Throw in pasta. Bingo: dinner.

We eat more pasta every year, and it's good for us. It's a complex carbohydrate which gives us six of the eight essential amino acids. There's only a gram of fat in a cup of cooked pasta, and only 210 calories. And word has it that eating pasta releases serotonin, a chemical in the brain that tells you that you're feeling relaxed and calm. That means there is scientific proof that pasta is comfort food. So that means also that those crafty people at Kraft have figured out a way to keep us feeling comfortable.

So what about the little blue box of Kraft Dinner? It is a success story based on smart marketing. Back in the 1930s, during the Depression, Kraft was selling grated cheese in little 2-ounce (56-gram) packages to add to soup or baked dishes. A macaroni salesman for Tenderoni Macaroni in St. Louis tried to figure out how to sell more of the little elbows. He tied one of the Kraft cheese packages onto the macaroni package with a rubber band, and convinced retailers to sell them as a unit. The first blue boxes were 19¢ (this was 1936, when steak was 26¢ a pound) and the slogan was "Make a meal for four in nine minutes." Because of the Depression, there was a huge need for inexpensive meatless meals, and Kraft sold 9 million boxes the first year.

Kraft Canada says that if all the boxes of Kraft Dinner sold each year in Canada were lined up end to end, they would stretch more than 16,000 km, or from Ottawa to Melbourne, Australia. In fact, Canadians eat 245,000 boxes a day.

What are our favourite foods to enjoy with KD? Kraft's Consumer Response Department says that vegetables, ground beef, tuna and hot dogs are the most popular KD enhancers. The purists add nothing. Why is KD still so popular? Convenience and price are important, but nostalgia plays a big part in the sales of KD too. Lots of people who grew up eating KD keep a box in their cupboard just in case. You never know when you'll need comfort and convenience.

122.

My mom says that putting vinegar in the water you use to boil eggs will keep them from cracking. How does this work?

At the risk of saying that perhaps your mother isn't always right, the truth is that putting vinegar in the water will not stop the eggs from cracking. But it is still a good thing to do.

The wider end of the egg contains an air sac, and this air expands when it gets heated. If it expands really quickly, the pressure will crack the egg's shell. The way to stop this from happening is to make a tiny hole in that end of the egg with a sharp needle, before you cook it. The hole will allow the expanding air to escape, without cracking the shell.

But your mom was on the right track, as there is a reason to put a few drops of vinegar in the water before you cook your eggs. It makes the egg white coagulate so that if the shell *does* crack, less of the white will seep out of the egg when you're cooking it.

• How can you tell if an egg is hard-boiled? Try spinning it. If it spins freely and uniformly, then it's cooked. But if the spin is wobbly, it's raw.
• Did you know that eggs are one of nature's most perfect foods? The only vitamin they lack is vitamin C.

123.

Why do hot dog buns come in packages of twelve when hot dogs only come in eight?

This seems pretty dopey, especially if you live someplace where hot dogs come in packages of ten and buns in eight or twelve.

What's going on? Basically, it's because the two industries don't think about each other much. The meat packers like things in neatly measured quantities like 500 grams, a kilogram or a pound. (The metric system is used everywhere in the world except the U.S. There are 2.2 pounds to a kilogram, so packages are most often either 454 grams, which is exactly a pound, or 500 grams, which is 1.1 pounds or 0.5 kilos.) If you look at your package of wieners, the net weight is likely one of these even numbers, and they have packaged the number of wieners that make up that weight. In the U.S. the wieners are generally one-tenth of a pound, so come ten to the package.

Then what about buns? Bakeries tend to sell things by the dozen or in eights, and that's really all there is to it. It also has to do with the size of the pans. (Plus, bakers have been going with a system based on "a dozen" for centuries.) So the explanation is as dopey as the problem: two industries that need each other for sales but never seem to think of each other when they figure out the really big questions in life, like how many buns or hot dogs to put in a package.

124.

Why does eating asparagus make urine smell funny?

Asparagus is really good for you but, *whoo, boy,* that smell can be bizarre. Why? Urine removes waste products from the body and provides valuable information about your urologic and general health. You pass more urine when you drink more liquids and eat more foods that contain more water, such as fruits and vegetables.

The normal smell of urine comes from the acid in it. In diabetics, urine may have a fruity odour due to the presence of excessive glucose. Or if the patient has a urinary tract infection, the urine may have a foul smell. Certain foods may create a characteristic odour as well — things like coffee, asparagus and some vitamins.

But about this particular smell. It is indeed true that eating asparagus can cause some people to produce urine with a temporarily odd smell — sort of a rotten cabbage smell. Back in 1702 a Frenchman, Dr. Louis Lemery, stated in his *Treatise of All Sorts of Foods*, "Sparagrass eaten to Excess sharpen the Humours and heat a little, and therefore persons of a bilious constitution ought to use them moderately. They cause a filthy and disagreeable Smell in the Urine, as every Body knows." The story even goes that at a venerable British men's club there is a sign reading:

DURING THE ASPARAGUS SEASON MEMBERS ARE REQUESTED NOT TO RELIEVE THEMSELVES IN THE HATSTAND

Why that really awful smell? Because two sulphur-containing compounds in asparagus convert during digestion in your body into a closely related compound that has that very distinctive cabbage-ish-sulphur-ish-ammonia-ish rotten odour!

The weird thing is that it doesn't happen to everybody. For years it was assumed that this happened to anyone who ate asparagus, but a study conducted with asparagus eaters indicated that of 800, only 344 produced the odorous substance. The researchers concluded that only about 40% of people have a gene that somehow causes this reaction. In fact, they think that every body excretes methanethiol (the compound that stinks), but that the ability to detect its odour varies from person to person. Apparently this is also an inherited trait. By the way, if you are in that unlucky 40%, you don't have to eat much asparagus. As few as five or six spears is enough to produce a pronounced odour.

So, in fact, there can be four responses to eating those succulent green stalks of asparagus: There are those who can both make it and smell it, those who can make it but not smell it, those who can smell it but not make it themselves, and those who neither make it nor smell it. Who says life is dull?

- Asparagus was a delicacy in Greek and Roman times. It was so popular and expensive that many people had to be content with another early spring vegetable, leeks, which were called "poor man's asparagus."
- The ancient Egyptians were so keen on asparagus that they offered it to their gods.

125.

Why are beans the musical fruit?

This phrase comes from a charming ditty:

Beans, beans, the musical fruit:
The more you eat, the more you toot!
The more you toot, the better you feel,
So let's have beans for every meal!
I ate my beans and they were loaded,
Went to bed and they exploded!

This rhyme is said to have come from the time of the Depression, when there wasn't much money to spare, so beans, being cheap and a good source of protein, were a popular but often eventful meal. (As so often happens with oral history, this kind of rhyme rarely gets committed to paper when it first surfaces, so its origins are a little hazy.) But one thing is certain — eat too many beans, and you'll make music, hence the rhyme.

The following rhyme was collected in the 1960s in New York state:

Beans, beans, are good for your heart!
The more you eat, the more you fart!
The more you fart, the better you feel,
So let's have beans for every meal!

It may thrill you to know that the average grown-up passes gas around ten times a day. Eat beans and you've got a 500% better chance of getting gas. Mostly it's because of chemicals (non-absorbable carbohydrates called oligosaccharides) found in many legumes, that can't be broken down in the digestive system. The bacteria in the intestine try to break down these oligosaccharides, and in the process cause them to ferment, which can produce very smelly gases.

There are ways around the problem. Cool it on lima beans and navy beans, as they are the worst offenders. Try drinking more water. Before cooking, soaking beans for several hours in water that you change a number of times helps break down the chemicals. Or you could take Beano, a product with an enzyme that may help break down the chemical and prevent the stinky gas. But it doesn't work for everyone.

You will notice, however, that beans aren't the only musical food. Broccoli, cabbage and cauliflower all contain some amounts of oligosaccharides too. The catch is that all these foods are very good for you, so you don't want to avoid them. But you might have to get used to them, or at least work up to the amount you eat.

Passing gas, by many other names:

air biscuit

anal announcement

body burp

cut the cheese

fart

flatulence

fluff

stink bomb

toot

trouser gas

trouser trumpet

wind

126.

Who invented chewing gum?

Yum, yum, gum. We can all take credit for our ancestors inventing chewing gum.

Humans are built to chew, and archaeologists have dug up masticated wads — complete with teeth marks — of whatever was available for our ancient ancestors to chew on. Tree resin, gristle, pencil eraser — we love chewing. It relaxes us, helps us digest food, soothes our nerves and prevents seasickness.

Packaged chewing gum, however, first showed up in 1848. It was made of spruce resin, something Native Americans had chewed for centuries. John Curtis and his brother cooked it up, calling it State of Maine Pure Spruce Gum, and despite the bitter taste, the low price got things moving. Then Curtis got into flavoured paraffin wax gums.

Around that time an exiled Mexican general, Antonio Lopez de Santa Anna, brought a huge chunk of chicle with him when he settled on Staten Island, New York. (*Chicle* is the name of the gum made from the latex that's extracted from the tropical sapodilla tree, *Manilkara zapota*.) Santa Anna showed it to Thomas Adams, a former photographer and inventor, who imported more chicle to sell. A few years later, in 1871, Thomas Adams received the first patent to produce a gum-making machine. Chicle was better than wax . . . which was better than spruce gum . . . but none of them tasted great. Adding flavour helped. Adams's key ingredient was licorice flavouring — Black Jack, which you can still find today, was born.

A soap salesman, William Wrigley Jr., got into

the act in the 1890s and his early inventions, Wrigley's Juicy Fruit and Spearmint, have been perpetual bestsellers ever since they hit the market in 1893.

Frank Fleer came up with bubble gum in 1906, although he and brother Henry's first attempts were disastrous. Even the name was a problem: Blibber-Blubber Bubble Gum. The gum was so wet you were blibbering and blubbering when you chewed it, and only turpentine and scrubbing would get the sticky mess off your skin. They never sold it. It took until 1928 for the company accountant, Walter Diemers, who was playing around with the recipe, to get it right.

And why is it always pink? Because that was the only colouring left when Mr. Diemers first made a successful batch of Dubble Bubble. Henry Fleer had an easier time. He put a hard candy coating around chicle to make the Chiclet.

It is hard to be discreet when you are smacking away at a juicy wad of gum. Of course the etiquette books of the day loved to hate gum-chewers. They called gum chewing vulgar and encouraged chewers to limit the gusto. Today Miss Manners calls gum chewing a pleasure that is never proper.

Tasty, though. Yum, yum, gum.

Baseball cards were packaged with tobacco until 1933, when the Goudy Gum Company got into the act and produced 239 cards to go with their "Big League Chewing Gum." If you had a complete set of those cards today they could be worth nearly $100,000.

127.

Who invented peanut butter?

If you guessed that a child invented peanut butter, you are wrong. It wasn't even invented *for* children! Despite that, peanut butter has become the yummy brown glue that holds kids everywhere together.

Peanuts have been around since prehistoric times. They're not really nuts, but legumes that grow below ground. Ground-up peanuts have been used in cooking for centuries: we enjoy the delicious Indonesian satay sauce and African peanut stew. Peanuts came to the United States from South America in the 1700s and were used to feed chickens, the poor and the slaves. They were called goobers, from the Bantu word *nguba* (ground nut). In the 1880s circus showman P.T. Barnum came up with nickel-size bags of roasted peanuts to sell at the circus, and they were a huge hit.

In 1890 two physicians came to the same conclusion about peanut butter at the same time. An unknown St. Louis physician figured out that grinding peanuts in his kitchen grinder and spreading the mixture on bread made a great high-protein meat substitute for elderly patients with no teeth. At the same time another doctor, John Harvey Kellogg (of the cereal company family), was looking for vegetarian foods for patients at the sanatorium where he worked. Kellogg and his brother put 4.5 kilos of roasted peanuts in a pillowcase and pounded them a bit to loosen the hulls, then fed them through grain rollers to make peanut butter. Kellogg was a fanatic about the stuff, and even published a book about it called *More*

Nuts — Less Meat. This was the beginning of what has become a big sticky business.

The credit for peanut butter most often goes to George Washington Carver from Alabama — but that wasn't until 1896, six years after the other two men. Carver was researching the lowly peanut, and made peanut ice cream and peanut butter cookies and by-products like mayonnaise, cheese and soap — even paper made from the peanut skins.

Each year Canadians eat 2.7 kilos of peanuts per person. Americans, according to some sources, eat even more — 2.8 kilos.

While it is too high in calories for most adults to indulge in much, peanut butter is an ideal food for children. It's relatively economical. About 45 mL of natural (unsalted and unsweetened) peanut butter contains 4.5 g of protein, all the essential amino acids your body needs, and small amounts of the elements iron and zinc. Peanut butter builds brains and tastes great.

128.

What percentage of kids are allergic to peanut butter?

Peanut allergies affect about 2.4% of children in Canada. Unfortunately, the peanut allergy is one of the most common food allergies. It can be very serious, but up to 25% of peanut allergy sufferers grow out of it as adults, so re-testing is recommended.

You may have heard at school about kids who are allergic to peanuts, so you don't take peanut butter sandwiches for lunch. It goes further than that — if someone is severely allergic, even a tiny trace (1/44,000 of a peanut) can give them hives or make it hard for them to breathe. It is really difficult but absolutely necessary for these people to avoid peanuts, so you are being socially responsible by not including PB and J in your lunch.

129.

How long ago were potato chips eaten?

By me? Yesterday. But for everyone else
— it all started not too long ago at all, just
about 150 years. That may seem like a long
time, but when you consider that folks have
been growing potatoes for at least 4500 years,
it took the world a while to figure out how to
deep-fry them.

French fries came first. They had been
popular in France since the 1700s, and came to
America with Thomas Jefferson after his stint
as an ambassador in France. But how do we get
from there to potato chips?

The story goes that one night in 1853 at
a fancy resort in Saratoga Springs, New
York, a wealthy diner sent back his
french fries, claiming they were too
thick. The chef, George Crum, tried
to make a thinner fry, but the picky
patron sent those back too.

So then Crum got really fed up
and sliced a potato so finely
you couldn't even pick slices
up with a fork. Surprise
— the guy liked them. So
did everyone else, and
they soon became known
as Saratoga Chips.

Crum went on to
open his own restaurant,
but potato chips didn't
become a widely

available snack food until 1925, when a mechanical potato slicer was invented that could cut potatoes 1.5 mm thick. Waxed bags came along right about then too. So next time you get to the bottom of a delicious bag of chips and see Crum's crumbs, remember this story.

130.

How many potatoes does it take to end up with a kilo of potato chips?

The folks at Frito-Lay say it takes almost 4 kilos of potatoes to end up with 1 kilo of chips, since potatoes have so much moisture in them. Get rid of the moisture by cooking them, and you are left with the solid potato chips. Frito-Lay uses more than 2 billion kilos of potatoes a year.

Sniglets are made-up of words that one day might make it into the dictionary. (Rich Hall has a great collection of them in *Sniglets: Any Word That Doesn't Appear in the Dictionary, But Should*). Here are a few of Hall's snack food Sniglets:

◉ snackmosphere: (noun) the air that takes up 95% of the space inside bags of potato chips

◉ charp: (noun) the green, mutant potato chip found in every bag

◉ cheedle: (noun) the residue left on one's fingertips after consuming a bag of Cheetos

---

131.

Why is root beer called root beer?

Because that's what it is, a beer made of roots — it has its *roots* in beer! But it isn't the kind of beer North Americans expect. Here, "beer" usually means the alcoholic drink, which is made with water, fermented grain and hops. (The hops are cultivated flowers responsible for the beer's bitter flavour, which counteracts the sweet malt.)

The word *beer* can also mean a non-alcoholic drink that is flavoured with the extract of a root. This is a very old-fashioned use of the word, but there are four of these beers available today: birch, ginger, spruce and root beer. Root beers have evolved over the years. The recipe has included up to twenty-five ingredients including allspice, birchbark, ginger, cherry bark, sarsaparilla, vanilla beans, molasses, licorice, wintergreen and sassafras root, plus carbonation. Unfortunately, a cancer-causing agent was found in sassafras, so the makers had to replace it with an extract. Most of the root beer we drink today has either an artificial flavour or includes wintergreen and vanilla.

You can buy a root beer mix and combine it with water, yeast and sugar to make your own home brew. Given the chance, this mixture could ferment and produce alcohol, but it would likely be nowhere near as tasty as your root beer. Follow the recipe very carefully though, because getting the yeast to make carbon dioxide and give you the perfect amount of fizziness in your root beer is a precise science.

132.

Why does chocolate give you zits? And what *are* zits, anyway?

Eating chocolate does not give you zits — never has, and it likely never will. Zits are acne, which tends to come on with the power surge of teenage hormones, mixed with sebum and bacteria. So what does that mean?

Everyone has hormones called androgens. They stimulate the oil glands in our skin to get bigger and to make this yucky stuff called sebum. Sebum is the fatty gunk — dead skin cells mixed with skin oils — that your sebaceous glands produce. All of this is normal, but if you are prone to acne, your sebaceous glands overreact to your seemingly normal androgens, and produce too much sebum. Blackheads occur where a plug of sebum and bacteria clogs the hair follicles in your skin. And if that isn't gross enough, if the blackheads don't darken with oxidation, they'll stay white and become pustules, or open up and become lesions or inflamed acne cysts.

The good news is that there is decent medication, and usually acne clears itself up in a few years. Everybody's different, but one rule is universal — don't pick your acne. (Do wash your hands.) And don't worry about diet affecting acne, especially chocolate. There have been lots of studies, and it's just a myth that chocolate gives you acne. In studies where everyone ate chocolate, most people's acne stayed the same, some got better and some got worse. Being a teenager is tough enough without denying yourself something as delicious as chocolate. Enjoy.

133.

What's the difference between a yam and a sweet potato?

Sweet potatoes frequently tend to be called yams, but the two are very different from a botanical point of view. And neither belongs to the potato family (Latin name: *Solanum tuberosum*) at all.

If you put them side by side, the "true" yam is usually dark orange, with a distinct starchy taste and rough scaly skin. It is actually a tropical herb native to Asia and West Africa. It belongs to the Yam or *Dioscoreaceae* family, and can grow up to almost 2 m long!

The lighter "potato" is the sweet potato (*Ipomoea batatas*), part of the *Convolvulaceae* or morning glory family, which comes originally from South America and is grown in the U.S. It is lighter-coloured than the yam.

To confuse things further, there are two variations of sweet potato. The really pale kind with red or magenta skin and white flesh is generically called Boniato or "Cuban sweet potato." The darker variety (most common and most often mistakenly called a yam) has thicker, copper-coloured skin and deep-orange flesh. Sweet potatoes are available year-round and they are popular throughout the world.

In the United States a sweet potato tends to be called a yam. And canned "yams" are usually sweet potatoes. Why this mix-up? When the darker orange of the sweet potato varieties was introduced to North America, African slaves called them yams (from their word *nyami*) since that was what they were used to, and the name stuck.

134.

Why do you stir the plum pudding for good luck before you bake it for Christmas? And why are little prizes like coins baked into it?

Sometimes cakes are filled with more than sweet delicious ingredients (and calories). Your family may not do this exact thing with your Christmas pudding, but many of the cakes we eat on special occasions involve other rituals.

The ritual of stirring the Christmas pudding is this — everyone who takes a turn stirring makes a wish. That gets everyone involved . . . and also helps ensure that there is no bad luck in the home where the Christmas pudding is being made — which, if you are superstitious, is always a good thing.

Hiding "charms" like toys or coins or a button in a dessert is an extremely old custom. The person who gets the charm will surely get good luck.

You probably know the rhyme:

Little Jack Horner
sat in a corner
eating a Christmas pie.
He stuck in his thumb
and pulled out a plum
And said, "What a good boy am I!"

Jack Horner got the charm — or in this case, the plum. In other words he got good luck from the cake.

Other charms which have been wrapped in paper and hidden in cakes over the years are coins (which means you will have wealth soon), rings (marriage is coming) or buttons (no marriage).

Cakes themselves have also been used as prizes, and that's where the expression "to take the cake" comes from.

135.

Why are hamburgers called that if they aren't made of ham?

Because they came from Hamburg, Germany. Sort of. Actually, the original hamburgers didn't look a lot like a Big Mac. They were more like a steak. It all started with a group of nomads called the Tatars or Tartars, who invaded eastern Europe and central Asia in the Middle Ages. They liked their beef raw, and even today some people enjoy a dish called "steak tartare" (essentially, ground or chopped raw meat) that was named after them. When the Tatars showed up in Germany, the locals decided they preferred their pulverized beef cooked with some spices. The Germans started to call the fried or broiled meat a Hamburg steak, and took along this taste treat when they emigrated to the United States. The sandwich was introduced at the 1904 World's Fair in St. Louis and was an instant hit with Americans. You can now get a hamburger almost anywhere in the world, and although folks think it is an American invention, you now know better. Adding the bun is American, but the Germans can claim the patty. Oh, and frankfurters came from Frankfurt, Germany. But that's another story.

136.

Why does it burn if I eat a pepper that is too hot?

When you think hot peppers, remember the name Scoville, as in Scoville Units. The more of them you have, the hotter the pepper. How do you get something like this named after you? Come up with something that needs ranking, figure out a way to do it and see how it flies.

Wilbur Scoville did just that, and since it was 1912 there were no fancy computer programs to analyze things. He asked a small group of tasters to eat different peppers and tell him how hot they thought they were. Of course, nowadays food scientists use high performance liquid chromatography (a computerized process) to get their results, but they still call the units Scovilles.

Where do you get that heat? The burning feeling comes from capsaicin, a chemical unique to peppers. And capsaicin knows exactly how to get to you. It goes for the special sensor cells in your nose, mouth and throat, making them feel pain. Then your body shoots out endorphins to try to let you relax, but they haven't a hope. Eat a habañero pepper and your ears will feel like they are blowing off and you will break out in a cold sweat . . . And your tongue? It hurts to even think of it.

What's the point of eating these hot babies if they burn your mouth in such a memorable way? Some people believe that in hot countries people need to perspire to keep their body temperature regulated and stay cool. Eating hot peppers is also said to blow a cold or sinus problem out of your system. Others, though, think this is utter nonsense. They simply like the taste and love the feeling of relief after they have finished eating hot peppers.

There is no disputing the fact that peppers are low in fat, packed with vitamins A and C, and include calcium, phosphorus, iron and potassium. The taste is worth it all and you get all those extra benefits — what a deal in a tiny package.

If you are going to try hot peppers, know this in advance: you can ease the burn with yogurt, milk or sour cream. Bread or rice help too.

Cool Facts About a Quick Burn

Chili peppers are ranked according to their heat or "pungency" level:

Scoville Units	Pepper varieties
0 - 100	Bell and Sweet Peppers
500 - 1000	New Mexican
1000 - 1500	Espanola
1000 - 2000	Ancho, Pasilla and Poblano
1000 - 2500	Cascabel and Cherry
2500 - 5000	Jalapeño and Mirasol
5000 - 15,000	Serrano
15,000 - 30,000	de Arbol
30,000 - 50,000	Cayenne and Tabasco
50,000 - 100,000	Chiltepin
100,000 - 577,000	Habañero*, Scotch Bonnet and Thai
16,000,000	pure capsaicin

* Some Habañeros are as low as 100,000 Scoville Units, but others max out at 350,000 - 577,000 Scoville Units.

137.

What's the difference between baking soda and baking powder?

Baking soda and baking powder both help make baked goods rise. Baking soda doesn't work unless it is added to a mixture containing acid, like sour milk, lemon juice, buttermilk or vinegar. The baking soda reacts chemically with the acid to produce carbon dioxide (CO^2), which is released as bubbles — that's what causes the cake or bread to rise.

If you look on the ingredients list for baking powder you'll see baking soda (its chemical name is sodium bicarbonate or bicarbonate of soda). There are other ingredients in baking powder to make food rise, like cream of tartar. When you add water to baking powder, carbon dioxide is released. When you mix it into dough you're creating gas pockets while you mix. By popping the batter into the oven or onto a griddle, the heat releases more carbon dioxide and expands the trapped CO^2, making more pressure and swelling the gas pockets, which expands the food being baked. You get the idea.

Really fresh baking powder is the key to better baking. You can try this freshness test at home: pour 250 mL (¼ cup) of hot tap water over 2.5 mL (½ tsp.) of baking powder. If the mixture barely fizzes, it's time for some fresh baking powder.

To make your own baking powder: for 5 mL (1 tsp.) use 2.5 mL (½ tsp.) cream of tartar, 1.25 mL (¼ tsp.) baking soda and 1.25 mL (¼ tsp.) cornstarch. (You can leave out the cornstarch if you are going to use the baking powder right away.)

138.

What is the difference between a fruit and a vegetable?

A simple answer to this question might be: Fruit has seeds or pits and vegetables don't. But immediately your mind wanders toward exceptions to this fruit/vegetable seeds/no seeds idea. What about peppers or tomatoes? Are they fruit? Yes, they are, at least from the point of view of botanists, the scientists who study plants.

Botanists will tell you that a fruit is the fertilized seed of a plant, which develops after the flowers are finished. By this categorization, all of these are fruit (although we commonly refer to them as vegetables): beans, corn, cucumbers, eggplants, sweet peppers, peas, pumpkins, tomatoes and zucchinis.

So what determines that a plant is a vegetable? Botanists don't even use that category. Here's how they divide what *we* consider to be the vegetable world:

tubers (potatoes)
flower buds (cauliflower and broccoli)
stems (celery)
roots (radishes and carrots)
leaves (lettuce)
fungus (mushrooms and truffles)

There is only one vegetable that we commonly call a fruit: rhubarb. It is actually a stem.

Cooks divide the world into vegetables, which we eat with the main course, and fruit, which we eat for dessert or as individual pieces.

139.

I heard a rumour that there was once cocaine in Coke. Is this true?

It's not a rumour — it's a fact.

Coca-Cola is now the most recognized trademark in the world. The name came from two of the syrup ingredients: *coca* from coca leaves (the source for cocaine) and the *kola* nut (a source of caffeine). Back in 1886 when a pharmacist brewed the first syrup, he put it together as a "brain and nerve tonic" and sold it for a nickel a glass.

There was only the teensiest smidge of cocaine in Coca-Cola — perhaps 1 part in 50 million — but once cocaine began to be associated with crime after the turn of the twentieth century, it was wise to lose the association. People even wrote articles saying that there ought to be a law against drinking Coca-Cola. So the producers started to use only coca leaves that had already had the cocaine extracted. Then they dropped the notion of their drink being a cure for headaches, and instead marketed it as a drink that refreshes.

Coke (as we call it today) still packs a punch . . . but a weak one.

Beverage	Volume needed to get the same amount of caffeine
Coffee	1 cup
Tea	2 cups
Coke	5 cups

How were candy canes invented?

and Other Festive Facts About HOLIDAYS

140.

How were candy canes invented?

Like all good (and tasty) traditions, this one comes with a host of plausible stories. Which one is true is up to you. What is a candy cane? A white peppermint stick striped with red, in the shape of a cane . . . or is it the shape of a shepherd's crook? There's a legend about a candy maker running out of room on his baking pans, and bending the candy sticks out of necessity. There is another story that someone thought they should be able to hang up the candy sticks on the tree. Hence the crook. And since it is Christmas candy, maybe it is the shape of a J, for Jesus.

Spangler Candy Company in Ohio makes 2.7 million candy canes a day. They say that candy canes date back to Germany 350 years ago. The candy started out as plain white sugar sticks used to pacify babies, and apparently to reward kids who sang in church choirs. The story goes that the choir master at a cathedral back in the 1600s came up with the idea to shape the sticks into crooks like the ones the shepherds carried at the time of Jesus' birth. He did it to keep the boys in the choir quiet during the long Nativity ceremony. A brilliant idea.

Eventually the smaller sugar crooks became Christmas tree decorations. Around the early 1900s the red stripe was added, and peppermint flavouring too. Small candy stores handmade them for their customers, and by the 1950s large candy companies mechanized the process of producing hard-pulled sugar candy into cane shapes. Now we see them everywhere.

141.

Who got the idea of having Christmas trees, and what does holly have to do with Christmas?

December 25 worked out nicely as a Christian festival to celebrate a new life, because a number of pagan festivals honouring a similar thing already existed for that time of the year. The Romans honoured their god Saturn between December 17 and 23, at the *Saturnalia*. It was the time of the winter solstice and of celebrating the fact that after the shortest day comes the rebirth of light. On January 1, along with a new year's feast, there was *Juvenalia*, the festival of childhood and youth. Add to that the Jewish festival of lights, (Chanukah or Hanukkah, which takes place in December), Yule (a Baltic and Scandinavian winter festival in honour of the gods Odin and Thor), and *Sacaea* (a Middle Eastern festival to welcome the new year). You can see that there were already a number of customs involving gift exchanges, game playing, eating and general merriment, before Christmas celebrations became common.

The Christians went in for decorations too. But why the shiny, green, prickly-leafed holly bush, or Christmas trees? It's a big and serious reason: they are *ever* — as in, always — *green*, and so are seen as symbols of life in the dark of winter. The Romans had had these life symbols too, and Christians incorporated the use of evergreens into their beliefs of everlasting life.

Holly has been a popular winter decoration for thousands of years. The Romans had a custom of bringing evergreens to people during winter celebrations, because evergreens meant good luck. Before Christianity, holly was a pagan symbol of immortality. In ancient times holly was thought to protect your house and bring you good luck and long life. The Romans thought that the prickles would stab and repel witches, demons and evil spirits.

The Christians considered the prickles to be like the crown of thorns that Christ wore at his crucifixion, so the holly's festive red berries came to represent the drops of blood where the thorns had pierced Christ's flesh. (In Denmark, holly is known as Christ-thorn.)

There were also lots of superstitions and beliefs about hanging holly:

◉ Holly was considered to represent the male and ivy the female. Because holly was the male symbol, only men could bring it into the house.

◉ If you nailed up a sprig in the cowshed, your beasts would thrive.

◉ A berried sprig was the ideal ornament for the top of the Christmas pudding, and a scrap was preserved and burned under next year's plum pudding, as a charm for continuity.

What about Christmas trees? Trees were originally decorated as a peace offering to the spirits who supposedly took off with the leaves in the winter. People would drape the bare branches with painted cloth and coloured stones, and what do you know, it worked! The leaves came back in the spring!

The Germans first erected trees at Christmas, and covered them with decorations lit with candles. The first Christmas trees were oaks, because early German pagans were keen on them — in fact, they worshipped the mighty oak. As was often the case, rather than trying to ban a custom, the Christian missionaries adopted the idea. But Christians went for the fir because of its triangular shape. The triangle is the sign of the holy Trinity (the Father, Son and Holy Spirit).

142.

Why do kids hunt for Easter eggs at Easter?

In almost every culture there is some sort of celebration of the arrival of spring, and for thousands of years the egg has played its part as a symbol of life. The ancient Greeks, Romans, Egyptians, Persians and Chinese gave eggs as gifts during the spring rituals. The egg stands for the universe and new life, and was believed to have special powers. Early Christians saw it as a symbol of the resurrection of Jesus and the rebirth of man, so the egg became part of Easter celebrations.

There's a Polish legend that tells of Mary giving eggs to the soldiers at the cross when Jesus was crucified. As she wept, her tears fell on the eggs and spotted them with dots of brilliant colour. Another Polish legend says that when Mary Magdalene went to take care of the body of Jesus, she carried a basket of eggs for her meal. When she uncovered the basket, the white eggs had turned the colours of the rainbow.

Egg decoration has all sorts of variations. Greeks dye the eggs crimson red to symbolize the blood of Christ. Slavic people like Ukrainians and Poles decorate their eggs with elaborate patterns. These are called *pysanki* eggs. Some of the designs have special meanings, and are handed down in a family from generation to generation.

In England people would write messages and dates on the eggs they gave as gifts. In the 1800s candy eggs started to be given instead of real eggs. Some were very elaborate, with windows and tiny scenes inside.

The goldsmith Peter Carl Fabergé made the most famous Easter eggs. Russian czar Alexander III gave his wife, Marie Feodorovna, the first Fabergé egg in 1886 as an Easter gift. It was made of platinum, and opened to reveal a smaller golden egg inside. The smaller golden egg opened to display a golden chicken and a miniature version of the Imperial crown. The tradition of giving an "Imperial Egg" continued for the next three decades — every year there was great anticipation to see what design Fabergé had come up with. Each egg was more magnificent than the last.

- The world's largest Easter egg used to be in Vegreville, a small Ukrainian town in Alberta. Built in 1975, it's decorated in traditional Ukrainian style. The egg itself stands 5.5 m tall.
- The largest decorated Easter egg, in Pomerode, Brazil, is more than 15 m tall.
- An Easter egg over 8 m high was built out of chocolate in Belgium in 2005.

143.

How did the tradition of giving gifts on Christmas start?

You'd expect the answer would be because of the three wise men offering gifts to the infant Christ — but gift-giving goes back way before that. A gift exchange is an ancient midwinter custom. It goes back to the stone age, when the practice of farming was widespread enough that there was a slight food surplus. Extra food would be put into storage and brought out daily, and when the halfway point of the winter was reached, they knew they were going to make it through the long cold season. They could relax, so they had a celebration.

Each farmer had his own specialty, or what he grew best, so there was a big food exchange along with the feast. Sort of like a potluck dinner, with doggie bags. Or similar to the potlatch tradition of the Northwest Coast First Nations, where they redistribute wealth. And as the centuries rolled on — but still before Christianity — the gift-giving got more involved. In ancient Rome the ceremonies at winter solstice, *Saturnalia,* got very elaborate. Popular gifts were honey, fruit, lamps and gold coins. Failure to give presents was said to bring extremely bad luck.

The early Christians apparently tried to end this pagan gift-giving ritual, but people weren't keen on letting it go. They made it a sacred thing instead. Gift-giving would symbolize Christ's birth as well as the gifts from the wise men. It fitted with the Christian ideal of unselfishness in giving to the poor and the needy too, so the gift swap continued.

The rather lavish gift exchange we see today began around the same time as the modern Santa. It was all part of the nineteenth-century commercialization of Christmas. Along with that came the wrapping of presents. Handmade presents were the norm at first, but around 1900, people started to give store-bought, manufactured gifts. They were less personal than handmade gifts, so retailers encouraged shoppers to have their purchases gift-wrapped.

People often joke that Christmas cards and wrapping paper were a Hallmark invention. That's not quite true . . . but it's close. The first creator of a commercial Christmas card was John Calcott Horsley, an English artist who sold his first work in 1843. It was a drawing of a family sitting down to a feast, and it said *Merry Christmas and a Happy New Year to you.* Cards became very popular in the U.S. when lithographer Louis Prang set up business in Boston in the 1870s.

Enter Joyce Hall, a boy from Nebraska who went to Kansas City in 1910 to sell picture postcards. Hall developed a system for distributing to dealers — an idea that was an innovation at the time. Within four years he gave up postcards and went into greeting cards, with a special focus on Christmas cards. Hallmark Cards was born. Norman Rockwell created Hallmark's most famous Christmas cards, but over the years Hallmark bought designs from other famous artists. Today the company prints over 8 million cards every day.

The first thing Hallmark added to their line of cards was special gift-wrapping paper. During the Christmas rush in 1917 they ran out of tissue wrapping paper, so they tried selling some old envelope-lining papers from their warehouse, at 10¢ a sheet. Customers went wild, so they began manufacturing all kinds of designs . . . and there's been no turning back.

144.

Why is a bunny connected with Easter?

If you've ever kept rabbits, you'll know that they can produce lots of babies in a short amount of time. The rabbit has been a symbol of birth and new life during the spring season for thousands of years.

The Easter bunny tradition seems to have started in Germany — there it's called *Oschter Haws*. There are writings about it from as far back as the 1500s. One legend tells about a poor woman who had no food and no gifts for her children at Easter, so she dyed some eggs and hid them in a nest. The next morning when the children went hunting for the eggs, a big rabbit leapt out of the nest and hopped away. The story spread that the rabbit had brought the Easter eggs for the children. German immigrants brought the Easter bunny idea to America in the 1700s.

Children would build nests out in the gardens around their homes and wait for the Easter bunny to come and lay its coloured eggs. This is where Easter egg hunts — that other Easter tradition — come from.

In 1989 the Eveready Battery Company brought us one of the most popular rabbits around today, the Energizer Bunny. This famous pink bunny got his start in a series of television commercials that use the slogan "keeps going and going and going." It's been one of the most popular ad campaigns of all time. Now you can buy Energizer Bunny stuffed toys, mechanical toys, T-shirts and even screen savers for your computer.

145.

On Hallowe'en some children call out, "Shell out, shell out, the witches are out." How common is this? What else do kids say?

First let's get this tradition sorted out. The Hallowe'en we celebrate is the result of a big witches' brew of traditions that has been stirred up over the ages. The earliest Hallowe'en was in fact a big Druid festival named for the Lord of the Dead, Samhain. (It was the end of the Celtic year, and Samhain means "summer's end.") Folks dressed up in the masks of animals, and at the end of the festivities was the original Hallowe'en bonfire. But in those days, the Druids burned criminals too, with the idea that they were warding off evil spirits.

The conquering Romans hated this and every other Druid custom, so they came up with their own fall festivals, but the bonfire part carried on. The Christians condemned Samhain as well, but folks still continued to keep up bits of it. Eventually, in 835, Pope Gregory IV made a sort of compromise. He moved a May celebration called All Saints' Day or All Hallows' Day to November 1, figuring this would make the day more religious and prayer-filled. But old habits die hard. The festivals continued on the night before November 1 — October 31, or All Hallows' Eve. The name was eventually contracted to Hallowe'en.

It was a scary and superstitious night, so farmers in the British Isles would carry torches to frighten away witches. Irish children carried candle-lit lanterns made from turnips, to protect themselves from evil spirits. (Their "o'lanterns" were the forerunner of today's jack-o'-lantern. (The Jack part of the word involves a long tale about a fellow who lost his soul to the devil, who then let him light his way to Hell with a coal stuffed into the turnip he had been eating.)

And then there were — and still are — Guy Fawkes celebrations on November 5. Children would dress up a dummy as a historical rebel named Guy Fawkes and beg "a penny for the guy" from strangers. (His name is where our word "guy" comes from.) There is a related Irish custom of soliciting contributions in the name of Muck Olla on the Eve of Samhain. Muck Olla was a shadowy figure who would be sure to wreak vengeance on the selfish. Eventually, his vengeance turned into the wrath of goblins. Disappointed (treat-less) humans might just come up with a few pranks and tricks of their own — and that's how we got the idea of trick or treat.

The tradition of children parading around in costumes is a twentieth-century addition. However, it too may have evolved from some older customs. On All Souls' Day (November 2), costumed children used to go door to door, offering to pray or fast for the dead in exchange for money or gifts. There are parts of England where people would hand out small cakes called "soul cakes" to the petitioners, and in Yorkshire it was even called "Cake Night." Carollers would travel from house to house on Cake Night singing:

> *Soul! Soul! for a soul cake!*
> *I pray, good missus, a soul cake!*
> *An apple or pear, a plum or cherry,*
> *Any good thing to make us merry,*
> *One for Peter, two for Paul,*
> *Three for Him who made us all.*

So what about Hallowe'en hollers? In many places children call "trick or treat." Some believe that you have to give the little ghosts and goblins a treat, or they will perform a trick on you. And in other places adults ask children to perform a trick to earn their treat. Other calls include "Hallowe'en apples" and "Shell out, shell out, the witches are out," but "Shell out" seems to have mostly died out about forty years ago. In the prairies in the 1950s, kids used to say "Apples, nuts or candy, or over goes your shanty." (They meant they'd tip over the outhouse.) That one can't exactly be used today, in most parts of the country. Nowadays kids also say "Trick or treat, smell my feet, give me something good to eat!"

146.

How fast does Santa have to travel? Like, what Mach? How does he manage to get presents everywhere on time?

A scientist named Roger Highfield wrote a book called *The Physics of Christmas: From the Aerodynamics of Reindeer to the Thermodynamics of Turkey*, which is a very cool read. He has tackled this topic thoroughly and figured out the following:

When Highfield wrote his book, there were over 2.1 billion children under age eighteen in the world, and for the sake of argument, Highfield assumed that Santa would give to *everyone*. He would have to make 842 million stops, (figuring on 2.5 children per household) on Christmas Eve, travelling 355 million km in one night. The good news is that, working with the time zones and travelling against the Earth's rotation, Santa actually has forty-eight hours to make his rounds — a little over 1/5000 of a second to reach each house and deliver the presents.

This means that from a standing start, he is going from 0 to 4116 km per second in 1/5000 of a second, an acceleration of 20.5 million km per second per second, or 20.5 billion m per second per second.

According to Dr. Highfield, Santa achieves speeds of around 6395 times the speed of sound (which is 330 m per second) or Mach 6395. But he is not breaking any cosmic speed limit because the speed of *light* is 300 million m per second. In fact, Santa is poking along at 1/145 the speed of light. Even so, the speed at which Santa has to travel is why we never see him . . . and maybe why he is so appreciative of all those snacks.

147.

What is Mrs. Claus's first name? What's her maiden name?

That's a fine question, and brings up another: What's Santa Claus's full name? Actually, Santa is a title, not a name. It's a simple way of saying "Sinter Klaas."

Santa Claus is the descendent of impressive ancestors. One, Saint Nicholas, was a bishop in the fourth century. He is considered to be the patron saint of children, and is said to have had a generous nature. In the twelfth century he became connected with a Christmas tradition of giving gifts to children. In different countries, Christians had their own version of Saint Nicholas, like Holland's Sinter Klaas. The idea of Sinter Klaas followed the Dutch who started settling in America after 1609. Over the years the name evolved to Santa Claus.

But that wasn't what you asked.

Mrs. Claus has had numerous handles over the years, proving that there is more than one legend to her life. It looks like Mrs. Claus was first introduced as *Goody* in an 1899 book, *Goody Santa Claus on a Sleigh Ride*. (*Goody* is short for *Goodwife*, which is really a title, not a name.) That book was part of a set of thirty-two books written by Katharine Lee Bates, who composed the song "America the Beautiful." Other contenders for Mrs. Claus's first name are Jessica (from the movie *Santa Claus Is Coming to Town*), Anya, Martha, Betsy and Anwyn.

Since no one knows for sure, I suggest that Mrs. Claus be known as Mary Christmas from here on in.

148.

Why isn't Canadian Thanksgiving on the same day as American Thanksgiving?

In the United States, having a feast to give thanks for the harvest has been happening each fall since the year after Pilgrim settlers arrived in Plymouth, New England. Local First Nations had been celebrating harvest ceremonies there long before the arrival of settlers. The idea of setting aside time to give thanks spread throughout the American Colonies, but there was no set "day" for the celebration — it just depended on the state of the crops and what suited the community. In 1789 U.S. President George Washington declared November 26 to be a day of national thanksgiving. At the same time the Episcopal Church was pushing for the celebration day to be the first Thursday in November. In 1863 President Abraham Lincoln proclaimed the last Thursday in November to be the ideal day. Then in 1939 President Theodore Roosevelt bumped Thanksgiving yet again, this time to the fourth Thursday in November. His plan was to help retail businesses by giving them a little longer window for Christmas shopping, since many Americans tend to have a shopping blitz between Thanksgiving and Christmas Day. In 1941 the U.S. Congress made Thanksgiving Day a federal holiday.

The first "Canadian" Thanksgiving — though Canada wasn't called Canada then — was in 1578 in the eastern Arctic, when explorer Martin Frobisher celebrated the safe journey from England to the New World. And Loyalists who moved north from the United States after the Revolutionary War brought the Thanksgiving custom to Nova Scotia in the mid-eighteenth century. The Canadian Parliament adopted a national Thanksgiving holiday in 1879, and moved it around almost as much as the Americans had done: from the last Monday in October . . . to the third Monday in October . . . to the same week as Armistice Day (November 11) . . . to its final spot, the second Monday in October, where it has been celebrated since 1957. Canadian Thanksgiving also gives thanks for the harvest, but is celebrated closer to the actual harvesting time. Many Canadians who have cottages use this weekend to close up for the winter after their big meal. That's because one thing that hasn't changed much is the idea of a feast, and some of the favourite foods — turkey and pumpkin pie.

149.

Who invented April Fool's Day and when and why?

April 1 is an annual excuse for practical jokers to try out their best tricks on potential April fools. This jesting goes on throughout North America, Great Britain, France and Germany. There is a similar tradition in India, where the last day of their March feast (Holi) is heralded with jokes and general mischief. In ancient Rome, March 25 was the festival *Hilaria*.

So what's so hilarious about this time of the year? No one is exactly sure, but it probably has something to do with the equinox and the coming of spring (March 21). Nature has a tendency to "fool" us with great weather and then retreat back into foul days. And it might have something to do with the cuckoo bird (the fool's symbol) arriving in April too.

In 1790 this poem was written about the confusion of the origin of April Fool's Day:

The first of April, some do say,
Is set apart for All Fools' Day.
But why the people call it so,
Nor I, nor they themselves do know.
But on this day are people sent
On purpose for pure merriment.
— Poor Robin's Almanac (1790)

The other explanation commonly accepted involves the calendar we use today, which changed about four hundred years ago (it is called a Gregorian calendar now). In the 1580s the King of France, Charles IX, decreed that New Year's Day must be celebrated on January 1.

However, some people just didn't want to change from the long-established custom of celebrating the New Year between March 25 and April 1. Those who adapted to the change in France began taunting the *"poisson d'Avril"* (the April fish or April fool) who continued to celebrate on April 1. (Unfortunately, the fish/fool connection has been lost through the years.) These "April Fools" became the target for annual practical jokes, and over the years everybody got in on the All Fool's Day act.

Every year people are coming up with trickier April Fool's pranks. Be wary of what you read (a lot of newspapers run bogus stories), hear and watch. But the old standards still work too. If someone tells you to watch out for the elephant coming up behind you, you can be sure that you'll be called an "April Fool!" if you look.

In parts of Canada, the tradition is that all tricks must be finished by noon, but in Scotland the tricks can go on for forty-eight hours! So wherever you live, keep your sense of humour . . . and watch out for that elephant!

April Fool's Facts

- "The first of April is the day we remember what we are the other 364 days of the year."
  — Mark Twain
- Napoleon married Marie-Louise of Austria on April 1, 1810, and earned himself the nickname: Poisson d'Avril or April Fish!

150.

What's the connection between gingerbread and Christmas?

Ginger is pretty great stuff. It's almost up there with salt and sugar as valued commodities go. Ginger can flavour your food and preserve it too, and it can be used as medicine for stomach problems, flatulence and hangovers. The ancient Romans were keen on it, but after the fall of the Roman Empire it became expensive and rare. By the eleventh century it was more readily available throughout Europe, and fifteenth-century spice traders made ginger even easier to acquire. Nuremberg, Germany, became the heart of the medieval ginger business. The city was even home to a guild of *Lebkuchen* (gingerbread cakes and cookies) bakers.

The taste is great, but the fact that gingerbread can be cut into all kinds of shapes — like gingerbread houses and gingerbread people — combined with its preservative qualities, allows for Christmas decorations that can be used for a month or so, and then still be a yummy treat.

Speaking of Spices
Salt was once such a rare and precious commodity that it was traded for equal amounts of gold. The word salary comes from the Latin word *salarium*, which was a wage given to Roman soldiers to purchase salt.

151.

What's up with kissing under mistletoe?

It's a strange custom, that's for sure. And stranger still when you learn that mistletoe is a parasite — it grows on other trees, most commonly the apple tree. The Druids, who were the learned class of ancient Celts, regarded mistletoe as extremely swell stuff. They thought it was magical, brought peace and cured all kinds of things (they actually called it "all-heal"). Like holly and ivy, mistletoe was also green at Christmastime, so it made a special decoration.

The kissing part likely had its origins around the fourteenth century in Britain. In churches where the custom was not discouraged — it had been forbidden from the fourth century right through the Middle Ages — mistletoe was used as greenery around a small display of Mary, Joseph and the baby Jesus that would be hung in a small hoop inside the doorway. Visitors were embraced and blessed as they crossed the threshold, by the priest or by family members.

After some years, the Church decided that they weren't keen on these models of the Holy Family, so the "people" were removed but the decorations were allowed to remain. By the sixteenth century kissing got added to the doorway ritual. For a while the rule was that for every kiss, one of the white mistletoe berries was removed. When they were all gone, no more kissing. That custom got lost somewhere along the way, and the hoops were lost too. What remains today is the custom of kissing under just a sprig of mistletoe.

Who invented the peace symbol?

and Other Intriguing Facts About INVENTIONS

152.

Who invented the peace symbol?

The peace symbol was invented in 1958 when there was a huge campaign for nuclear disarmament in Britain. Bertrand Russell, the famous pacifist, philosopher, mathematician and Nobel Prize winner, was the head of the campaign. He figured that the movement needed a symbol or sign for its big Easter march to Canterbury Cathedral, where participants were going to protest the Atomic Weapons Research Station at Aldermaston. So the committee hired Gerald Holtom, a commercial artist, to create a symbol. He knocked around lots of ideas and came up with a crow's foot sign. But it has nothing to do with crows and everything to do with semaphore, the flag signaling system that most of us forget after our time in the scouting movement (if we ever knew it at all).

Take an *N* for "nuclear" and a *D* for "disarmament." The *N is* an upside-down *V* in semaphore, and *D* is straight up and down. Put them in a circle, and you get the peace sign. Upside down, it's like an ancient symbol for death and despair. It also looks like someone putting up their hands in defeat.

Since February of 1958, when Holtom finished his design, people have suggested other origins and have reinterpreted the meaning: the circle means eternity, and so on. The peace symbol became hugely popular with the peace movement of the hippie era, and now a whole new generation has incorporated the nuclear disarmament symbol on their fashions.

153.

Who created the Oscars? Was it someone named Oscar or something?

The Academy Awards were started in Hollywood in 1927 as a way of honouring achievements of members of the Academy of Motion Picture Arts and Sciences. That's the professional association of folks who work in film. This gang needed some sort of trophy for their awards dinner, and that's where Oscar came in. A sculptor in Los Angeles came up with a knight. He's standing on a reel of film with a sword in his hand. At first he was solid bronze, and now he is made of an alloy, britannium, plated with gold. He is 34.3 cm tall and weighs 3.8 kilos.

Why Oscar? It's a little unclear. One story goes that the knight looked like the academy librarian's Uncle Oscar. She told the staff this story and they started calling the little guy Oscar. By the sixth year of presentations, a columnist referred to what's officially known as the Academy Award of Meritas, as Oscar. The academy officially adopted this nickname in 1939.

What started out as a little award dinner for 270 members has turned into an internationally broadcast tradition for the six thousand members of the Academy. Almost three thousand Oscars have been given out, most looking exactly the same, but in 1938 Walt Disney got a regular Oscar and seven mini Oscars for *Snow White and the Seven Dwarfs.*

Take a Bow!

When she was six years old, Shirley Temple won the first Academy Award ever presented to a child for her performance in *Bright Eyes*, the movie which introduced her signature song, "On the Good Ship Lollipop." The mini Oscar came with the message, "This award is bestowed because Shirley Temple brought more happiness to millions of children than any other child of her years in the history of the world." That's a hard act to follow!

154.

What year was the bikini invented?

The bikini was invented after World War II, when the world was at peace. People still had war on their minds, though. Women had been wearing two-piece bathing suits (which looked more like shorts and a halter top) since 1935. In 1946 a Frenchman named Jacques Heim designed the "world's smallest bathing suit." It was a two-piecer which he called The Atome, referring to the atomic bomb which was being tested at that time.

Then Louis Reard, a Renault car company engineer from France, got into the act. He went further and came up with what he called "smaller than the world's smallest bathing suit." But he couldn't settle on a name. Then, four days before he was to show his suit, the U.S. military set off a nuclear explosion near Bikini Atoll in the Pacific, and the name came to Louis Reard.

The bikini was so skimpy Reard couldn't find a Paris model to wear it, so he found a showgirl to introduce his outrageous fashion on July 5, 1946. The gimmick was that it could only be a bikini if it was "small enough to pull through a wedding ring."

Bikini

Ring

Pull

This was hot stuff — too hot to handle for many years. Even freewheeling Hollywood mostly shied away for a long time.

In 1956 French actress Brigitte Bardot wore the skimpiest of bikinis in the film *And God Created Woman*. In 1960 the now-famous song came out: "Itsy Bitsy Teenie Weenie Yellow Polkadot Bikini." The bikini wasn't really accepted in North America for almost another decade — not until 1965, when *Beach Blanket Bingo*, starring Frankie Avalon and Annette Funicello, was released. Since then the skimpy suit has gone in and out of fashion, but in one form or another the bikini is here to stay.

155.

How was Velcro invented?

Once upon a time a long time ago (the late 1940s) a Swiss inventor named Georges de Mestral went for a walk. He came home and discovered cockleburs on his dog and on his pants. He was dismayed at these brown things gripping stubbornly to his trousers . . . and then, being the scientific type, he looked at them more closely under his microscope. Those darned burrs had hundreds of tiny hooks and — what do you know? — the fabric in his pants had hundreds of tiny loops. When those hooks and loops came together — bingo, you've got Velcro. Generically speaking, you have a hook-and-loop fastener, but de Mestral himself came up with the brand name, Velcro, from *velour*, the French word for velvet, and *crochet*, the French for hook. In 1978 the patent for Velcro expired, and there have been lots of competitors ever since.

Originally hook-and-loop fasteners were just used for clothes and domestic items. Now there are thousands of applications, using hundreds of different types of fasteners — everything from the regular nylon variety which holds your pockets closed, to an injection-molded nylon style with stiff arrowhead-shaped hooks used in the automotive industry to hold everything together (cushions, headliners and carpets). The fasteners are inexpensive, strong, resistant to vibration and can be heat-resistant and fireproof too.

156.

Where did Silly Putty come from?

It came from the mind of a Scottish engineer in New Haven, Connecticut, during World War II. James Wright was working at General Electric on a contract for the U.S. government, trying to come up with an inexpensive substitute for synthetic rubber. Silly Putty was a fluke — a remarkable outcome of his experimenting, and one that he certainly never expected.

Wright noticed that when he dropped boric acid into silicone oil he got goofy pink goo that stretched and bounced more than rubber. And the bonus was that the stuff could pick up images from comic books or newspapers. It could be molded, too. But . . . what could they do with it? Nothing. It was no good as a synthetic rubber substitute — it was just . . . well . . . nutty. Maybe that's why GE called it "nutty putty."

Things began to change when some scientists started taking it to parties. In 1949 at a cocktail party with a bunch of executives, a toy store owner happened to watch people stretching, bouncing and shaping the stuff. Advertising copywriter Peter Hodgson, a Montrealer by birth, was at that party too. Hodgson and the toy store owner decided it would be smart to put a description in the toy store's catalogue and sell it for two dollars as an adult's toy. It sold fabulously, but the toy store just wasn't interested in marketing it further.

Hodgson, who had been calling it "Gupp" until he came up with "Silly Putty," decided to go for it. He took a risk and bought 9.5 kilos of the goo for $147.00 (which he had to borrow!). Since Easter was coming, he hired a student to help him chop it up into small portions and put them into coloured plastic eggs, with the slogan, "The toy with one moving part." The markup was huge: he sold his 672 eggs for $2.00 each — that's about $1.78 profit per egg (minus labour and the eggshell).

At first, sales were mildly successful — just 300 eggs a day — but what made them take off was a mention in *The New Yorker*'s "Talk of the Town" that August. In four days Hodgson had a quarter of a million orders. He quickly got into mass manufacturing the stuff, shipping the eggs in egg cartons, and becoming a very wealthy man. Eventually he moved into a mansion that folks called "Silly Putty Estate." And all that success was in marketing just to adults!

Hodgson quickly figured out that there was a huge market for children, but the kids were getting putty stuck onto carpets and their clothes. By 1960 the manufacturers replaced the formula with one that was non-sticky. Today Silly Putty is mostly thought of as a kids' toy. Hand an egg to most adults, though, and they know what to do with it.

Silly Putty can be used for:

◎ cleaning keys on piano or computer keyboards

◎ keeping tools from floating around in zero gravity
(if you happen to be an astronaut)

◎ removing lint from clothing

◎ steadying wobbly tables

◎ taking casts of footprints

◎ plugging leaks

157.

Why and where was the pretzel invented?

Think about the shape of the pretzel. Think Middle Ages. Think monks. Thought of anything yet?

The story goes that an Italian monk invented the pretzel during the Middle Ages. He rolled long strips of bread dough and shaped it to resemble arms crossed in prayer. After baking, he gave them out as treats to children who had memorized their prayers.

It's also possible that the word comes from the Latin *pretzola*, which means "little reward."

You can make your own big soft pretzels and treat your friends, whether they memorize something or not.

Make Your Own Pretzels

250 mL water

1 8-gram package active dry yeast

30 mL sugar

5 mL salt

750 mL all-purpose flour, unsifted

15 mL butter at room temperature

1 beaten egg yolk

coarse salt

Mix 230 mL of the flour with the sugar, salt and undissolved yeast.

Heat 230 mL water and butter for 35 seconds in a microwave.

Gradually add to dry ingredients; beat
2 minutes at medium speed of mixer.

Add 100 mL flour.

Beat at high speed 2 minutes.

Stir in enough additional flour to
make a soft dough.

On floured board, knead 5 minutes.

Set in greased bowl; turn over to grease top
of dough.

Cover and let rise in warm, draft-free
place for 40 minutes.

Preheat oven to 190°C.

Divide dough into 12 equal pieces.

Roll each into a 50-cm rope.

Shape into pretzels or other shapes.

Place on greased baking sheets.

Cover; let rest 5 minutes.

Mix egg yolk and 20 mL water; brush on pretzels.

Sprinkle with coarse salt.

Bake 15 minutes, or until done.

Cool on racks.

158.

How were M&M's invented?

Like many inventions, you could never guess
how this sweet treat came into being. Forrest
Mars Senior of Mars Candies was travelling
in Spain during the Spanish Civil War. He saw
soldiers eating what looked like pellets of candy.
They were chocolates in a hard sugary coating.
Sound familiar? The coating was there so the
chocolate wouldn't melt. Mars thought this was
a great idea and went home to invent the recipe
for M&M's plain chocolate candies.

The public first saw these in 1941, but

American GIs serving in World War II had tried them before because M&M's were included in their food rations, packaged in tubes. The military liked this snack, since it travelled well in many climates. By the end of the 1940s M&M's were popular with the public, and the tube gave way to the familiar brown pouch. In 1954 M&M's Peanut Chocolate Candies were introduced, and that same year came the M&M characters and the slogan, "the milk chocolate melts in your mouth, not in your hand."

M&M stands for Mars and Murrie, after Forrest Mars and Bruce Murrie, who developed the candy.

159.

What the heck does "PEZ" mean?

It's a shortened form of the German word for peppermint: *pfefferminz*. PEZ has been around since 1927, when it was created in Vienna, Austria. At first these mini-sized, soap-shaped candies came in only one flavour — peppermint — and they were meant for adults. They arrived in the U.S. in 1950 in a plain dispenser. No Garfield heads, snowmen or cellphone replicas. By 1952 the manufacturers added fruit flavours and cartoon heads, beginning with Popeye. Now the folks at PEZ (who call their product the pioneer of "interactive candy") have produced hundreds of dispensers over the years, spawning collectors galore. PEZ sells over 3 billion candies a year in the U.S. alone — no peppermint flavour anymore, though — as well as in sixty countries around the world.

160.

When Ben Franklin invented electricity and he got electrocuted, why didn't he die?

Benjamin Franklin was born in 1706, the fifteenth child of seventeen, and the youngest son. He went to school in Boston for only two years because his family could not afford to pay for his education. He taught himself algebra, geometry, navigation, logic and science. He also learned French, German, Italian, Spanish and Latin, and became one of the best-educated men of his time.

Franklin was one of the first people to experiment with electricity, but he was very lucky that he was not killed while flying his famous kite. Franklin suspected that lightning was a form of electricity, so on June 10, 1752, he decided to test his idea. There are lots of misconceptions about this experiment because Franklin never wrote about it. He did tell his colleague, Joseph Priestley, and Priestley wrote it down — but not until 15 years after it happened.

Franklin made a kite from a large silk handkerchief and two cross-sticks, with a wire pointer fixed to it. He attached a metal key to the bottom of the kite's string. The string was made of hemp (a weak conductor) on the upper portion, and silk ribbon (a non-conductor) on the lower.

With the help of his son he launched the kite during an approaching thunderstorm. After a while he noticed that some of the threads on the hemp

215

part of the string were sticking straight out, so he touched his knuckle to the key and observed an electric spark. The kite and hemp string had collected the electric current in the air and then charged the metal key. This confirmed Franklin's idea that lightning is actually a large electric spark.

Franklin wasn't stupid. He had suspected that lightning was a very powerful electric force. That's why he launched the kite just as the thunderstorm was approaching. Had a lightning bolt actually hit his kite he probably would have died instantly. So Franklin wasn't really electrocuted while doing his kite experiment.

Franklin used his knowledge of lightning to invent the lightning rod. It's a metal rod that is attached to the roof of a building. A wire made out of copper or aluminum runs from the rod into a conductive grid buried in the ground. If the rod is struck by lightning, the system carries the electrical current down the rod, through the wire and into the ground — without causing damage to the building.

Franklin's experiments did involve risk, though. One time he tried to kill a turkey with an electric shock, but instead *he* got shocked. He said, "I meant to kill a turkey, and instead, I almost killed a goose."

- When you see a flash of lightning, start counting the seconds until you hear thunder, and then divide the number of seconds by 3. That will tell you, in kilometres, how close the lightning is to you.
- Lightning kills about twelve people in Canada each year, and ten times that many in the U.S.

161.

Who invented the first video game system?

Credit for the first video game goes to Steve Russell. In 1962 Russell was a computer programmer at the Massachusetts Institute of Technology (MIT), which had received a donation of a computer from Digital Equipment Corporation (DEC). DEC wanted to see what the bright young programmers at MIT could do with the Digital PDP-1 computer. Little did they know that a game called Spacewar would be the result!

There was one big problem though. The computer that ran the game was a mainframe computer that took up the floor space of a small house! It was also very expensive (several million dollars), and only the biggest corporations and universities could afford it. Spacewar was a two-player game that involved spaceships firing photon torpedoes at each other. (Pretty simple stuff compared to what you can now do on a laptop or a handheld device.)

Credit for getting the arcade video game industry going goes to Nolan Bushnell. In 1971 he took over his daughter's bedroom to develop a much simpler machine that could play the Spacewar game. (His daughter had to sleep on the couch.) The computer business is all about timing, and Bushnell's timing was just right. The silicon computer chip had just been developed, making it possible to build smaller and cheaper computers. He called his arcade game Computer Space. Unfortunately it was a total flop, mostly because people didn't know how to play it!

Bushnell realized that he needed to develop a game based on one that people already knew. So

Pong (based on ping-pong) was born. Pong was introduced at a bar in Sunnyvale, California, in 1971. The game was such a hit that the machine became too full of quarters and broke down!

Bushnell then started a company called Atari, after the word a samurai uses to warn his opponent that he is about to be attacked. Atari sold ten thousand copies of Pong. Lots of other companies imitated it, and it became the most popular coin-operated game around. In 1975 Sears sold the first home version of Pong, to be played on a television set. People lined up outside stores for hours to get their hands on a game, just the way we do for new computer gadgets now. For many adults, video games were our first introduction to using computers, and have been credited with getting computers into our homes.

Can you go deaf by listening to rock concerts?

and Other Weird Notes About MUSIC

162.

Why is it so easy to remember words to a song, even years after you first heard it, when it's nearly impossible to remember lines of a poem you have to recite in class, or a list of facts?

It's true, songs are relatively easy to remember. There are two main reasons for this. The first reason is the song itself. A song is often a very organized and catchy piece of work with lots of rhymes, and usually with some repetition too. The rhymes, the words and the repetition are all "cues" to help you retrieve it from your brain. Chances are that if you like a song you listen to it over and over, and this repeated listening also helps you recall it. The second reason is that music is a very emotional experience. We enjoy emotional experiences like this very much. The key here is that we remember experiences having positive emotions far more easily than traumatic or nasty experiences. (If something really nasty happens, we can have a very hard time remembering it.)

So the positive emotions, combined with a song's cues and its structure, make it much easier for us to remember words to a song, even many years later.

Try putting lists of facts, or poems that you want to remember, to a favourite tune — it can't hurt, and might help you to do a much better job of remembering.

and d.. polished up the handles of the big front do

163.

Can you go deaf from listening to rock concerts?

One loud rock concert isn't going to damage your hearing permanently. But repeated attendance at live concerts can definitely do damage. The sensitive hair cells (cilia) in the inner ear are destroyed by repeated exposure to loud noise. Once damaged, these hair cells cannot be repaired, ever. Concerts are often as loud as 100 to 115 decibels, and the closer you are to the speakers, the louder and more damaging the sound gets. As a comparison, a single exposure to gunfire that is over 150 decibels can cause permanent damage to your hearing.

When the music is loud, you get a temporary hearing loss — things seem muffled or you have ringing in your ears — which is a warning sign. One problem with this is that people turn up the music to compensate, and make it even worse for their ears.

You don't have to go to a rock concert to encounter music this loud. School dances are often over 100 decibels. Ask to have the music turned down. It is still enjoyable and easy to hear when it is turned down. Plus, your voice won't be hoarse from yelling at your friends, which is another problem.

Try some earplugs at concerts. There are special earplugs for musical concerts that don't change the way the music sounds, they just make it quieter.

164.

Why can people who usually stutter manage to sing without stuttering?

A big problem for stutterers is tension in their vocal cords. Vocal cords lock up, and stuttering is one way to loosen them up. Now think about singers — their vocal cords move constantly, so they can't tense or lock up. Add that to the fact that when you sing you aren't thinking of something to say, you are singing words that you know and have memorized. And the singer can think about the music rather than just the words.

Stuttering seems to be related to a faulty link between the left side of the brain, where words are initiated, and the voice mechanism. Since music is connected to the right side of the brain, the stuttering doesn't kick in. Many stutterers also use musical tricks to avoid stuttering. Winston Churchill, the former Prime Minister of Great Britain, would hum before he made a speech, and that let him get through without stuttering.

165.

What makes people tone deaf?

There isn't a simple answer to why some people are tone deaf. First of all, what does tone deaf mean? Basically, it means not being able to hear the highness or lowness of a note of music, so it is impossible to sing it on pitch.

Pitch means how high or how low a note is. Think of a piano — each key is a different pitch. Sometimes you don't hit the note right on pitch when you are singing — you fall between the keys. You can be sharp or flat because your aim is off or your sound production is bad.

Tone is the quality or resonance of your pitch. So if you're tone deaf you don't hear where the note is supposed to go. You don't hear the C or whatever note you're aiming for — so you can't match the pitch because you can't perceive the difference.

If someone is missing the pitch, they can be trained to produce better quality sound and to hit the note they're aiming for. But it doesn't work if they can't perceive the sound. These folks are tone deaf and aren't physically able to do it. The worst part is that they think they are singing on pitch because they can't hear themselves singing flat or sharp, so it can be awful for anyone listening.

Tips for Better Tone

@ If you don't want to wreck your voice, don't whisper or yell.

@ Don't drink really cold water because it shocks your voice muscles.

@ Milk can encourage some people's bodies to make phlegm, which interferes with the clarity of their voice.

Why are people so terrified of giving a speech?

and Other Unusual ODDS AND ENDS

166.

Why are people so terrified of giving a speech?

Fear of public speaking is many people's number-one fear. Standing in front of a crowd is scarier for these people than the fear of death and disease, or even the fear of falling off a cliff. Why? Because it's performance, and the accompanying anxiety is totally normal.

Think of the last time you gave a speech. Were you trembling or sweating, did you have clammy hands, was your heart racing, your tummy queasy, your voice shaking? Were you blushing, a bit confused, losing your train of thought? All of these are symptoms of performance anxiety. It might be a fear of failure, a fear of making a fool of yourself, or just a general fear.

The crowd doesn't have to be an auditorium full of people. You might get scared doing an oral presentation in front of your class. The good news is that you can get over performance anxiety . . . but it will take a while. First you have to stop avoiding speaking in public. Then try some small things to get you more comfortable. Try asking a few questions in class. Read out loud at the dinner table in front of guests, or do a little presentation somewhere. Ask for some help from your teacher or your parents. These coaches will remind you to relax and help you to structure your ideas, to rehearse, and to breathe! Being well prepared and calm is the key to feeling confident enough to soar through a performance.

167.

Why do golfers yell fore (or is it four?) when teeing off?

This is a warning: you are forewarned. (That is a hint.) You wouldn't want a golf ball to whack you when a golfer hits it with a huge amount of force. So golfers yell "Fore!" to warn you that it is coming.

Golf has been around since the fifteenth century, and something has been yelled in warning ever since. "Fore!" is likely a shortened form of the military phrase, "Ware before!" (from "Beware"), which was used to mean "Look out ahead!" or "Duck!" because guns were going to be fired over your head.

168.

Why are so many cars black, red, white, blue or grey?

When Henry Ford built the first Model T in 1908, he told customers that they could have it in any colour, as long as it was black. Things have progressed since then, and today there are dozens of choices. Colours change with fashion too. Blue and grey were once very popular with fleets like delivery cars and rentals. Red and white were the most popular for private buyers.

Dark green once rivalled white, which has been the long-time favourite (especially in warm climates since it doesn't absorb much heat, and it looks clean and simple). White is still the lead colour for luxury cars, and trucks and vans. More natural colours like tan, and light greens like sea foam, have been popular at times too, as well as aqua, silver and purple.

People like a change, and colours have cycles of popularity. The DuPont Corporation, a huge supplier of automotive paints, does a lot of research on colour preferences so that car designers and stylists can try to predict what colours will be most popular in the future.

60% of men and 50% of women aged eighteen to thirty-four say that colour is an important factor in their car purchasing decision.

169.

Why is a car's performance measured in horsepower?

James Watt, a Scottish engineer, invented the steam engine. Because horses had been the main method of power before his invention, he came up with the idea of horsepower to compare the power of his engine to the power of horses. Watt was trying to establish the rate of doing work. He figured out how much coal a horse could haul in a minute, by what he called a foot-pound — how much work it took to move one pound the distance of one foot (about a third of a metre). He worked out that one horsepower is 33,000 foot-pounds of work per minute, or 746 watts.

So what did that mean? Mostly it meant that a standard for comparison had been established. When the steam engine gave way to car engines and electric motors and other powerful devices, there was a way to compare them. A car engine's horsepower lets you know how powerful your car is — how fast it will go from 0 to 100 km per hour. Most high-end sportscars go up to 600 horsepower.

170.

What did we use before toilet paper?

The oldsters always refer to using pages from a Sears Roebuck or Eaton's catalogue, or pages from old books or newspapers — but that was after paper and printing were cheap. What about before that, or for folks who didn't read? Corncobs. Yes, the cob that corn comes on. Eat the corn and you have a cob that could be dried and hung in an outhouse to be used for cleaning up. Throw it down the hole and it would compost nicely. (This makes catalogue pages seem very hygienic and convenient, not to mention soft!) And when you are camping, leaves seem to be the t.p. of choice. Just be sure to avoid stinging nettles.

In some countries people use nothing but water to clean themselves after going to the bathroom. The left hand is always used for cleaning. That's why in India you must only use your right hand for eating. To do otherwise would be gross and very impolite.

171.

What does the post office do with all the letters addressed to Santa Claus, and why did kids start writing to him in the first place?

Canada Post gets just under one million letters to Santa a year, because everyone knows that Santa lives at the North Pole, which is in Canada. Kids from all over the world write to Santa Claus, North Pole, Canada H0H 0H0. All across the country, Santa has hundreds of helpers. Every letter is answered. Volunteers, mostly retired postal workers, are the ones who actually reply to the children's letters. If a letter is in another language, it is translated.

There are helper letter-from-Santa writers in other countries too. In the United States, many of the children's letters are sent to Santa Claus, Indiana, and returned with the town's postmark.

The most famous Santa letter was written in 1897 by eight-year-old Virginia O'Hanlon of New York City. She wrote to the editor of the *New York Sun*.

Dear Editor,

I am eight years old. Some of my little friends say there is no Santa Claus. Papa says, "If you see it in *The Sun*, it's so." Please tell me the truth, is there a Santa Claus?

Virginia O'Hanlon

And this was part of editor Francis Pharcellus Church's response:

Yes, Virginia, there is a Santa Claus. He exists as certainly as love and generosity and devotion exist, and you know that they abound and give to your life its highest beauty and joy. Alas! How dreary would be the world if there were no Santa Claus! It would be as dreary as if there were no Virginias. There would be no childlike faith then, no poetry, no romance to make tolerable this existence. We should have no enjoyment, except in sense and sight. The external light with which childhood fills the world would be extinguished.

Not believe in Santa Claus! You might as well not believe in fairies. You might get your papa to hire men to watch in all the chimneys on Christmas Eve to catch Santa Claus, but even if you did not see Santa Claus coming down, what would that prove? Nobody sees Santa Claus, but that is no sign that there is no Santa Claus. The most real things in the world are those that neither children nor men can see. Did you ever see fairies dancing on the lawn? Of course not, but that's no proof that they are not there. Nobody can conceive or imagine all the wonders there are unseen and unseeable in the world.

172.

Is it possible to dye your hair with Kool-Aid?

It is, but we don't recommend it, because the stuff will stain everything. Your bathtub could stay Purplesaurus Rex for weeks. People who have used Kool-Aid say their hair stays a good strong colour for only one to three days, then it will be a faded version of that colour for about a week. (The good thing is that their parents probably got over it sooner than if they used real hair dye.) You absolutely have to use the unsweetened stuff. Pre-sweetened Kool-Aid makes a huge sticky mess.

Kool-Aid works best on light hair — the blonder the better. If a dark brunette put Great Bluedini Kool-Aid on his hair it would look like his hair was growing mould — an icky, dull green mould.

People who have dyed their hair with Kool-Aid say you need about three packets for short hair. They dump the Kool-Aid into a small bowl or dish — glass is best as it won't stain the way plastic will — and add a tiny amount of water to make a paste (sort of thick, like tomato paste). The true colour won't be obvious at this point. Then they slap the paste all over their hair and try to comb it in until their hair dries. It is hard and clumpy and messy, even with a large-toothed comb. They leave the Kool-Aid on all day for intense colour, but some people say it works even if you leave it for just an hour or two. Then they wash the

231

paste out of their hair . . . and start scrubbing out the shower after they rinse out the paste. Stain City!

Remember, it's not recommended that you actually try it on your hair, but it can work on other stuff. You might try dyeing some wool yarn. Mohair works best. Wash it in Ivory Liquid first so the dye will take or set better. Pour hot water (enough to cover the wool) into a container, then mix in the Kool-Aid powder. The more packages, the stronger the colour. For example, add a small amount of wet yarn to one packet of cherry Kool-Aid mixed with a few cups of water in a glass mason jar (uncovered). Zap it in the microwave for just a couple of minutes — don't boil it! Leave it in the microwave until it cools down, and the yarn will be a fabulous intense red. It smells great too — just like cherries.

A Nebraska salesman invented Kool-Aid in 1927. He hated selling soft-drink syrup in bottles; the bottles were heavy and kept breaking. So he eliminated the water, got rid of the bottles, and sold the drink powder in handy little envelopes. He called his new product Kool-Aid. At first, there were just a few flavours — grape, lemon-lime, cherry, orange, raspberry and strawberry. Now there are dozens of flavours with wacky names like Man-o-Mangoberry and Stompin-Strawberry-Kiwi.

Some people use JELL-O to dye their hair too, but it has sugar in it as well as gelatin. Talk about messy — this stuff is unbelievable. But they can really sculpt their hair with JELL-O if that's the look they're aiming for.

173.

Why did people create money?

Money didn't have to be in the form of the coins and bills we use today, but something was needed to exchange for goods and services. It could have been chickens — but that would be a bit messy. Bricks are too heavy, and feathers would fly away. Get it? Money is really an idea or concept, more than an object.

The first humans didn't need money, but as the population increased there was a need for more food. Families would travel to hunt and gather food. They began trading with other families — maybe skins for meat or fish for shells, whatever they had for whatever they needed. They would trade goods for goods, which is called bartering.

But things started getting complicated. What if you needed food but the farmer who grew the food didn't need what you produced? That's when people started using objects as money. It could be *anything* as long as people agreed on its value. Salt was used as money in many parts of the world because it was valuable for flavouring and preserving foods. Shells, tobacco, blankets, tea and barley were also used, in different places.

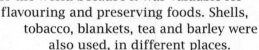

They can be a little hard to transport though — they get heavy. And salt can melt in the rain. There was definitely a need for something else.

Almost four thousand years before Christ, the Sumerians thought something needed to be done, so they started using silver bars as money. As trade started to spread around the world, ideas were exchanged as well as goods. People liked the metal money that the Sumerians had invented, so most countries began to use silver.

Coins came next. They were easy to use, and could be stamped with pictures of the country's leaders. Coins came in all sorts of metals — copper, bronze, silver and gold. In 1295 Marco Polo came back to Italy from a trip to China with the discovery that the Chinese had been using paper money for hundreds of years. But it took a long time for Europeans to catch on to paper money. Coins felt safer because the metal would always have value. Sometimes citizens didn't really trust the governments who printed the paper money.

In the colonies of North America, settlers used coins as well as things like corn and fish and wampum (belts or bracelets and necklaces made of shells, used originally by some First Nations). Mints were eventually built to produce the coins or bills we use as money, and there has been no turning back.

Now many people use debit or cash cards for money. When a debit card is used to pay for goods, the amount of money is immediately transferred out of the purchaser's bank account. Cash cards (which are called smart cards in some places) can be "filled" from someone's bank account, then used until the cash value is used up (like phone cards), and then "refilled."

Debit cards, and sometimes cash cards, are also used for parking meters and movie tickets, so people need actual cash less often. So, who knows just how long the Sumerians' invention will stick around in the future?

174.

Why do drivers in some countries drive on the left, and others on the right?

Road rules are a mishmash all over the world, except on the ocean where one rule rules: ships of all sizes keep to the right (starboard side, green light), and traffic passes on the left (port side, red light). The saying goes: "Green to green or red to red. Perfect safety, go ahead." Too bad it isn't so simple on roads. It totally depends where you are whether you drive on the left or the right.

It all started back in the old days, when travellers had to worry about being attacked on their journeys. Since most human beings are right-handed (only ten per cent are left-handed), they wanted to walk on the left in order to pass oncoming people on their right, because they carried their swords in their right hands. That way they were always at the ready to do battle. Think of a knight on a horse with his lance in his hand — he kept to the left too. This was only a custom to begin with, but it was made official in 1300 by Pope Boniface VIII, who wanted no fighting among the pilgrims on their walk to Rome during that year of jubilee celebrations. He said to keep to the left, and people stuck with this ruling in Britain when they began driving.

When settlers first came to the United States they also drove wagons on the left, because that had been the custom in Europe. Some people think they eventually switched over to rebel against the Old World customs, but the truth is a better story.

It's actually about how covered wagons, called "prairie schooners" or Conestoga wagons, work. There was no front seat, so the driver controlled the horse or oxen team by sitting on the left rear animal. That was the best position for a right-handed person to handle a whip. When two wagons approached each other, they would veer to the right, so each driver could clearly see the passing wagon's wheel hub, and avoid collision. In 1792 a law was passed confirming the stick-to-the-right custom. A hundred years later, automobiles were invented, and the steering wheel was placed on the left, the same side used by Conestoga wagon drivers.

It was the same in France. Freight wagons there were similar to the Conestogas, and also drove on the right. In Britain, however, the wagons had a driver's seat in front of the load, and drivers sat on the right side, just where the British now mount their steering wheels.

Because Canada is a Commonwealth country, most people drove on the left until the 1920s. The last place to make the switch was Newfoundland, which changed over at midnight on January 2, 1947, two years before joining Confederation. One reason Canada switched is obvious — it is so close to the United States that it would be confusing to switch sides of the road at the border.

How many countries are on each side? Of 232 countries in the world, 73 drive on the left and 159 on the right; 69% of the vehicles on the road drive on the right, and 31% on the left.

175.

What did people use before toothbrushes and toothpaste?

The first toothbrush was a twig, likely a licorice root, about the size of a pencil. One end of the stick was frayed to make it soft and fibrous; it would be rubbed against the teeth.

In some places, chew sticks are still used. Some African tribes fray twigs from the *Salvadore persica* or "toothbrush tree." The American Dental Association has discovered some remote areas of the U.S. south where twig brushes, mostly from white elm, are used. Twig brushes can work as well as our nylon toothbrushes.

Picks have been popular since Roman times. Quills could be used, or special brass or silver toothpicks made.

The first bristle brush like the ones we use today came from China in 1498. It was made of hand-plucked bristles from the backs of the necks of hogs, fastened into handles of bamboo or bone. The Europeans went in more for horsehair toothbrushes. Dr. Pierre Fauchard, who is considered the father of modern dentistry, said in his 1723 textbook that horsehair brushes were too soft. He figured a better way was to rub teeth and gums vigorously with some natural sponge.

After Louis Pasteur, a nineteenth-century scientist, proved that animal-hair toothbrushes could be a breeding ground for bacteria and fungus, people looked for an alternative. When the DuPont company created the nylon bristle toothbrush in 1938, there was no turning back.

As long as four thousand years ago a sort of toothpaste was used. In 2000 B.C. doctors made a paste of powdered pumice stone and strong wine vinegar. It must have smelled very strong, and it was very abrasive too. People would brush it on with a chew stick. Perhaps the strangest "toothpaste" used was urine. The early Romans used human urine because they thought it would whiten teeth and fix them more firmly in the sockets. And it gets worse. Upper-class Roman women would pay big bucks for Portuguese urine that was said to be the strongest on the continent. Urine continued to be an active component in toothpastes and mouthwashes into the eighteenth century. It was actually the ammonia molecules in urine that did the cleaning. When people figured this out, ammonia was used instead of urine.

Artificially whitening teeth is a big business today and it has been since the fourteenth century. A barber-surgeon would file the teeth with a coarse metal tool, then dab them with *aquafortis,* a solution of highly corrosive nitric acid. The teeth looked great for a while, but the acid eventually destroyed the enamel, and by mid-life people's teeth would be a decayed mess. Vanity rules, though — these acid treatments were done until the eighteenth century!

Toothpaste today contains fluoride that helps protect teeth against cavities. The abrasive is often silica that polishes and cleans the teeth. Glycerine is used to keep the paste creamy and prevent it from hardening. Then there is a bit of an artificial sweetener, a colourant, and flavouring like mint or wintergreen. If you don't like all these ingredients, try some baking soda with a little cinnamon added for flavour. It's simple and does a good job.

People who performed "dentistry" were jacks of all trades. You could get your hair cut, your teeth extracted, your beard trimmed and your blood let all at the same time and place.

176.

How big does a hill have to be before it becomes a mountain?

You would think that there should be a simple answer to this. There is sort of a simple answer. Hills are less than 305 m above the surrounding area, and have to have a distinct summit or point. But they are not just small mountains. It has to do with how hills were formed.

A hill has to be constructed from loads of built-up rock or sand that has been put there over the years by glaciers and wind. Or a hill can be a big raised bump in the earth that has then worn down.

A mountain, though, has steep slopes, and sharp or rounded peaks or ridges. And mountains often have more than one climate zone, which means that plant life that grows at one altitude won't grow at the next.

Mountains form in lots of ways. Some are volcanoes, which means that after each eruption more layers of hard lava build the mountain. Some have been created because of folding and uplifting of the earth over the past millions of years. The Rocky Mountains stopped uplifting about 70 million years ago.

So it is possible to have a hill that is higher than a mountain — it depends how it was formed. But after 305 m, it is called a mountain no matter how it was formed.

177.

Are the Yellow, Red and Black Seas actually yellow, red and black?

Actually, two out of three are true to colour. The Yellow Sea between mainland China and Korea is yellow because of a yellow silt deposited by the Yellow River. The Red Sea, which separates northeastern Africa from the Arabian Peninsula, is red because of reddish seaweed in the water. The Black Sea (inland, between Europe and Asia) is quite dark in colour, but it is called that because it is really a stormy place with a dark and nasty character.

> The Dead Sea isn't a sea at all, but a lake filled with so much salt that almost nothing can live there.

178.

What's the difference between a sea and an ocean?

It is an understandable confusion. We go on an ocean liner and eat seafood. Sea horses live in the ocean. We go to the seashore, and it might be the Pacific or Atlantic Ocean.

For starters, how many oceans are there? Turns out that that is a trick question. One answer could be that there is only one ocean, a huge thing that covers 72% of the Earth's surface and surrounds all of the land masses on the planet. But although there is one great ocean, called the "world ocean" or the "global ocean," the other answer is that it's usually divided into four parts or four oceans: the Pacific, the Atlantic, the Indian and the Arctic — although some geographers disagree and call the last one the Arctic Sea. (What about the Antarctic Ocean? It's not officially an ocean, but an extension of the southern part of the Pacific, Atlantic and Indian Oceans.) When you think about it, splitting up the ocean makes navigating and describing where you are going a lot easier.

So what's the difference between an ocean and a sea? It's another trick. The dictionary will say that the words are interchangeable. The encyclopedia says that too. Geography books make it even more complicated, so let's straighten this out.

There are four major oceans, and within those are smaller bodies of water called seas. In the big oceans, the major seas are the Caribbean and the Mediterranean, which are part of the Atlantic. The Bering and the South China Sea are in the Pacific.

So sea and ocean can be interchangeable, but you'll do better if you use the right term for the right body of water.

Which ocean is biggest? The Pacific, by far. It holds 46% of the Earth's water and it covers more area than all of the land on the planet put together.

179.

What's a snow dome?

Those marvellous scenes in a dome, that you turn over and shake to make it snow merrily inside, are called snow domes. They can also be called waterdomes, snowstorms, water globes, shake'em-ups, waterballs, snowscenes or blizzard weights.

The first snow domes showed up at the Paris Universal Exposition in 1878. French glass artisans made paperweights of hollow balls filled with water and white powder. The first scene inside the dome was added in France too. A ceramic Eiffel Tower on a little square base was shown at the 1889 Exposition. *Voilà, un souvenir.* Within years, lovely blown-glass globes were being made in Bavaria in Germany, plus Czechoslovakia, Austria and Poland. These were a big hit in Victorian England, often showing scenes from fairy tales. Dome-mania made it to North America in the 1920s, mostly via Germany. The globes sat on cobalt-blue bases hand-inscribed with the names of local towns. First produced in Pennsylvania in 1927, these globes showed up in mail-order catalogues as a "new and clever novelty." Within a year the Japanese copied the Pennsylvanian designs, and the globes were everywhere. Round, square, squat, tall, with bases made of everything imaginable and encasing every scene imaginable. In 1950, when plastics became popular, oval-shaped domes were developed. Soon domes started to be made in Hong Kong, and their prices plummeted.

Thousands of serious snow dome collectors focus on all sorts of themes. Some concentrate

on World's Fair domes (widely available since
the 1939 New York World's Fair), hand-blown
domes only, cartoon figures, presidents, cities,
countries, Christmas or religious themes,
globes with moving bits inside. The very
collectable are the domes that contain bloopers
or mistakes, just as "blooper" stamps or coins
are rare and valuable. Watch for scenes with
bald bathing beauties, or Eiffel Towers labelled
Puerto Rico.

180.

Why is Humpty Dumpty always shown as an egg when there is no egg mentioned anywhere in the rhyme?

Humpty Dumpty sat on a wall,
Humpty Dumpty had a great fall.
All the King's horses and all the King's men
Couldn't put Humpty together again.

Kate Greenaway, a children's illustrator,
once drew Humpty Dumpty as a young child
sitting on a high wall, dangling his legs,
leaning forward and gazing into space with a
forlorn expression. What happens to him seems
worse if Humpty Dumpty is shown as a child.
Normally he is portrayed as an egg with human
characteristics. Why is that?

Maybe it has to do with superstition. Eggs
occur in many mythological tales as creation
symbols. They are also used in some magical
practices. There are many superstitions
associated with eggs (such as breaking one egg

accidentally being bad luck). There's even an
old rhyme:

Break an egg, break your leg,
Break three, woe to thee,
Break two, your love's true.

In the nineteenth century it was believed
that having eggs on board a ship would cause
bad winds that would blow you off course.
Some fishermen wouldn't even allow them
on their vessels. Even today there are people
who believe strongly in brown over white eggs
or vice versa, even though both colours are
identical in food value. Some people believe
that double yolks are lucky.

Is this egg superstition why Humpty
Dumpty is portrayed as an egg? No. The fact
that he's an egg is the answer to the rhyme's
riddle. All the king's horses and all the king's
men couldn't put Humpty together again
because once an egg falls and breaks, it can't be
repaired. This riddle is thousands of years old.

There is an equivalent name
for Humpty Dumpty in dozens of
cultures: gigele gagele, humpelken
pumpelken, hillerin lillerin.

181.

Little kids in lots of countries figure that when they dig a hole they are "digging to China." Where do kids in China think they will end up?

Nobody knows why we say we are digging to China. Maybe it is because, in earlier times, China seemed to be about as far away from North America as possible. There are lots of places in the world where children believe that they are digging to China: Canada, the United States, Australia, New Zealand and France, for starters. Childhood beliefs are pretty widespread.

None of this makes much sense — you can't dig through the earth because it's too hot in there. The earth has a molten interior, so if you dug straight down you'd get fried.

A person from China told me: "It's interesting to find out such an expression as 'digging to China.' When I was a kid, sometimes I told my friends we were heading for Brazil!" When he was older he realized that if he could go right through the earth from where he lived in southern China, he'd actually emerge in Chile . . . but that's pretty close to Brazil.

How do you figure out where you might emerge if you could dig straight through? For a rough idea, you could buy a cheap, small plastic globe and stick a knitting needle through it. But math comes to the rescue again. Look at a globe or an atlas for the latitudinal and longitudinal co-ordinates of where you live. For example, if you live in Toronto, the co-ordinates are 43 degrees 40 minutes north and 79 degrees 23 minutes west (43° 40'n, 79° 23'w). The latitude part is simple, just the opposite of your starting point. For the longitude, though, you need this equation: 360° – (79° 23' + 180°). So, if you headed from Toronto straight through the centre of the earth, you would come out at 43° 40' south and 100° 37' east. (Remember that each degree is 60 minutes — that's why the 23' and 37' add up to 60', or 1°.) Those co-ordinates would put you in the southern part of the Indian Ocean, about 1500 km southwest of Perth, Australia. Not China.

If you live in Australia or somewhere else in the eastern hemisphere, you have to add a minus sign before the longitudinal co-ordinate when you do the calculation.

182.

Why did people start imagining aliens on Mars, not some other planet?

Maybe it's the reddish glow Mars gives off that has made it an object of fascination since ancient times. Red stood out in the night sky, and the planet didn't move along the same arc as most of the other planets and stars. In fact, the ancient Egyptians called it "the backward traveller" because after moving in one direction for months, it would appear to reverse direction and travel backwards across the sky. The Greeks and Romans were also fascinated by Mars, and came to associate it with war, probably because it is red — the colour of blood and the colour associated with rage. (The Romans' name for their god of war was Mars.) The truth is, Mars is red from rust — it's covered with oxidized minerals that are rich in iron.

The first science fiction writing about space journeys and life on other worlds is from the seventeenth century. By the end of the nineteenth century Mars was a favoured "destination" in science fiction. In the 1800s there was a lot of fascination with the "red planet." Italian astronomer Giovanni Schiaparelli drew maps of the *canali* (the Italian word for "channels") he observed on Mars. English-speaking people thought he meant "canals," and soon people came to believe that there were artificially constructed waterways on Mars . . . and that had to mean there was life on the planet. What Schiaparelli had actually meant was that there were grooves in the surface!

Astronomer Percival Lowell built a private observatory in Flagstaff, Arizona, and started making observations of Mars in 1894. He was convinced that the *canali* were real, and eventually mapped hundreds of them. He believed they were created by a race of intelligent Martians, to carry water from the polar caps to the equatorial regions.

Influenced by Lowell's ideas, in 1898 H. G. Wells published the famous *The War of the Worlds,* in which the Martians — who have been spying on Earth for years — finally invade it.

Astronomers knew that on August 23, 1924, the proximity of Mars and the Earth would be the closest since the beginning of the 1800s, and many people believed this would be the time that Martians would try to contact Earth.

Military stations monitored the airwaves for unusual radio signals, but nothing happened.

One of the best remembered Mars "experiences" came on Hallowe'en night, in 1938. Orson Welles, who had a contract with CBS to provide a weekly radio broadcast of adaptations of well-known classics, broadcast *The War of the Worlds* on a radio program. Because it sounded like a news broadcast, many people believed that the Martians actually *were* invading Earth, and there was mass panic. Cars jammed the highways, trying to escape the cities. People had heart attacks. The National Guard was called out. It took days for the Red Cross to convince people that it was safe to return home.

There were movies made about Martians, too: *Flash Gordon: Mars Attacks the World* in 1938, *Abbott and Costello Go to Mars* in 1953, *Robinson Crusoe on Mars* in 1964 and *Mars Attacks!* in 1996.

It turns out that it is possible there was life on Mars, and that Martian life forms have been landing on our planet for billions of years. Scientists have found what they believe is fossil evidence of life that existed on Mars, in meteorites found in Antarctica. The catch, though, is that the fossils are the remains of teeny tiny bacteria — nowhere near the invading *aliens* we've imagined all these years.

The recent space missions to Mars will continue to give scientists much to research and to ponder.

183.

Is it legal to do your income tax in Roman numerals?

People *can* do it, but the tax department doesn't really like it. (People who pull a stunt like this usually do it because they aren't happy about paying taxes. They just want to irritate the tax department.) If people do use Roman numerals, the income tax officials will pull out their form for "translation" and it will take extra time to have it processed, but it is, technically, legal.

The word taxation actually means "forced exaction." Taxes have been around for about six thousand years. There are Egyptian murals showing people being whipped for not paying their taxes. Throughout history people have not been amused about giving up a part of their wealth, no matter how happy they are about using the services their tax money pays for (like roads, schools, hospitals and water).

Apart from the Egyptian murals, another reason we know so much about taxation is the existence of the Rosetta Stone, from 200 B.C. It discusses how Egyptian king Ptolemy V reduced some taxes and abolished others.

In 1913 the United States joined a number of other countries which were already taxing incomes: Japan, New Zealand, Australia, the Netherlands and Germany. It took until 1917 for Canada to begin taxing personal income. Most governments consider income tax their single largest source of revenue.

Over the years the tax department has seen tax cheques written on all kinds of things — even a shirt.

184.

Where and what is the Holy Grail?

There's a good chance you know something about Arthurian legends. You might have read *King Arthur and His Knights of the Round Table* or maybe you've seen the movie *Camelot* or *The Sword in the Stone*. There are thousands of stories based on the legend of King Arthur, the hero of many of these medieval romances. Whether he ever existed, though, is questionable. It is also unknown how, where and when the stories started, though Wales is commonly assumed to be the original setting, perhaps in the sixth century. The whole phenomenon is a fascinating web of history and fable.

It started with one basic tale. Uther Pendragon was king, and when he died all of the knights wanted to claim his crown. Merlin the Magician proposed the idea that the person who could pull the silver sword, Excalibur, out of the stone must be the true king of England. None of the knights could do it, but Arthur could, so he was obviously Pendragon's successor.

During the Middle Ages the legend began to be about other characters from King Arthur's court: Sir Lancelot and Queen Guinevere, Tristan and Isolde, Galahad, Gawain, Perceval and the Holy Grail.

A grail, probably from the old French word *graal*, is a fairly plain dish or platter — but in medieval literature it became a holy vessel made of gold and inlaid with precious stones. In that story young Perceval, a rather naïve, bumpkin-like knight in Arthur's fellowship, visited the castle of the wounded Fisher King, keeper of the grail. There he saw the beautiful grail in a mystical procession, but because he had been warned not to talk too much, he didn't ask about it. It turned out that if he had asked about the grail, he would have cured the Fisher King, who had been wounded by a poisoned spear through the thigh (or the genitals). That's because the grail held a single wafer that could mysteriously sustain life indefinitely. (This might sound familiar too if you've read Susan Cooper's series *The Dark is Rising*, which has lots of Arthurian echoes.)

Because Perceval failed to cure the Fisher King, he had to go on a quest for the grail. Eventually he figured out that the Fisher King was his cousin. Lots of things happened to Perceval because he was so naïve about responsibility and chivalry, but he learned all sorts of life lessons along the way, and grew from simpleton to Grail Keeper because eventually he made it back with the grail, and cured the Fisher King. In other versions of the stories, Perceval had a lesser role, and a knight named Galahad became the grail hero.

The Holy Grail has been a topic of fascination for centuries. It represents a mystical experience that many people, including T.S. Eliot; Alfred, Lord Tennyson; and T.H. White have written about — the struggle between the forces of good and evil for possession of the grail, the most sacred of vessels. There are reams of interpretations of this story too. One is that the knights of a round table are Jesus' disciples, and when they search for the grail they're actually looking for a sacred relic, the cup Christ used at the Last Supper — the same cup that collected drops of divine blood during the crucifixion.

185.

How do mood rings work?

As fads from the 1970s go, the mood ring was right up there with the pet rock for silliness and for massive but short-lived sales. Basically, a mood ring is a heat-sensitive liquid crystal "quartz" stone that changes colour according to your mood. Or so the producers would have you believe. (Notice that only one colour shows any glee in your life, so they should have been called "Moody" rings.) Here's what the colours were supposed to show about your mood:

COLOUR	MOOD
blue	happy
greenish-yellow	dull
purple	moody, erratic
reddish-brown	insecure
black	desperate, down, gloomy

Joshua Reynolds invented the mood ring. Reynolds was a student of biofeedback (a way of controlling your body's reaction to stresses) and called the mood ring a "portable biofeedback aid." A widely read astrologist wrote about the rings, so when they went on sale, the public went crazy. Fall of 1975 saw 15 million mood rings sold, from $5 knock-offs to $250 gold versions.

In truth, body temperature makes the crystals change colour — the warmer your body, the happier you were said to be (or so your blue ring indicated). The fad was all over in a matter of months, which was a good thing because the liquid crystals tend to stop working after a couple of years.

Why do girls get taller before boys?

and Other Mysteries About THE OPPOSITE SEX

186.

Why do people close their eyes when they kiss?

Why not? When you think about it, kissing is so weird anyway, smashing lips together. Why not noses or forearms or ears? Most people do close their eyes when they kiss. It is sort of a reaction to the nice, comfortable warmness of the moment. And you don't want to be distracted.

But there is a more practical reason. You can't really keep your eyes open and look at your partner without going cross-eyed. The trick is to close your eyes right after you lock lips, because if you do it before you might mash noses. Done right, kissing is lovely, but it isn't worth worrying about the eyes closed/open thing. It will just come naturally.

By the way, the kiss as a romantic act is fairly recent. It only dates back to medieval times.

Some kissing superstitions:
- If your nose itches, a fool will kiss you.
- If you are kissed by a chimney sweep, you'll have good luck.
- Sneeze on Tuesday, you'll kiss a stranger.
- Kiss a deck of cards before you play, and you'll win.
- Kiss over a gate, you'll have bad luck.

187.

Why do girls get taller before boys?

Girls start earlier for sure. Girls get a growth spurt when they are around ten and a half, while boys take until twelve or thirteen to get growing. So if you look at a Grade Six or Grade Seven class picture, the students are all different sizes — they don't grow evenly. The girls are often ahead of the boys, but the girls don't all start at the same time, either, and of course they will end up different heights.

Whenever your body gets around to making these changes, that time is called puberty.

And that growth spurt in puberty is because of rising levels of hormones called androgens. Both boys and girls have androgens, as these hormones come from the ovaries, testes and adrenal glands. Androgens make your bones grow, and your shoulders broaden. Androgen levels start to rise in girls before they do in boys, and that's why girls start their growth spurt before boys.

Estrogens, another type of hormone, also influence how much bones will grow, in both boys and girls. Girls' bodies make more estrogens than boys' do, and when estrogen levels get high enough, bones stop growing, so girls usually don't grow as big as boys. Estrogens also cause fat to be added on girls' breasts and hips.

None of these changes hurt much — they are all natural — but you will find you need lots more sleep to let your body do its thing.

188.

Why do boy babies get dressed in blue, and girls in pink?

Long ago, many people believed that evil spirits hung around the nursery, but that these spirits were repelled by certain colours. The most potent colour was blue, associated with the heavenly sky. Blue was believed to frighten away demons and rob them of their power. So blue on a baby was not only adornment, but also seen as a very necessary precaution.

Now this was a long time ago, when girls were considered inferior, so boys got the really potent blue colour — it didn't matter what colour girls got. The assumption is that later generations chose pink for girls to symbolize that new rosy all-over-pink look.

189.

Why do men have nipples?

Why women have nipples is obvious — to feed their young. We're mammals and, like other mammals, we have nipples and we have hair. The nipples may be hard to find on some mammals, and the hair may be microscopic, but it is there. (The exception to this mammal rule is the platypus, which doesn't have nipples. The babies lick up the milk that oozes out of the mother's pores.) Platypus aside, why bother with the nipples on the guys?

It is because humans all start out the same at the embryo stage. If you get an X chromosome from each of your parents you will be a girl, and if you get an X from your mother and a Y from your father you will be a boy. Genitalia (ovaries or testicles) start to develop at five to ten weeks. But even before then, everyone gets what are called milk ridges, two lines of tissue running from your underarms to your groin area. Eventually these ridges mostly disappear, leaving just two nipples, although some people have three or more, all along where the ridge was. Nothing more happens with human breasts until puberty, when they become developed in females, but not in males. Nipples on men (and on every male mammal) are completely non-functional, just a reminder of how we are made.

Right after they are born, both boy and girl newborns can secrete a tiny bit of liquid from their nipples. It is sometimes referred to as witches' milk.

190.

When did men start cutting their hair short and why?

Parents' complaints about their kids' hair length and changing hair fashions have been a part of life for much of history. Hair length has gone up and down for centuries because of age, marital and social status, religion, occupation and other reasons. Here's a brief history of hairstyles:

In ancient Egypt, shaved heads and hairless bodies were signs of nobility. The Egyptians even had a barber god, and wealthy men could afford to have barbers come to their homes. As time went on, the Egyptians would wear heavy black wigs for special ceremonies. Sometimes they would also wear false beards.

Barbershops were popular in ancient Greece and Rome. Men would meet to exchange news while they were being shaved or having their hair styled, or having a massage. The most popular hairstyle for Roman men was short, brushed forward and arranged in curls that were made with curling irons — even the older men wore it like this. Men would even use perfume and face paint to beautify themselves.

The Gauls, who lived in what is now France, believed that long hair was a sign of honour. When Julius Caesar conquered them in 50 B.C., he made them cut their hair to demonstrate their submission.

The Bible mentions barbers during the time of Ezekiel. Female barbers have never been as popular as male barbers, maybe because of the story of Samson and Delilah. Samson was an ancient biblical hero who was forbidden to cut his hair, the source of his strength. But the doomed Samson fell in love with a woman named Delilah, who betrayed him to his enemies by cutting off his hair while he slept.

In the Middle Ages longer hair was popular, and most men had beards. Bowl haircuts and the pageboy — where chin-length hair is curled under — were the most popular men's hairstyles. During King Henry VIII's reign, men wore their hair longer and there was more variety in the styles.

In France, cutting off a king's hair was thought to take away his power. But in the sixteenth century, after Francis I of France accidentally burned his hair with a torch, men wore short hair and grew short beards and moustaches. In the seventeenth century upper-class men's hair got longer and wigs gained in popularity. Some of them were extremely tall and curly. Poorer people wore shorter, uncurled haircuts under caps.

Wigs for men were still popular in the eighteenth century in Europe and the American colonies, but they were not as extravagant. The most common style of wig had a ponytail at the back that was either tied with a ribbon or tucked into a bag. For special occasions the wigs were made with white hair or were powdered to be white. Wigs that are still worn by some judges are based on these styles. During the French Revolution in the late 1700s, men returned to more classical Roman hairstyles. In the nineteenth century men kept their hair quite short and seldom wore wigs, but most had some kind of facial hair, either sideburns, beards or moustaches.

259

During the first half of the twentieth century, most men wore their hair short and were clean-shaven, probably because of the military influence of the First and Second World Wars. In the 1950s Elvis Presley appeared with a shiny black pompadour hairstyle and long sideburns, and in the 1960s the Beatles and other rock-and-roll groups had a big influence on men's hairstyles. Now almost anything goes! No matter how you wear your hair, you ought to be able to show your parents that at some point in history it was "all the rage."

No matter the culture, a person's hairstyle can tell a lot about them:

◎ Age: In many cultures a child's hair is cut to symbolize that they are entering a new stage of life. In England, young boys would receive their first haircut at about age three — the same time they got their first pair of long pants.

◎ Marital status: In some African countries a woman's hairstyle shows not only if she's married, but whether or not she has children.

◎ Occupation: In most cultures, soldiers have the same hairstyle to show their obedience and to signify that they are part of a group.

◎ Religion: Some religions require that their followers shave or cover their hair, or wear a special hairstyle. Buddhist monks, who believe strongly in having no attachment to material things, keep their heads shaved to avoid distracting themselves from their meditation and prayer.

◎ Fortune: In Nigeria, children born with thick, curly hair are thought to bring good luck to their parents.

◎ Reverence: Some tribes in Papua New Guinea believe that your ancestors' spirits live in your hair, so you shouldn't cut it.

191.

Why do so many blond or light-haired men often have darker beards?

Before we attack the topic of colour, let's look at facial hair in general. Men grow beards for all sorts of reasons: to be fashionable, to be unfashionable, to be a rebel, or to hide behind. (Or maybe because it hurts their skin to shave.) It's important to know that Gillette didn't invent the safety razor until just before World War I. Shaving was much easier after that, and gas masks fit better on a clean-shaven man.

Over the centuries, facial hair has gone in and out of fashion. Back in the second century A.D., Hadrian the emperor grew a beard to conceal some scars, and bingo — Romans copied their emperor. And that's been the pattern: beards have been pretty common, with little surges of popularity when influential men wore one. Today, movie stars rather than emperors often lead the trends.

You have to admit, a beard is one accessory that any man can afford. Sideburns too. They are named after Ambrose Burnsides, an American Civil War general who sported the odd hairline extension. Back in the sixteenth century, there were intriguing descriptive names for beard styles. The Sugar Loaf was long and rounded, wider at the top than bottom. The Bush, French Fork, Swallow-Tail, Needle, Screw and Fan-Tail all have names that describe them well.

The goatee is a beard with an odd history. When you think about it, representations of the

261

good guys in the Bible (like God, Jesus and Moses) all have big beards like Santa Claus. Yet the devil is usually shown with a goatee. His beard doesn't join up with the sideburns. It's basically a moustache and a goatee (a short, pointed beard) that don't meet. It can disguise a disappearing chin, or maybe add sophistication . . . but mostly it makes a man look menacing. Moustaches also seem to have a fairly sinister reputation, as over the years bad guys wore them.

But let's talk colour, finally. The fact is, doctors and scientists don't really know why so many blond or light-haired men have darker, often ruddy beards. (And remember that what you see may not be entirely true, because you have no idea who is dyeing their hair these days.)

Hair and beard colour differences may or may not relate to the apparent age of the follicle. Hair on your head ages first. It gets lighter and thinner and disappears first because the follicle shrinks. Partially that is because of too much time in the sun without a hat. And density seems to decrease from the top down. It's sort of like the places where people go grey first. Most people grey in the area in front of the ear, not behind it or above it. But this doesn't apply to everyone.

- The man sporting the longest recorded beard was Hans Langseth. It measured 5.33 m when he died in 1927.
- Whisker facts: The average man's beard contains 15,500 hairs, which grow 0.038 cm each day, or 14 cm a year. During his lifetime the average man will spend 3340 hours shaving off 8.4 m of whiskers. He will shave off nearly half a kilogram of whisker hairs every sixteen years.
- Superb words to toss around are pogonotrophy (beard growing) and pogonotomy (beard cutting).

192.

Why do men have Adam's apples?

That lump on men's necks, the outer part of the voice box or larynx, is called an Adam's apple. Women have one too, but a man's Adam's apple is at a sharper angle and seen more easily.

The Adam's apple is named after Adam, who the Bible says was one of the first two people on the earth (along with Eve, his mate). The legend is that Adam ate some forbidden fruit from the Garden of Eden and a piece of it got stuck in his throat. That throat bulge has been with men forever, supposedly to show that men can be weak and give in to temptation.

The medical explanation is that men have stronger larynx muscles, hence deeper voices, and the Adam's apple is where those muscles are stored.

193.

Is it true that the lifespan of a woman is longer than a man's? Are there more males or females in the world? Why?

Indeed it is true. In most developed countries of the world, women outlive men by 5 to 9 years. In 2016 the life expectancy for females in over 40 nations was at or exceeded 80 years. In Canada life expectancy for women is 82 years and for men, 77 years. That beats the U.S., where life expectancy for women is 84.7 years and for men is 80.9 years. The World Health Organization reported in 2016 that there were 7.4 billion people in the world, and the average global lifespan was 72 years.

Records for things like lifespans started to be kept in the 1500s, so we know that at least since then women have lived longer than men. Cavemen probably only lived to be about 18. Over the past hundred years life expectancy in developed countries has increased for both women and men — mostly due to better nutrition and better health care. Throughout the world, there are nine times more women than men who are over 100 years old. The death rates for women are lower than those for men at all ages, even before birth.

Some scientists believe that females are genetically programmed to live longer so that they can raise their children and maybe even their grandchildren. Sex hormones probably have a

lot to do with lifespan — males have a hormone called testosterone that experts believe is linked to aggressive behaviour and which puts men at higher risk for heart disease. Females have estrogen, which doctors believe protects them from heart disease and strokes until later in life, though rates of heart disease for women have been increasing.

You might assume, then, that the world would have more women in it. But it isn't true — according to the United Nations' statistics for the year 2019, there are 3,889,035,000 males and 3,824,434,000 females worldwide. The sex ratio was 101.7 males per 100 females. If girls live longer than boys, how can this be?

It all comes down to the fact that more males are conceived and born than females. According to the same 2000 statistics, at birth, there were about 106 male babies for every 100 female babies. And although more males than females die in every subsequent year of life, it doesn't quite balance out. Between the ages of 15 and 24, males are three times more likely to die than females — and the most common cause of death is from motor vehicle accidents, followed by homicide, suicide, cancer and drowning. Even between the ages of 55 and 64, men in the U.S. are twice as likely as women to die in car accidents. So boys — be careful!

Some scientists believe that life expectancy will continue to rise. Some even think that there is no maximum age, because of medical advances, and that in the future, people will die only because of accidents, not from "old age."

194.

How come tortoiseshell cats are always girls?

Tortoiseshell and calico cats have a combination of orange/red colouring from one parent, and black, tabby or other non-orange colouring from the other parent. Red, black and cream tortoiseshell cats are almost all female. Same thing with calico cats which are more than half white, with patches of red and black. Funny, isn't it? Only five in one thousand are male, and those males are sterile — they can't reproduce. Why?

It all comes down to the way chromosomes work. Females have two X chromosomes (XX) and males have an X and a Y (XY). Turns out that the gene that controls orange/red is an X chromosome, as is the gene for non-red. Since females have the XX pattern, only they can have the two colours. The rare male tortie is a result of an extra X chromosome (an XXY combination) where the male gets all the female colour characteristics with the two XX chromosomes, plus the Y for the male characteristics.

Because of the rarity of male torties, for many centuries it has been considered good luck to own one. In England it was even believed that you could get rid of warts by having the male tortoiseshell cat's tail rubbed on your warts in the month of May. Japanese fishermen, who would use them to protect their ships from storms and the crews from ghosts, also keenly sought out these cats.

195.

What is a courting candle?

Courting is an old fashioned term for seeking affection — dating, wooing or romancing. And a courting candle is a relic of the times before electricity, when parents were very strict with their daughters' affections. The courting candle comes from the nineteenth century, and looks a bit like a candle stuck into a heavy bedspring. The deal was that the suitor could stay only until the candle burned down to the level of the top of the holder. Since different kinds of candles burn at different rates, and since the girls' parents could also choose how much of the candle to let stick above the holder, there was room to manipulate the courting situation. A young man would know his girlfriend's parents thought he was okay if the candle was high above the holder and took a very long time to burn down. He got a nice long visit!

196.

Why does hair fall out and why does it only happen to men?

Male or female, you lose up to 125 hairs a day. New hairs will replace the lost ones — unless you're balding. And it doesn't just happen to men. Both men and women lose hair density as they grow older, but far more men than women go completely bald.

Why do you go bald? Your hair follicles start shrinking. When those hair follicles can't produce new hair to replace the hair that falls out every day, you have a net loss. Your hair follicles shrink because of hormonal changes, and men have a typical type of balding (called "male pattern baldness") caused by the male hormone testosterone. Researchers also know that your age, your sex, and whether or not your parents were baldies play a part. Basically, don't get too attached to those locks, guys.

197.

Is it true that only boys can be colour-blind?

No, but while 8% of boys can't distinguish various colours and shades, less than half of 1% of girls are colour-blind. The professionals call it colour vision deficiency, which describes the problem better — difficulty determining various colours and shades.

We all have cones and rods at the back of our eyes that help us detect the differences in colours and degrees of brightness. If you are colour-blind there are varying degrees of problems with those cones, or just fewer cones. Mostly you are born with this, but some older adults develop troubles distinguishing one dark colour from another as they age, or if they develop a retinal disease.

The most common problem is red-green colour vision deficiency, which means there aren't enough red and green cones. So in lower light, folks with this problem might think those colours are brown, or that the green object is red.

Likely you will figure out if you are colour-blind during your school years. And if one of your family members is colour-blind, you have a greater chance of being colour-blind too. It's not considered a disability — more a social inconvenience. If you are affected you may need help coding your clothing to make sure it doesn't clash badly. And figuring out traffic lights will take some training too. So many guys have this problem that it makes you really wonder why red and green are used for warning signals. And remember: be sensitive to your colour-blind friends — they absolutely won't be able to play laser tag with you.

Why can't you tickle yourself?

and Other Strange Stories from SCIENCE

198.

Why is it so hard to get rid of hiccups?

Hiccuping (or hiccoughing — that's a clue) is a funny and rather rude reflex action, sort of like coughing or sneezing or even vomiting. Maybe you ate or drank too fast, and swallowed some air. It might be a stomach problem and you need to get rid of some gas. It might be that you have a tickly throat, or maybe the nerves that control your diaphragm are a bit jumpy. Whenever one of these things happens you can react with a hiccup.

Most people hiccup for a minute or two. It can be somewhat annoying, but is usually quite funny. Sometimes, though, people can't stop. One man in Iowa started hiccupping in 1922 and stopped in 1990. That's sixty-eight years! In the meantime he got married twice, had eight children, and led a normal life. Obviously he even figured out how to sleep.

If you are just a regular hiccupper, a loud "Boo!" can often make you stop. It'll scare the extra breath out of you. What happens is that the shock of the scare distracts your nervous system and it "forgets" to hiccup. If you sneeze, the same thing can happen. But getting yourself to sneeze is pretty hard. You can gargle, tug on your tongue, or try drinking water upside down. But mostly, when your hiccups want to stop, they will.

I-HICC-do

199.

Why do we get electric shocks in our fillings when we chew on aluminum foil?

This makes my teeth hurt just thinking about it. You may not have this problem, but your parents might. It is a shocking experience indeed when your filling — which is made of an amalgam (a mixture) of silver or tin and mercury — touches aluminum foil. Suddenly you get an electric reaction. That's because when you put two different kinds of metals together, in the right circumstances, you can get a quick zap of electricity.

A man named Count Volta discovered this in Italy in 1800. That's where we get the word "volt" from — it is a measurement of electrical current. Count Volta stacked up a tall pile of discs: copper, cardboard soaked in salt water, zinc, then copper, soaked cardboard, zinc, etc. again. Then he touched the top and bottom discs on the stack at the exact same time and got a shock. What he had created was, in fact, the first battery, but at the time they called it a voltaic pile.

In your mouth the aluminum foil and your filling are the two metals. Then your saliva works like the salt water, which is needed for the charge. Contact is made when you bite, and a small current gets going, which the nerves in the teeth can feel. That's how you get the shock.

200.

Why do WintOGreen Lifesavers spark in the dark?

Try this yourself. Stand in the dark in front of a mirror. Put a WintOGreen Lifesaver in your mouth. (It has to be a fresh one; if it is soggy you get no sparks.) Crunch down hard on the Lifesaver and bingo — sparks! Bluish sparks will burst from your mouth. It's a fabulous sweet spark. Tiny but impressive.

Why does this happen? It's called *triboluminescence*. That's what happens when crystals fracture. Triboluminescence is the light that is the result of crystals crushing or tearing.

Here's what happens.

Everything around us is made up of atoms like carbon, nitrogen, hydrogen and oxygen. The atoms are made up of tiny particles — electrons, protons and neutrons. Atoms cluster together in groups called molecules. When you crunch the sugar crystals in a Lifesaver, electrons break loose and zip around. Invisible nitrogen molecules that are in the air can detect an opening where the electrons have broken free, and zoom into that spot. All this happens very fast. The electrons that broke off the sugar crystals in the first place decide they want to return to the fold, but since the nitrogen molecules are already there, the electrons crash into the nitrogen. They re-combine with a bang. And that crashing together results in light — in fact, in ultraviolet radiation. It's totally safe; you can't get a sunburn from this tiny spark. But it is impressive.

Add the fact that this ultraviolet radiation

has hit the wintergreen flavouring (which is called methyl salicylate) and you get the bluish tinge to the glow. You can actually get almost all crystal sugar candy to give you a bit of light when it is crushed. This was first noticed in Italy in the seventeenth century. But for most crystal candy it is a rather dim light. It takes wintergreen to really light up your life.

It's probably much more scientific than you need to know — but now you do. The important thing is that it's fun. And it is a good party trick too — just don't break your teeth!

201.

How are marbles made?

Perfectly spherical marbles are really pretty things. They are favourites of collectors, and have been toys for thousands of years. Archaeologists have even found clay marbles in the pyramids of Egypt. Marbles are called marbles, by the way, because in the early seventeenth century they were made of marble, ground into spheres. There were also aggies made of agate, and commies (for common-ies) made of inexpensive clay. But now marbles are mostly made of glass.

Marbles are either made by machine or by hand, worked off spun-glass rods. The glassmakers heat the rods until the glass is molten and then cut it and round it off. In the middle of the nineteenth century a German glassworker invented marble scissors that made mass manufacturing of marbles a possibility. These scissors were a simple cupped tool that rounded a hot glass marble in one step, instead of having to round them by hand. You would form the shape by pressing the hot end of the glass into the cup of the marble scissors, and turning it several times. The scissors were then pressed together and twisted slowly until the rounded glass was separated from the glass cane. Then the slightly hardened marbles were rolled in a wooden barrel where they gradually cooled and become more round.

Today most marbles are made by machine. Glass (which is made of sand, soda ash and lime) is melted at between 1300° and 1400°C for up to twenty-eight hours, until it is the consistency of molasses. This batter is poured, cut and put through rollers, then cooled and made into little balls. It's a bit like cookie dough — but a lot hotter.

Different technologies have made it possible to make different kinds of marbles: clearies or purees, which are one clear colour; various coloured and patterned swirls; corkscrews in various colours; bumblebees (black and yellow); and Vaseline glass that is fluorescent in colour. In the 1950s the Japanese came up with cat's-eye marbles that are clear, except for a vein of brightly coloured glass. How do you get those sparkling swirls or spirals in marbles? You take a striped glass rod and twist and twist it, and then shape it as usual.

202.

How was duct tape invented?

You know what is said about duct tape: You only need two things in life: WD–40 to make things go, and duct tape to make them stop.

Duct tape is the handyman's secret weapon. Need to fix your canoe, your car or your sneakers? There are thousands of uses for this great, sticky grey tape.

Duct tape was invented during World War II to meet an important need. At that time, it was called "duck" tape. The American armed forces needed a strong, waterproof mending material that could be ripped by hand to make quick repairs to Jeeps, aircraft and other military equipment. There was also a need for something to keep moisture out of ammunition boxes.

Johnson & Johnson were already producing adhesive tapes for medical uses, so they just added a rubberized waterproof coating. Waterproof, like a duck . . . and *voilà* — duck tape.

After the war there was a housing boom in the United States. Many of the new homes had fancy new heating and air-conditioning units with ductwork. The military tape was perfect for binding and repairing these ducts. The tape began to be produced with the rubberized topcoat in a sheet-metal grey colour (so it would blend in with the ducts) and duct tape was born.

This handyman's secret weapon is no longer a secret. There are entire books devoted to describing zillions of uses for duct tape, there are jokes about duct tape, and even Web pages about it. In fact, the Web is where these words of wisdom were found: "Duct tape is like the force, light on one side, dark on the other. It holds the universe together, and if not handled properly, becomes a sticky mess."

203.

How are hurricanes named?

A hurricane or a typhoon is actually a strong tropical cyclone. That's a huge storm with very heavy winds — winds, in fact, that are higher than 119 kph, often with large amounts of rainfall. Less than 119 kph is called a tropical storm. For a hurricane to get started the ocean-water temperature has to be over 26°C. That means these storms usually come in the late summer and early fall in the tropics. Hurricanes can also start tornadoes, and the wild winds and rain can cause huge increases in sea levels, and flooding too.

The quiet centre of a hurricane, called the eye, shows up on satellite images. It can be 16 to 48 km wide. But surrounding the peaceful part are wild winds at speeds up to almost

300 kph. To whirl the core of the winds that fast takes 500 trillion horsepower! That's the equivalent of exploding an atomic bomb every ten seconds.

Before this century, hurricanes were named after the saint's day on which the hurricane appeared. Now, an alphabetical list of twenty-one names is made up by the World Meteorological Organization in Geneva, Switzerland. Since 1971 the names have alternated in gender from male to female, and skipped the letters Q, U, X, Y and Z because there aren't many names that start with those letters. The people who make these decisions choose names for the remaining twenty-one letters, names that are distinctive, not too long, and easy to pronounce and remember. The names on the North American list are also international — English, French or Spanish — because those are the three languages most used in North America.

The further along in the alphabet a hurricane name comes, the more hurricanes there have been that year. For example, in 1996 there were hurricanes called Opal and Pablo — it was a bad year. If the list only gets to Gordon, like in 1994, there weren't many hurricanes.

When there is a really fierce hurricane which is highly destructive and costly, the name will be retired for at least ten years. So far almost forty names have been retired, names like Anita (1977, Mexico), Cleo (1964, Lesser Antilles, Cuba, southeast Florida), Gilbert (1988, Lesser Antilles, Jamaica, Yucatán Peninsula, Mexico), Hugo (1989, Antilles, South Carolina), Katrina (2005, New Orleans) and Paloma (2008, Cuba and Cayman Islands).

Tropical Cyclone Names Worldwide

Caribbean Sea, Gulf of Mexico and the North Atlantic Names

2020	2021	2022	2023	2024	2025
Arthur	Ana	Alex	Arlene	Alberto	Andrea
Bertha	Bill	Bonnie	Bret	Beryl	Barry
Cristobal	Claudette	Colin	Cindy	Chris	Chantal
Dolly	Danny	Danielle	Don	Debby	Dorian
Edouard	Elsa	Earl	Emily	Ernesto	Erin
Fay	Fred	Fiona	Franklin	Francine	Fernand
Gonzalo	Grace	Gaston	Gert	Gordon	Gabrielle
Hanna	Henri	Hermine	Harold	Helene	Humberto
Isaias	Ida	Igor	Idalia	Isaac	Imelda
Josephine	Julian	Julia	Jose	Joyce	Jerry
Kyle	Kate	Karl	Katia	Kirk	Karen
Laura	Larry	Lisa	Lee	Leslie	Lorenzo
Marco	Mindy	Matthew	Margot	Milton	Melissa
Nana	Nicholas	Nicole	Nate	Nadine	Nestor
Omar	Odette	Otto	Ophelia	Oscar	Olga
Paulette	Peter	Paula	Philippe	Patty	Pablo
Rene	Rose	Richard	Rina	Rafael	Rebekah
Sally	Sam	Shary	Sean	Sara	Sebastien
Teddy	Teresa	Tomas	Tammy	Tony	Tanya
Vicky	Victor	Virginie	Vince	Valerie	Van
Wilfred	Wanda	Walter	Whitney	William	Wendy

The lists are used in rotation. Thus, the 2020 list will be used again in 2026; the 2021 names will repeat in 2027, and so on.

204.

Do astronauts use a key to start the Space Shuttle?

Like a key to start a car or a snowmobile? No, at least not the sort you might put on a key ring or hang around your neck. Space Shuttles are entirely controlled by a computer. The reason a key isn't used is that the computer has to time the launch events really carefully. It has to be incredibly precise, as exact as thousandths of a second. Keys and humans just aren't precise enough.

The launch countdown starts forty-three hours before the launch. There are hundreds of things to do to get ready: checking the software, checking the propellant line systems (which carry the fuel that gets the rocket going), loading the liquid hydrogen and liquid oxygen into the external tank. Then the crew needs to get on board.

At T-9 minutes (T minus nine, or nine minutes to takeoff) the computer, called a ground launch sequencer, takes over. Then at T-26 seconds the ground-support equipment gives control of the orbiter to the four on-board computers that control the order of the launch. The computer on the ground and the computer on board the Shuttle talk to each other and cooperate in opening and closing valves, turning on and off switches, and ensuring that takeoff happens on time, to the fraction of a second. The pilot and commander just watch all the data.

Some ferries, which hold 500 cars and 2000 people and are the length of 2 football fields, have 4 engines that are 500 horsepower each. A computer controls the start-up of these ferries, just like on the Shuttle.

205.

Why can't you tickle yourself?

Have you tried? It just doesn't work. Tickling is all about surprise, and about losing control. When someone tickles you, you spend most of your time giggling and trying to get away at the same time. There is a bit of danger there — someone is attacking you, but your brain figures out that it is just in fun, so you start giggling. The reason you can't tickle yourself is because there is no "danger" and no surprise — so no giggling. It's just the way it is.

206.

Why does snow sparkle?

Here's a hint: What else sparkles like snow? Crystals. In fact, it would be more accurate to call snowflakes by what they really are: snow crystals. And a snow crystal is simply an ice crystal. Each crystal is formed when the water vapour on particles of ash, dust or pollen inside a cloud freezes. What defines a crystal is the way the molecules line up in a hexagonal lattice formation, so every crystal has six sides. Every snowflake is different, but they can be sorted into crystal types, which vary because of the temperature and humidity occurring when they formed. An International Commission on Snow and Ice came up with a classification system for solid precipitation in 1951. They defined seven principal snow crystal types: plates, stellar crystals, columns, needles, spatial dendrites, capped columns and irregular forms. And there are three more types of frozen precipitation:

graupel (which look like round pellets), ice pellets and hail. Frozen raindrops are called sleet.

Frozen crystals can combine to make a snowflake that looks as if it's made of just a few crystals, or like a puffball with thousands of tiny mirror-like sparkling crystals. A snowflake's sparkle occurs when light reflects off the many angled surfaces and catches your eye.

Snow sparkles most when it is fresh — melting dissolves that property. When snow melts, all the surfaces dissolve and the crystals lose their shape. The result is fewer angled surfaces to catch the light . . . and the snow loses its sparkle.

The largest snowflake ever recorded was 20 x 38 cm. Ranch owner Matt Coleman discovered it in 1887.

needles

plate

star

column

dendrite

column capped with plate

207.

Why does the ocean have salt in it and how did it get in there? About how much salt is in the Dead Sea?

The salt in the ocean is a far cry from your average table salt. It is actually a very complicated solution containing more than fifty natural mineral salts. Sodium chloride (table salt) is the most abundant, with much lower concentrations of others such as calcium salts (calcium carbonate or lime, and calcium sulphate), potassium salts (potassium sulphate) and magnesium salts (magnesium chloride, magnesium sulphate and magnesium bromide). Plus there are dissolved sediments and rocks from the ocean floor, decayed matter and water. Dissolved salts are carried to oceans from rivers and streams — to the tune of almost 4 billion tonnes a year.

Scientists think that the total amount of salt in all the oceans may be almost 50 million billion tonnes. Most seawater has a salt concentration of thirty-five parts per thousand, which means that 3.5% of seawater's weight comes from the dissolved salts.

The exception is the Dead Sea, which is actually a salt *lake*, not a sea. It is up to ten times as salty as the oceans, and is located on the very lowest point of the Earth's surface, about 400 m below sea level. It is called the Dead Sea because nothing — not even seaweed — can survive in the water or around the shore, which is white from the salt crystals that cover it. If a fish swims into the lake from one of the streams that feed it, the fish dies instantly. This incredible lake got so salty because the

Jordan River and some small mountain streams feed it, but there is no drainage out of it. The only way water can leave the lake is through evaporation, and that makes the salt even more concentrated.

Most table salt comes from mines rather than from salt in the sea. Sometimes iodine is also added to it to prevent an enlarged thyroid gland called a goiter. Since manufacturers began adding iodine to table salt, goiters are rarely seen in industrialized or first world countries, but they are still common in developing nations.

208.

How old is the oldest living thing that is still living?

It's nothing cute or fuzzy, nor is it a relative of a dinosaur or a gorgeous prehistoric-looking plant. The oldest living thing is probably — get this — some bacterial spores that were found in 2000 near Carlsbad, New Mexico. The spores (genus *Bacillus*) were floating in liquid brine inside a salt crystal. Perhaps the find isn't too exciting sounding to us, but it is a *huge* discovery to scientists. They calculated that the salt likely dates back about 250 million years, and it looks like these spores are ten times older than anything ever discovered before. But, as with all scientific claims, these records have to be independently substantiated.

The bacteria is called 2-9-3, which isn't much of a name for something that may help to uncover the beginnings of life. So far, the scientists know that the same kinds of crystals were found in a meteorite in 1999. They also know that both Jupiter's moon Europa and the planet Mars at one time had oceans, and possibly the same kind of salt formations.

By the way, these bacteria could win the age race by hundreds of millions of years. Before 2000, the best contender for "oldest living thing" was some 25- to 40-million-year-old bacteria which were found inside the stomach of a bee encased in amber. You may wonder just what scientists were doing inside that stomach. Well, they were looking for the oldest living thing.

Some scientists don't believe the spores are so old, and say the oldest living organism is a *quabena* aspen in Utah, U.S., that is eighty thousand years old.

209.

Is soapstone really soap, and if so, then can it be used like bathroom soap?

Soapstone isn't soap at all. (Doesn't this kind of thing drive you crazy?) There is usually some vague connection between two words like this. In this case it is because soapstone has a bit of a soapy/slippery feel.

Even weirder is the fact that soapstone is mostly made of talc, the *softest* of minerals. Talc gets a 1 on the Mohs Scale of hardness; diamonds rate a 10.

It turns out that miners and drillers use the term "soapstone" for any rock that has a soft soapy/slippery feel, whether it has talc in it or not.

Mohs Scale	
1. Talc	6. Orthoclase
2. Gypsum	7. Quartz
3. Calcite	8. Topaz
4. Fluorite	9. Corundum
5. Apatite	10. Diamond

While you can't use it as bathroom soap, there is a small chance your sink or countertop might be made of soapstone, since it makes beautiful fixtures for bathrooms and kitchens. But in truth, since you hardly want a sink that gets scratched every time a pot or fork touches it, a "soapstone" sink is likely made of steatite. That's a harder rock (3 to 4 on the Mohs Scale) and is 40% or so talc. Soapstone can also be used for fireplace surrounds because another of its qualities is its ability to absorb and distribute heat evenly.

Many Inuit carvings are said to be made of soapstone, but in fact most are made from steatite or serpentine, both harder than soapstone.

What have we learned from this soap/soapstone puzzle? Often things aren't what you think they are, or as they are labelled. Keep asking questions!

210.

What exactly are Mexican jumping beans anyway?

They're from Mexico, and they do jump, but they're not really beans. What we call a Mexican jumping bean is actually the seed capsule of the shrub *Sebastiana pavoniana*. It's a fairly ordinary shrub with dark green leaves that turn red in the winter months, but those seed capsules or "beans" make it something special. These little beans can writhe around, rolling and hopping like a happy puppy in a roomful of ping-pong balls.

What's really happening is that a type of moth that is particularly active while hatching has hatched a marketing sensation. The female small grey moth, commonly known as the jumping bean moth (*Laspeyresia saltitans*), lays eggs on the flowers of the shrub. When the eggs hatch, the tiny larvae dig into the seed capsules, eating out parts of the interior and living there until the end of the summer. At that time the seed drops to the ground, since it can't produce a flower without some of its crucial parts. Then the hollowed-out seed containing a healthy fat moth larva starts jumping around. The warmer it is, the more the larva — and therefore the bean — jumps.

Then as the weather gets colder the larva spins a cocoon around itself and cozies in for the winter months. It is becoming a pupa now and it stops jumping. The next spring the pupa pushes out of the capsule through a hole it cut the fall before (while it was still jerking around), and becomes a moth.

Once just a simple act of nature, Mexican

jumping beans have metamorphosed into a
big export item over the years. As pets go they
are pretty interesting, not too expensive, and
you don't have to feed them. But timing is
everything when buying this item. The beans
will wiggle and groove for weeks or even
months in their container (if they have air —
punching holes in the lid of a shoebox or jar
will do it). By putting them on your hand or any
other warm object you can get them jumping
even faster. But as the larva begins turning
into a pupa, your purchase becomes rather
useless. Suddenly you'll have a crop of moths,
but unless you have jumping bean shrubs in
your garden for the moths to lay their eggs
on, so that the cycle can continue . . . no more
jumping beans. So enjoy the novelty, because it
doesn't last long.

Do animals dream?

and Other Fascinating Facts About SLEEP

211.

Do animals dream?

It seems that they do. Watch your dog or cat sometime, and you can tell it is dreaming of running after something. Its eyes twitch, sometimes it moves its paws — something is happening in its dreams. Scientists think that most warm-blooded animals dream. They have monitored goats, sheep, cats, dogs, rats, mice, monkeys and apes, and all had dream periods and symptoms — except the spiny anteater, which seems to be a dream-free mammal. Probably the animal that spends most time dreaming is the opossum.

Hunting animals like cats, dogs and humans spend more time dreaming than animals that are hunted, such as cattle, rabbits, sheep and goats.

212.

Why do people snore?

The noise that drives you bananas when your brother snores is the sound of air rushing through narrow air passages in his throat and nose. It vibrates against his tonsils, tongue or the soft tissue of his palate, or roof of the mouth.

This sound can get really loud, even louder than 90 decibels, which is defined as the highest amount of sound you can stand in the workplace. But lots of us do it: 30% to 40% of adults are snorers. Men snore more than women — half of men do. The worst culprits are overweight middle-aged men. Only around 30% of women snore, and even then they don't snore all the time.

If you sleep by yourself, snoring is no big deal. But couples sharing a bed, or siblings sharing a room, can have really bad nights (and bad fights) if one is a snorer. You have heard people call one another "mouth breathers," meaning stupid. Snorers are serious mouth breathers, but there are some ways to make them stop. If you can get snorers to change position, often you can stop the snoring, but that means you have to wake them up enough to get them to turn. People who sleep on their backs snore the most, so some books suggest tying tennis balls to the back of their pajamas so they can't sleep on their backs.

If snorers would lose weight that would help. So would avoiding alcohol at bedtime, since it clogs up your nose. Quitting smoking would help too. Sometimes snoring is a result of allergies, a broken nose, or a bigger than normal tongue, adenoids or tonsils.

There are a number of wacky-looking appliances on the market to try, which all hold the jaw and/or tongue forward to keep the airway open. Ow! It hurts even thinking about it. Snorers can also try laser surgery, but that sounds extreme. The other solution? Whoever has to sleep with a snorer can buy a large box of good earplugs.

213.

Is there another way to regain energy other than by sleeping?

Nothing comes even close to the power of a decent sleep. You can last longer without food than without sleep. Scientists don't quite know why humans are programmed to need sleep, but it's about restoring the body. Sleep is the ticket; resting just doesn't cut it. Sleep researchers say it doesn't have to be eight hours of sleep in a row — as you get older, you tend to sleep in smaller spurts anyway. You also have to get into a deep sleep — that means reaching stage four of non-rapid eye movement (NREM) sleep — before there is a release of the growth hormone that lets your body restore itself.

Think you can beat the system and stay awake? Think again. Rats deprived of all sleep lived for only three weeks instead of the usual two or three years. In driving tests, sleep-deprived adults score as badly as, or worse than, drunk drivers. Ask any new parent, or a student cramming for exams, about lack of sleep — it makes you punch-drunk and a little crazy. It would be nice if a cup of coffee or some other form of caffeine would help. In fact, it will give you a temporary energy boost, but it is not a replacement for sleep, and can actually interfere with it.

Strange Sleep Facts
- The average person falls asleep in 7 minutes.
- We will sleep for one-third of our life — about 24 years on average.

Sleep is by far the best method to *regain* energy, but there are ways to *conserve* energy too. Eating smaller meals helps. It takes a huge amount of energy to digest food and convert it to energy your body can use. That process is called metabolism. So if you eat a gigantic meal

— especially a fatty one — even though you gain energy from the food you've just eaten, your digestive system (a BIG part of your body) becomes metabolically very active and you don't have as much energy (in the form of glucose) immediately available for other things. Your stomach has a big job to do, producing acid and pepsin to break down the food, and contracting rhythmically.

What knocks you out each night but doesn't harm you? Sleep.

What do you call a sleeping bull? A bull dozer!

214.

Do bedtime tricks or routines help people sleep better?

Some people just go to the bathroom, brush their teeth and hit the hay. They fall right to sleep and that is that. But there are many who need to do certain things in a certain order to make themselves calm enough to get a good night's sleep. Some people need a snack, a warm bath, a good read . . . and maybe then they can get to sleep.

You need to sleep so that your body can rest, build up energy and stay healthy. People who don't sleep well get sick more easily; disease usually attacks the tired and weak. If you are ten to twelve years old you need about eight or nine hours of sleep every night. Researchers say that teenagers really need to sleep in, and that they don't do well in the morning. Tell your parents or your school that!

There are some tricks to getting a good night's sleep. Stay away from scary books or movies or TV shows before bedtime. You'll be riled up and you might get nightmares. Try not to do anything too frantic, like wrestling, but if you can do something that really tires you out, like swimming, you will be much happier. Hot baths are great for calming down. Some people like to write in a journal before bed, or write a list of everything that is bugging them before they sleep, so they won't be bothered by those thoughts all night long. Reading before bed is a nice ritual that can make you sleepy.

Of course there are bedtime and sleep superstitions too. Some people say you need to watch which way your head points. North means you will have short days, south means you will have a long life. If you want to be rich, point your head east, and if you want to travel, point west. Whatever it takes, just do it, because you always feel so much better after a good night's sleep.

When we are younger we all sleep on our belly or side much more, and as we get older we are all more likely to sleep on our back. The most common sleeping position for women is on their back. For men it is on their belly or their side.

215.

Is it true that if you didn't have dreams you would go crazy?

No one knows if this is true, because everyone dreams. We all dream every night, usually four to six dreams for every night's sleep. People who think they don't dream have actually forgotten their dreams. We know all of this because of studies in sleep laboratories.

Dreams are wild things. There are thousands of people involved in the industry of interpreting your dreams — academics, therapists and hobbyists. There are dream encyclopedias and dream dictionaries to tell you what the meaning of your dream supposedly is.

There are loads of superstitions involved too. Before analysts like Sigmund Freud and Carl Jung got into the act, people believed that dreams were your connection to the supernatural world, and could foretell the future. In some cultures it is believed that you dream because your soul leaves your body during sleep and goes out wandering.

There are many superstitions about dreams:

◎ Dreaming the same dream three nights in a row means that it will come true.

◎ You will have good luck if you forget your dream from last night.

◎ You can't tell your dream until after breakfast or it won't come true.

◎ If you have a dream on a Friday night and talk about it on Saturday it will come true for sure.

◎ In some cultures, whatever you dream, the opposite will come true. Dream of a funeral, for example, and a new baby will show up.

◎ To dream of the future, some people sleep with a key or a horseshoe under the pillow.

◎ If you go to a wedding and sleep with a piece of wedding cake under your pillow, you will dream of the person you will marry.

Sleep Facts

Some animals sleep a lot in 24 hours!

Little brown bat: 20 hours

Giant armadillo: 18 hours

Squirrel: 16 hours

Cat: 13 hours

Dog: 12 hours

Guppy: 6 hours

Horse: 3 hours

Tortoise: less than 1 hour

216.

Why do you drool when you nap?

Not everyone does this. It is fairly rare, and far from a desperate medical problem. We are constantly moving our tongues and circulating our saliva, and in our sleep we usually also swallow our saliva. But when some people are sleeping lightly, like during a nap, the saliva doesn't get swallowed. It is also possible that their heads are on a funny angle for napping, such as on the couch, so swallowing, which is an involuntary action, doesn't happen. Nappers get a low-quality sleep and a low quantity of sleep, and the drooling is proof that it is only a nap.

217.

Why do horses sleep standing up?

What does a horse do all those hours if it only sleeps for three? Grazing animals can spend up to eight hours a day in a sort of dozing state. They're not active, but they're aware enough to know if there's any danger, and can rouse in time to escape from a predator. Horses actually lock their legs so they can sleep standing up, but giraffes lie down to sleep (though they can doze while standing up).

> Why do horses sleep standing up?
> There wouldn't be any room in the bed if they all slept lying down.

218.

What is the crust in your eyes when you wake up?

Sleepies, and you have to rub it out! Some people call it sandman dust, sleepy seeds or eye gunk. It usually shows up on the little circular bump at the corners of your eyes, near your nose.

Your eyes have a lot of glands that make tears. When the tears have flowed over your eyes they drain near that bump in the corner (called a *commissure)* and go into your nose. Then you swallow them away.

At night when your eyes are closed, the tears slow down to almost nothing, but what tears there are roll down to the corner, expecting to drain out. Since your eyes are closed, the drain is closed too, and the tears, along with a bit of oil and sweat, make up the crust. Crusty, but no big deal.

Who invented the wave?

and Other Winning Facts About SPORTS

219.

What's the history of the seventh-inning stretch?

There are lots of ideas about the origin of the seventh-inning stretch, some more believable and more fun than others. Probably the best story is that in 1910 U.S. President William Howard Taft, a big fan of baseball, was at the season's opening game. He got up from his seat at the start of the seventh inning, and the whole crowd figured he was leaving, so got up to salute the president. And that turned into a tradition — the seventh-inning stretch.

220.

Who invented "the wave" in baseball, and where was it first performed?

Who? Well, two guys claim this fame, both believing they invented it in 1981. The more famous is "Krazy George" Henderson, a professional cheerleader with serious lungs who madly bangs a drum and can be quite obnoxious to opposing teams. He was at the Oakland Coliseum cheering an American League playoff game between the Oakland A's and the New York Yankees. George had an idea. He ran from section to section getting the fans to stand up, yell and sit down again quickly. Then the fans did it again and again, faster and faster. It was the start of something big. And something funny.

But a band director at the University of Washington claims he started the wave that same fall. Bill Bissell was at a Huskies football game, and led a cheer with a former student and cheerleader, Robb Weller, then co-host of *Entertainment Tonight*. They got different dorms and fraternities and sororities to stand up and sit down, and to do it faster and faster.

Krazy George usually gets the credit for the wave, and he still cheers for a living. You can watch for him on TV. The wave is now done all around the world, and at other sports like soccer and basketball.

221.

Why is tennis scoring so weird?

Tennis seems so simple — you hit a ball over a net, you hit it back. But the scoring isn't so simple. You don't get a point when you score — you get fifteen. Add the fact that tennis players start throwing around the words *deuce* and *love* and it can be quite confusing.

The scoring system comes from using the four quarter-hours of a clock (15-30-45-60). At 60 the game would be over, while 45 was eventually cut down to 40. No one really knows why "love" is used for a score of zero, but some think it comes from the French term *l'oeuf* for egg — a big zero. Or maybe it is from the notion that doing something for love is like doing something for nothing (zero). So if you keep playing and keep getting zero, you must really love the game.

222.

Where did the idea of cheerleaders come from?

Minnesota, or so the story goes. In 1898 the Gophers, the University of Minnesota's football team, were having an unbelievably lousy year.

The Gophers were in last place, the coach was hopeless and the fans were lifeless — mostly because cheering wasn't a natural thing then. Cheering was a half-hearted "The team's all right" sort of call when there was a goal — but there weren't many of those. So the crowd just sat there, making the team feel even worse. Someone wrote a letter to the paper to encourage fans to yell, but it didn't really help.

One young man, a first-year medical student, decided to lead the yells, and that was the beginning of cheerleading in the United States. Soon someone figured out that applauding individual plays, not just yelling randomly, was a good idea. Students started thinking up songs and appointing "yell captains." Words were added to old tunes like "Hello My Baby" and "There is a Tavern in the Town." It all worked. The Gophers played better and better, and word started spreading to other college teams. By 1900 cheerleaders and a group of two hundred young men who called themselves the Rooter's Club started using megaphones.

There was no turning back. Parades were added before games, as was blowing a whistle every time the team scored, and having a victory parade after every win. Eventually cheerleading for professional sports moved on to the women's domain. Short skirts and pompoms followed. But guys still do cheers on college campuses, as loudly as ever.

223.

Why are hot dogs so popular at baseball games?

Long before there were hot dogs in the United States, German butchers developed sausage making. Frankfurters were developed in Frankfurt, Germany, and wieners in Vienna, Austria. German immigrants brought the franks to America along with sausages. But it wasn't until 1900 that hot dogs came to be sold at baseball games. One cold day a man running the concession was having no luck with ice cream or soda, so he went out and got some "red-hot dachshund sausages," and the fans loved them.

One day a few years later, Tad Dorgan, a newspaper cartoonist who was watching a ball game, made a drawing of a real dachshund, smeared with mustard and stuffed into a bun. He couldn't spell *dachshund*, so he labelled the picture "Get your hot dogs." The name was so perfect that hardly anyone calls it a frankfurter or a wiener anymore.

Some people say "Hot dog!" to exclaim that they are excited about something. "Hot diggity dog!" is an even bigger exclamation. Since America came up with the term "hot dog," the world thinks it is an American invention. It is certainly one of the most popular foods in the United States, especially at baseball games!

224.

What do athletes do to bring good luck to their game?

Many, many things. Things you can't imagine that grown men and women would do. And they believe strongly in these superstitions and amulets or lucky charms, so strongly that some of them wouldn't play the game if they couldn't do the rituals they think bring them luck, or if they didn't carry their lucky charm or amulet.

Lucky Numbers

◎ Say you have a big success as number 7 on a team. You are going to want to be number 7 as often as possible — it is your lucky number for that sport. Another popular lucky number is 13.

◎ Some football players figure that double numbers on their uniforms (like 44) will bring good luck. They also think it's bad luck if a player takes a new number when he's traded to another team.

◎ Numbers aren't restricted to jerseys. Some golfers believe that you need to start your game with odd-numbered clubs. And they think they will have bad luck if they play using balls with a number higher than 4.

Lucky Food

◎ Some athletes have to eat the same meal before each game, like pasta or pancakes or maybe steak. Usually it is the same meal they ate right before they had a big win.

Lucky Clothes

◎ American tennis star Serena Williams ties her shoelaces the same way for every game.

◎ Michael Jordan used to wear lucky shorts. He put on University of North Carolina gym shorts under his uniform because in 1982 he was part of the winning team in the NCAA basketball championship.

◎ Mo Vaughn of the Boston Red Sox has a routine for dressing. He does it left to right: first the left sock, then the right; first the left pant leg, then the right.

◎ Many bowlers believe that they should wear the same clothes to keep a winning streak going.

Cowboy Superstitions
To have good luck:

◎ Saddle bronc riders always put the right foot in the stirrup first.

◎ Cowgirls often wear different-coloured socks on each foot.

◎ Some cowboys eat a hot dog before a rodeo competition.

What can bring bad luck:

◎ Never kick a paper cup thrown down at a rodeo.

◎ Don't compete with change in your pocket because that's all you might win.

◎ Never put your hat on a bed or wear yellow.

Necessary Routines

◎ Hockey star Eric Lindros is a neat freak. He liked things in his dressing stall just so. That was part of his routine before a game. His sticks had to be taped in the same way each time, and he ate the same meal of pasta and chicken before each game. He also had a two-hour nap before playing.

◎ Sidney Crosby of the Pittsburgh Penguins makes his team change hotels if they lost a game while staying there before.

◎ During games there are routines too. Many basketball players believe they must bounce the ball before taking a foul shot for good luck.

◎ Hockey players like to tap the goalie on the shin pads before a game.

◎ Baseball players like to spit into their hand before they pick up the bat — not to get a better grip, but to bring good luck!

225.

Can you hit a baseball farther with an aluminum bat than with a wooden bat?

Yes you can, at least in theory. Why? There are a few good reasons. Aluminum bats are lighter than wooden bats of the same size, so the batter can swing them faster. The weight is more evenly distributed, and the "sweet spot" is larger since the faster swing brings the centre of gravity closer to the batter's body.

What's a "sweet spot"? Find it on your bat and you'll know why it's so sweet. Hold the bat loosely just below the knob on its handle, and let it hang down from your fingers. Ask a friend to gently tap the bat with a hammer, starting at the bottom and working up. Every time the hammer taps the bat you should feel a vibration in your fingers — except when the tap is on the sweet spot. It might also make a slightly different sound. (This spot is also called the bat's centre of percussion.)

When a bat hits a ball, vibrations travel in waves up and down the length of the bat. If the ball hits the bat's sweet spot, the waves cancel each other out. You won't feel any vibrations in your hands, and since very little of the bat's energy is lost to vibrations, more energy can be transferred to the ball. Having a larger sweet spot means that even less energy is lost to vibrations. A high-quality wooden bat has a sweet spot roughly 7.6 cm in length. But an aluminum bat the same length has a sweet spot up to three times as large.

Because aluminum is a harder material than wood, an aluminum bat doesn't have as much "give" as a wooden one. So when the ball hits the aluminum bat, little of its kinetic energy is absorbed by the bat — and that energy is retained by the ball. A wooden bat will absorb more of a ball's kinetic energy.

A ball can go as much as 6.4 kph faster off an aluminum bat, and the potential distance it can fly is up to 10% farther than if it was hit with a wooden bat. When aluminum bats were first used by the NCAA (National Collegiate Athletic Association) in the early 1970s, batting averages rose thirty points and the number of home runs that were hit doubled.

226.

Who invented the skateboard, and is it true that skateboarders invented snowboarding and surfing?

Nope, skateboarders didn't invent surfing and snowboarding — surfers started it all. They nailed roller skate bases onto wooden planks so that they could sidewalk surf when the weather or waves kept them out of the water. This was back in the 1930s and 1940s. In 1958 when Bill Richards, a surf shop owner, and his son Mark started producing skateboards with wheels from the Chicago Roller Skate Company, sidewalk surfing took off. In 1963 about one hundred kids competed in the first skateboard competition at the Pier Avenue Junior School in Hermosa, California. A hit song by singers Jan and Dean called "Sidewalk Surfin'" followed in 1964 — a clear sign of how popular skateboarding was becoming.

All this excitement led to the first National Skateboard Championships in 1965. The fad quickly died out, though, partly because there was a lot of concern about reckless riding, which caused cities to start banning skateboards.

But it wasn't gone for long. In 1971 Richard Stevenson patented a newer version of a skateboard design, and in 1973 Frank Nasworthy invented polyurethane wheels that were perfect for surfing on cement. (Up until then the wheels had been made of metal or clay, which didn't grip the road very well.) Another skateboarding craze was underway!

By the late 1970s more than 40 million skateboards had been sold in the U.S. Even Fred

Astaire had one — and a broken wrist from falling off his board at the age of 77.

In the late 1970s, a man from Florida, Alan "Ollie" Gelfand, invented the "ollie" and started off a whole new craze of jumping over fixed objects like curbs, benches and walls, and using empty swimming pools and construction sites to skateboard in. Of course there were lots of injuries, and this got people even more worried than the first time around. They started banning skateboards in public parks and on streets and sidewalks. By the 1980s it was hard to find a place where you could use a skateboard.

But skateboarding's been back in a big way since the mid-1990s. And with it has come a whole skater culture: fashions, music, magazines and videos, and skateboard-only parks. According to some people, there are 6 million skateboarders in the U.S. alone.

Skateboarders, also called "riders" or "skaters," practise three skateboarding styles. Freestyle is where skaters do their tricks on level ground and rails, sometimes to music. In Streetstyle, skaters use the features of the urban landscape (curbs, stairs, benches and so on) to do their tricks. Vertical (also called ramp or half-pipe) is considered "extreme" skateboarding.

Some cool skateboarding terms:

- **Goofy:** You skate goofy if you skate with your right foot forward.
- **Sketchy:** When you just about — but don't quite — land a trick, you're sketchy.
- **Slam:** Basically, when you fall off your board and hurt yourself.

227.

Where did the "high-five" come from?

It seems so common now, but we've only been "high-fiving" since the 1970s. One story goes that Glenn Burke, a major league baseball player with the nickname of King Kong, invented the motion. It was September of 1977, and his team, the Los Angeles Dodgers, was down to its last game of the regular season. Dusty Baker, Burke's teammate, hit a home run and Burke ran to meet him at home plate. He congratulated Baker by leaping into the air and giving him the "high-five." A few minutes later Baker celebrated Burke's first major league home run with a "high-five," of course.

The other story that *Sports Illustrated for Kids* tells is that the "high-five" originated when female volleyball players were jumping to hit the ball during practices. They would often slap one another's hands by accident. Then they started doing it on purpose, to congratulate another player for a good move, or to build team spirit.

228.

Why is scoring three goals called a "hat trick" in hockey?

It certainly has nothing to do with pulling a rabbit out of a hat. And it has nothing to do with what was called a hat trick in the British House of Commons about a hundred years ago. (A member would save a seat for himself by putting his hat on it.) This hat trick is for a player scoring three goals in one game. But it is not originally a hockey term, nor is it originally Canadian.

"Hat trick" comes from the game of cricket about a century ago. A cricket bowler who got rid of three batsmen on three balls in a row would have a new hat bought for him by his teammates. By 1909 this term came into general use in many sports to celebrate a three-fold feat. And hockey picked it up early on in the game.

Why is 13 considered unlucky?

and Other Strange SUPERSTITIONS

229.

Why is 13 considered unlucky?

The number 13 has been considered unlucky for a long time, and by people all over the world. The early Romans thought 13 was a sign of death and destruction. And according to Norse mythology, if you sat 13 people down at a table, that was very unlucky. (Why? At a banquet of 12 people in Valhalla, an intruder — number 13 — caused the death of Balder's son Odin.) The number of people at the last supper of Christ and the twelve Apostles confirmed the superstition about the number 13 in Christian countries. And in the Middle Ages witches were believed to meet in "covens" that had 13 members.

The fear of the number 13 is called triskaidekaphobia. Many hotels have no room 13, and many buildings have no 13th floor. Next time you fly, see if there is a row 13 on the plane. As a date, 13 isn't too lucky either, especially when it falls on a Friday. That was always thought of as a really bad day to start a new project or to begin a ship voyage. Movers, doctors and dentists say their business drops on Friday the 13th. The good news is that a maximum of three Friday the 13ths can occur in a year, and sometimes there is just one.

Good Facts Associated with the Number 13

⊚ Composer Richard Wagner was born in 1813; he composed 13 operas – both good reasons to like the number 13.

⊚ Theatrical producer Florenz Ziegfeld preferred to open his shows on the 13th day of the month.

- One American president declared the number 13 to be lucky, while another refused to dine with a group of 13 people.
- According to one Texas superstition, a bag filled with 13 sow bugs tied around a child's neck will cure the child of thrush, or sores in the mouth.

Bad Facts Associated with Friday, the Number 13 and Friday the 13th

- A municipal bylaw in one Indiana town required all black cats to wear bells on Friday the 13th.
- Some Texans say never to cut any kind of garment on a Friday — if you do, it might never be completed.
- Greek philosophers called 13 an "imperfect" number.
- Thirteen pence halfpenny used to be the wage that would be paid to a hangman.
- Friday was a common day for people to be hanged.
- Some people won't buy a house with a street address including the number 13.

230.

Why are black cats considered unlucky?

The Egyptians of five thousand years ago actually considered cats very important and lucky. They were the first to believe that cats had nine lives. It was against the law to hurt or kill a cat, and when a cat eventually died it was embalmed, wrapped in linen and put in a mummy case made of bronze or wood. Because wood was expensive and rare then, we know that this custom was really important, and therefore that cats were considered important.

All cats were treated this way — black cats included. Archaeologists have even found entire cat cemeteries.

In later centuries, leaders in India and prophets in China kept cats. Until about five hundred years ago cats were not considered unlucky, but some people began to become suspicious about how independent, strong and stealthy cats were. (There was also the problem of huge population increases, since spaying and neutering weren't done.)

Then there was an uproar over the possibility of witches in Europe. Many people thought a lot of the old ladies were doing black magic, and that their black cats were witches too. In fact, black cats at night were thought to be human witches during the day. It doesn't make a lot of sense now, but in those times the rumours flew.

Strange as it may seem, the cat that had been revered by ancient people was now considered evil. So evil that, until King Louis XIII stopped the practice in the 1630s, thousands of black cats in France were being killed because people were so afraid of them.

Some people still think it's unlucky to have a black cat cross your path, but after Louis XIII's pronouncement, black cats started to be connected with a few good luck omens too.

- You can stroke a black cat and wish on it for luck. Sometimes sports teams keep one for luck.
- A visit from a black cat is supposed to bring you luck, but don't shoo it away or you will get bad luck.

231.

Why do people throw salt over their shoulder after spilling some?

Salt has always been a symbol of life. We know now that it is necessary to preserve the proper chemical balance in our bodies. In the past, people knew salt was an excellent antiseptic for wounds, plus a flavouring and a preservative for all kinds of foods. Without salt, we couldn't live. Salt was so important that it was once used as money, even as a sacrifice to the gods.

Salt has also come to represent good — some people refer to a good person as "the salt of the earth." That's why if you spill this "good" thing, it is bad luck.

What can you do to stop the devil from undermining your life if you spill salt? The devil is supposed to lurk over your left (or sinister) shoulder, so you toss salt over your left shoulder and hit the devil in the eye. He hates salt.

This salt-over-the-shoulder custom has been going on for thousands of years. The ancient Sumerians chucked salt. The Egyptians, the Assyrians and the Greeks did it. And it shows up in the Leonardo da Vinci painting of the Last Supper. There, Judas spilled the table salt, indicating that there was about to be a tragedy — his betrayal of Jesus.

232.

Why does a horseshoe bring good luck?

There are lots of reasons horseshoes are considered lucky, but here's a good one: There was a blacksmith called St. Dunstan. One day into his shop walked the devil, Satan, wanting shoes for his cloven hooves. St. Dunstan knew it was the devil, and convinced him that in order to have the shoes attached, he had to be shackled to the wall. The devil bought this, and St. Dunstan did a nasty job of putting on the shoes, hurting the devil really badly. Then he said he would only let the devil go if he would never enter a Christian's house again. The devil, in desperation, agreed, but wondered how he would know which houses were Christians'. St. Dunstan thought quickly and said that the sign would be a horseshoe over the front door. That's why it is good luck — it keeps the devil out.

More lucky horseshoe lore:

A horseshoe is also shaped like a crescent moon, is made from iron (which has magical powers), and usually has seven (a magical number) nail holes. To be really lucky, the horseshoe must be real, and a used one is better than new. If it comes from the near hind leg of a grey mare you are really in luck. If you find it on the road — bingo! You have to pick it up, spit on it and make a wish at the same time. Then you throw it over your shoulder, or nail it outside over the door to your house. You get extra luck if you use its own nails to nail it to the house, and if there is an odd number of nails. To bring good luck to the house, the points have to go up, so the luck won't "run out."

233.

Why does a bird in the house mean a death is likely to occur?

It is mostly because a bird is thought to be the returned soul of the dead. Since the beginning of time, birds have had all sorts of superstitions associated with them. But this is the most famous: if a bird flies in through an open window, it means the death of someone who is in that house. It is widely believed that a person's soul will go out with the bird.

234.

Why were twins considered so unlucky that in ancient times the second twin might be left to die?

We know now that identical twins are the result of the mother's fertilized egg splitting, so that two babies are formed instead of one. (With fraternal twins, two eggs are actually fertilized.) But people in ancient times figured that if there were two children there must have been two fathers, which was a sin, or that God or some spiritual being had been involved. They were highly suspicious of twins, so they did what they thought was right. They got rid of one or both of the babies, and usually punished the mother.

But different societies through the centuries have viewed twins differently. The ancient Egyptians were keen on twins. They actually worshipped twins called Osiris and Set. Ancient Romans were keen on twins, too. They had twin demigods, Romulus and Remus. These twins were the offspring of a god and a mortal. The ruler of the day wanted them drowned because they were the grandsons of his rival. Their basket was left on the edge of the flooding Tiber River, and was found by a female wolf who nursed the twins until a king's herdsman found them. He and his wife raised the boys. Eventually word got out who they really were. Remus got into crime and Romulus reluctantly had to kill his brother. Romulus went on to be the founder of Rome.

For the Tsimshian on Canada's west coast, the wind is the "breath of twins." And the Kwakwaka'wakw believe that twins can influence the weather and help the fishermen.

More recently, the fate of conjoined twins has been followed closely. These types of twins, which are extremely rare, are physically bonded through a malformation of a part of their body. The most famous pair was Chang and Eng, born in Siam (hence the old name, Siamese twins) in 1811. They were ordered by the King of Siam to be put to death when they were thirteen years old because the king believed they must be evil. Fortunately, a British merchant rescued them. They went on to work at a circus sideshow and then retire as farmers in North Carolina. Chang and Eng married sisters and had a total of twenty-two children between them. They died in 1874 within two hours of each other.

Superstitions about having twins:

- If a husband spills pepper, he has to throw some of it over his left shoulder or his wife will have twins.
- If a pregnant woman eats twin fruit (two pieces of fruit that have grown together), she will have twins.

235.

Why is it bad luck to open your umbrella indoors?

The word umbrella comes from the Latin word for shade, *umbra*. Umbrella superstitions come from Egypt. The Egyptians used umbrellas to shade themselves from the sun. Umbrellas were considered to be status symbols and religious objects. That's because Egyptians believed that the sky was in fact the body of the goddess Nut, who arched her body over the earth, sort of like a big umbrella. When you carried an umbrella, the shade it made was said to be special. Bad luck occurred when someone stepped into the shade created by your umbrella.

The umbrella came to England from Italy, where it was used to keep out sun and rain. The bad luck associated with opening an umbrella *indoors* comes from London, England, in the eighteenth century. Why bad luck? It was dangerous to open an umbrella indoors. Umbrellas were awkward, with nasty points, and if someone knocked over a lamp or candle (remember, this was before electricity) they could cause big trouble.

Opening an umbrella *indoors* was also thought to be dangerous because an umbrella was an *outdoor* thing, so it went against doing things "the right way" — the way people thought God intended.

They also believed that if you opened up your umbrella inside, it would rain outside, and you didn't want that. We still have a goofy belief that if we take our umbrellas to school or work, it won't rain, and if we leave them at home it might rain.

236.

What are the real rules on breaking apart a wishbone for good luck?

The wishbone is the forked bone overlying the breastbone of most birds. It is the most prominent bone, and easiest to retrieve from a chicken or turkey. It is called a wishbone because of the superstition that when two people pull the bone apart, the wish of the person who gets the longer bone will be fulfilled. Actually, a wishbone is a charm, like a horseshoe or a four-leaf clover. These are all objects you can make a wish on.

How? With a wishbone you have to dry it first for a few days — three is a good magical number — until it is brittle. Then two people (usually children) pull it apart by hooking their pinky fingers around the ends. The person who gets the longer piece will have his or her wish come true. Sometimes it takes some measuring, but there will always be a longer side. In some families it is said that the wish will only come true if it is not revealed to anyone. (The same belief holds for wishing on the first star each night, and the wish made before blowing out birthday candles.)

Before 400 B.C. the Etruscans killed a sacred fowl known as a "hen oracle." They dried the collarbone, and the person looking for an answer from the gods made a wish on this "wishbone" by stroking it and making a wish.

In the British Isles a wishbone was sometimes called the merrythought, as in, make a merry wish. Back in the seventeenth century a person would put a wishbone on the nose like a pair of spectacles. Then he would think his thought or make his wish and shake his head until he shook the wishbone off his nose. Then it was pulled apart, and the winner would get his or her wish.

Things then got even more complicated: the winner would put both parts into his hand and the other person would draw. The one who drew the long part got his wish, the other didn't.

It is said that wishbones were snapped at the first Thanksgiving in the United States in 1621. So an ancient Etruscan superstition has come a long way.

> Whoever wins the wishbone pull definitely gets "a lucky break," which is where that expression comes from.

237.

Why aren't you supposed to walk under ladders?

The obvious reason is that you might get hit on the head by the tools of some carpenter or painter who is up on the ladder. But the historical reason isn't so obvious. If you lean a ladder up against a wall you get a triangle — and that three-sided form is thought of as representing the trinity of the gods. If you walk through the triangle you break the Holy Trinity, putting you in league with the devil instead.

The Egyptians thought the ladder was good luck. It could be used to climb to heaven. But later, when Jesus Christ was crucified, his followers decided the ladder was bad luck because there had been a ladder resting against the crucifix to take him down from it.

Now ladders meant wickedness and death and betrayal, so you didn't want to walk under one.

So what should you do if you walk under a ladder by mistake? You could make the "fig" sign. Thrust your closed fist, with the thumb sticking out between the index and middle fingers, at the ladder to wipe out the bad luck. You could also spit through the ladder, spit over your left shoulder, cross two fingers and keep them crossed until you see a dog, or don't speak until you see a four-legged animal.

When criminals in France and England in the 1600s walked to the gallows to be hanged, they were made to walk under a ladder — as if they didn't already have enough bad luck. With those odd origins, the superstition began to take on lots of meanings: Do it and you will be hanged, or do it and you won't get married that year — a dangerous situation for a marriageable woman in times when single women were vulnerable or scorned.

238.

Why do kids save their baby teeth for the tooth fairy?

Why would the tooth fairy want all those teeth? What could she do with them? There are lots of ideas. Maybe she makes a necklace and wears it to the Dentists' Ball.

Let's think about it. The custom is really about an exchange: money for used teeth. That's a fair exchange, so this shows it's good magic, not evil.

We may not believe this today, but for thousands of years people did. Any body bits — whether hair or nail clippings or teeth — that were discarded by people were magically linked to their owners. Even if you could hide these lost body parts, they were still part of the owner, because someone could take that bit of you, do some magic thing with it, and hurt you. Like grinding up your tooth to give you a toothache.

In Germany there is a folk belief that says any new growth in your teeth will be like the teeth of whatever creature took away the lost tooth. So a rat or a mouse or even a beaver is most welcome to spirit away your tooth, because they have very tough teeth.

In England and North America, children usually put their teeth under a pillow or a mat, in an egg cup, on a clock or in a glass of water. The teeth are exchanged for a coin.

Why does the tooth fairy want the teeth?

Here are some more theories:

◎ The tooth fairy saves your teeth and gives them to new babies – that's how babies get teeth.

◎ The tooth fairy puts the shiny teeth up in the sky and that's how stars get made.

◎ The tooth fairy puts a magic spell on the tooth and turns it into a dime – that's where coins come from.

◎ The tooth fairy uses them to build her castle and her village.

239.

Who started chain letters anyway? And why are people afraid to break the chain?

Chain letters must originally have been somebody's idea of fun. They started just before the 1920s when people sent postcards with chain prayers. Then came postcards that said something like *Good luck, copy this out in the next twenty-four hours and send it to nine people. Do not break the chain or you will have bad luck — count nine days and you will have great luck.* The threats of terrible tragedies for breaking the chain started to become more outrageous, and the whole idea began to lose its innocent flavour.

Then another kind of chain letter surfaced, offering big material returns for not much effort. You got a letter that had a list of a certain number of people. You were supposed to send something to the person at the top of the list. Most often it was money, but sometimes books or pretty underwear — whatever the letter told you. Then you dropped off *their* name (which moved the second name to the top) and added *your* name to the bottom of the list. You sent out this letter to the specified number of people, and eventually you were supposed to receive lots of items or money in return. The instructions usually included some sort of guilt factor, because if you broke the chain you would never get any money or books — nor would anyone else.

If everyone followed through, you could potentially get a lot of stuff. This results from what is called a geometrical progression, and this assumes that no one breaks the chain. If you sent the letter to ten people, this is what could happen:

Level one (You are #10 on the list)
   People involved: 1
Level two (You are #9 on the list)
   People involved: 10
Level three (You are #8 on the list)
   People involved: 100
Level four (You are #7 on the list)
   People involved: 1000
Level five (You are #6 on the list)
   People involved: 10,000
Level six (You are #5 on the list)
   People involved: 100,000
Level seven (You are #4 on the list)
   People involved: 1,000,000
Level eight (You are #3 on the list)
   People involved: 10,000,000
Level nine (You are #2 on the list)
   People involved: 100,000,000
Level ten (You are #1 on the list)
   People involved: 1,000,000,000

So say you sent $10 to the person at the top of the list. When you got to #1 you would get 10 x $1,000,000,000 or $10,000,000,000 ($10 billion).

Sound too good to be true? Well, it is. The first chain letter asking for money appeared in Denver in 1935. Each person was to send in a dime, and the big payout would be $1562.50. It made the Post Office a madhouse — one day they had to deal with 285,000 letters by hiring dozens of new staff. The Post Office decided that chain letters were illegal.

And there are other problems. There is the

fact that people break the chains. Even worse, look at the final numbers. It would take years for the population to expand enough for there to be enough people to support the payout to you.

Another problem is that the chain letter is a classic example of a "pyramid scheme." It is gambling, it is a bad investment, and it is illegal in most places, mostly because somebody always loses — usually the people at the bottom of the list. So there is absolutely no good use for chain letters. If you want to get mail, write some letters. Your friends will respond, eventually.

240.

Why is breaking a mirror bad luck?

Seven years of bad luck is only the beginning. A lot of people believe that if you break a mirror there will be a death in the family that year.

So what's the deal with mirrors? We take them for granted now, but it wasn't until the fourteenth century that you could even get a reflective glass mirror like we know today, and then only in Venice, Italy (a major glass-making area). Before that, people used polished metal, and before *that*, any reflective surface was regarded with awe. When people saw themselves reflected in a lake, they thought that reflection was their soul.

Vanity has been regarded as a character flaw throughout the ages. Parents tried to tell their children that the devil would get them if they spent too much time admiring themselves. In an ancient Greek myth, a youth named Narcissus fell in love with his own image, and instead of hunting he just admired himself . . . until he starved to death. (That's why a seriously vain person is sometimes described as having a Narcissus complex.)

The Romans also came up with the notion of seven years of bad luck or bad health if you broke a mirror. Why seven? That was the time the Romans thought it took for life to renew itself. Since a mirror contains your image, or your "life," they applied the seven-year rule to the mirror. Go figure.

It was also believed that in the year a mirror was broken, you would see something tragic take place. That's probably where the death-in-the-family idea comes from. And then there's the fact that mirrors were incredibly expensive, owned only by the wealthy, so if a servant broke one it might take seven years of salary to replace it!

What other superstitions exist about mirrors and luck?

◎ The number of pieces into which a mirror is broken will show how many unlucky years you will have.

◎ To break a mirror means that you will lose your best friend.

And here's some counter-magic:

7

- ◉ After you have broken seven mirrors you will have good luck.

- ◉ Visiting a graveyard at midnight on a starless night can ward off bad luck resulting from a broken mirror.

- ◉ If you break a looking glass, bury all the pieces to prevent bad luck.

- ◉ To avert the bad luck that comes from breaking a mirror, throw the pieces of glass into a river and all your trouble will be washed downstream.

241.

Why do we knock on wood for good luck?

"Touch wood" or "knock on wood" are such common expressions that a lot of people forget that they are superstitions at all. Knocking on wood or touching wood is done to ward off evil, or simply to make sure that what you hope for will happen. It works when you say something like this: "My flu is getting better, knock on wood," and you knock on wood or touch something wooden while you say it.

Why? It ties in to our superstitious fear of boasting or getting too cocky about something, thereby "offending the gods" and making them want to do something to make you know your place — which is lower than theirs. (Greek and Roman mythology is full of stories about the gods cutting humans down to size.) We "knock on wood" so we don't tempt fate to do the opposite of what we want.

Why wood, though? It may be that this came from the pagan notion of powerful wood spirits that were believed to be protective, or from the fact that Christ's cross was made of wood. Wherever it came from, it is so ingrained in our culture that people now often don't even physically touch the wood. They believe that just saying it does the trick.

242.

Why does touching a toad give you warts, and what cures them?

This is a weird one, as toads are rather clean little fellows. Toads are actually considered lucky because the presence of a toad means there is water around — so no droughts, which generally means that good fortune is ahead. Warts, those annoying but not dangerous skin growths, are in fact from a virus, not from a toad. But since toads have bumpy and wart-like skin, and since the most common location for warts is on the hands, over the years toads have been given a bad rap as the source of warts. Not so. There is even a superstition about getting rid of warts by touching a toad. Also not so.

If you have a wart, talk to your doctor. He or she will likely tell you to use an over-the-counter ointment, to wear the wart down with a pumice stone, or get it surgically cut out or zapped with a laser to kill the roots. It will depend on the wart. There is no "best" treatment, and sometimes warts just go away.

Of course, there are all sorts of folk treatments too, and you never know . . . it might just work to try one of these:

◉ Never think of it or look at it.

◉ Show it to someone else and don't look
at it for nine nights.

◉ Rub it gently and repeat:
Anna, mana, meno, mike,
Paro, lono, bono, strike,
Mare, war-e, wallow-wack.

◉ Put some tears, produced from cutting
an onion, on the wart.

◉ Rub it with a penny and throw the penny away where
no one will ever find it.

◉ Steal a dishrag, go to the woods, turn around three
times and throw the rag behind you from your right hand.
Go home and don't go back to that place
for three weeks.

◉ Wash the wart in dew before breakfast, just as the sun
rises, on the first three mornings of May.

◉ Rub a snail on the wart.

◉ Put a piece of horse manure on a stump. When the
manure is gone, the wart will be gone.

◉ Tie a string around the wart, remove the
string and then hang it on the wall. When the
string rots the wart will leave.

Anna,
mana,
meno,
mike,
Paro,
lono,
bono,
strike.

243.

Why is a rabbit's foot considered lucky?

Since before 600 B.C., folks have thought the whole rabbit to be pretty special — it is both mysterious and lucky. But after St. Augustine converted the Britons to Christianity, pagan (pre-Christian) symbols were banned. Some people still believed in them, but did so in secret. So instead of worshipping the hare, many Britons carried a hare's *foot*, which they would hide in a pocket.

Later, rabbits were introduced from Europe, and the rabbit's foot — more easy to get — took over from the hare's foot.

And why the foot, specifically? It is a symbol of potency and speed, and the bone of the hare's foot was said to cure gout and rheumatism.

But why is the rabbit considered lucky? The ancient peoples in Europe thought rabbits had a direct line to nature spirits who happened to live alongside them. Since rabbits produce so many babies so often, people thought the spirits were using the rabbit as a symbol of prosperity and good health.

Add it all up, and the rabbit or hare was much revered in pre-Christian times.

To really work as a charm or talisman, people thought that the rabbit's foot had to come from the left hind foot of a rabbit killed at the full moon by a cross-eyed person.

To find out more, check out the Easter bunny info on page 191.

244.

What's the evil eye supposed to do to you, and how do you stop it?

You've likely heard the expression "giving someone the evil eye." This is one of the oldest and strongest superstitions around. Your eye was considered the window into your soul; people thought that by looking into someone's eyes they could tell what that person was all about.

It was also thought that if you gave someone the evil eye you could make them sick, give them lousy luck or even kill them. So it was in your best interest to stay away from those who had these powers. This might be anyone with blue or green eyes, or eyes that were strikingly different from the eye colour usually found in the region. It was definitely best to stay away from anyone with two different coloured eyes, and from folks with deep-set, uneven, squinty or crossed eyes. People with cowlicks and left-handers were suspect too. And some animals were said to have the evil eye — black cats, all black birds (like magpies and crows), black sheep and rams.

Belief in the evil eye was strongest at the height of the witch hunts in the seventeenth century. People even put glass "witch balls" into their windows in the hope that they would ward off spells, and keep out the bad sorts and bad luck. These were 15-cm blown-glass spheres, often with strands and swirls of colour inside, the hope being that this "web" might trap the spell.

If you happened to run into a person with the evil eye, it would be smart to have an amulet — an object worn as a charm against evil — on hand. The best amulets were shaped like the eye of a toad. Or necklaces of blue worry beads, a red ribbon, a piece of coral, horseshoes, or something with the fleur-de-lis design could help.

People whose aim was decent could spit in said person's eye or over their shoulder. Or they could put their middle two fingers down and using the pinky and pointer finger, show the other person the "devil's horn," or the "fig sign." Then they would be okay.

245.

Why is it bad luck to pass someone on the stairs?

Likely this superstition comes from back when staircases were very steep and poorly lit (or not lit at all). The chances of meeting up with an enemy on the gloomy narrow stairs were very good. Wider staircases and electric lighting have rid us of the superstition, but even today some people cross their fingers if they have to pass someone on the stairs, to save themselves from bad luck.

If you trip on the way up the stairs you are said to be in luck, and might even be getting married soon. In addition to falling down the stairs — which is doubly unfortunate because you will likely hurt yourself — tripping on your way down is bad luck. And whatever you do, don't change your mind halfway up the staircase. Go all the way to the top and turn around, or sit down, whistle a bit and then head back down. That should keep your luck intact.

246.

Why do we say "break a leg" for good luck with a play?

We only say this under certain circumstances — otherwise it is just plain rude. "Break a leg" is part of an elaborate series of superstitions used since the early 1900s in the theatre. Actors are said to be the most superstitious people around (next come gamblers, then jockeys and sailors). It's not surprising — live theatre is a chancy business. Actors figure that maybe there is a reason beyond their control why they performed badly or didn't get a part. If they can't blame luck, they'd have to blame their own acting abilities, and who wants that!

"Break a leg" is a negative sentiment. The idea behind using it is a very old superstition — never to outright tell someone to have good

luck. If you sent best wishes or good luck to your friends, you would tempt the Fates or evil spirits to do the opposite and do them harm. Also, by wishing someone good luck, you would be parting with the luck yourself. So instead, actors think they are tricking the Fates by doing the opposite and saying "break a leg." The phrase itself seems to be a mild translation of what German actors say: *Hals-und Beinbruch*, which means break a neck and a leg. This superstition might have started with World War I pilots, then spread to the German and finally to British and American theatres.

Some Chinese parents worry that if they tempt the Fates by "bragging" about a new baby's prettiness or intelligence, it might bring bad luck.

247.

Why do you say "God bless you" when someone sneezes?

Sneezing is something that everyone everywhere does. Over the ages, different beliefs have attached themselves to this rather bizarre act — it is like an explosion from within, a big-time nose relief. There were Native Americans who believed that sneezing clears the brain. Maoris of New Zealand thought their god of creation, Tiki, sneezed life into the first person. Others thought sneezing took the breath of life away.

Every culture also seems to have a need to say something after we sneeze — to somehow acknowledge the sneeze, which was considered to be dangerous. Whether it is the German *"Gesundheit"* ("Good health") or the Roman "Congratulations" (these cultures thought that sneezes ridded the body of the spirits from coming illnesses), few sneezes go unheralded. The Romans took this a step further. They believed that keeping in a sneeze would essentially kill you.

Christians and others believed that when you sneezed, the soul left the body, so if you asked God's blessing, the sneezer might be saved from the evil spirits or from getting the plague. That idea came from Pope Gregory the Great (540-604 A.D.). It made perfect sense at the time, since there was a horrible plague in Italy, and one telling symptom was relentless sneezing and then swift death. So the Pope encouraged anyone who heard sneezing to say "God bless you" to attempt to keep the plague from killing the sneezer.

Why does February have fewer days?

and Other Tantalizing Facts About TIME

248.

If people live near the International Date Line, do they get to celebrate their birthdays two days in a row?

The International Date Line isn't straight, but it is more or less along the 180th meridian, in the middle of the Pacific Ocean. Cross that line and you must change the date by one day. The key: it is one day later east of the line than west of the line.

If you are travelling west, say from Vancouver to Tokyo, your day gets one hour shorter for every fifteen degrees of longitude. When you get to the International Date Line though, you have to change the date a whole day ahead. That's because even though you're west of North America, the date line is east of Greenwich, England, the starting meridian for time. Too bad if it's your birthday, you've missed out.

What if you go the other way? If you start in Japan or New Zealand or Australia and head back to North America, you would be in luck and get two days of celebration. You get to repeat a day at the International Date Line.

To really stretch things out, you could stand on the little island of Taveuni in Fiji, where there's a signpost saying International Date Line, and step from east to west. Only problem is, it might be difficult to arrange for all your friends to get there for the party, and there aren't many locals! Not so great for a birthday party.

249.

How did February come to be the month with two (or three) fewer days than the other months?

Basically, some month had to take the short straw. Why? Mostly because of math and the moon. This started in the eighth century B.C. when the Roman calendar was figured out. Until then there were only ten months — no January or February at all.

According to some historians, it was Numa Pompilius, a Roman king, who decided to make a change and add two months. He worked the year out to 355 days (12 lunar cycles), which was close. The Romans were superstitious about even numbers, though, believing that these numbers were bad luck, so the Roman calendar had only 29- or 31-day months. To arrive at 355 days there had to be one shorter month, and February was chosen. March was the beginning of the year then, so February was the last month and in the dead of winter. Maybe the Romans also figured that if one month had to have some bad luck attached to it because of the even number of days, it might as well be a short month.

Julius Caesar gave the calendar another once-over much later, and bumped the total up to 365 days. He kept February short because it was a month that no one really liked. His calendar is called the Julian calendar, and was used until 1582. Then Pope Gregory XIII worked out his version, the Gregorian calendar, which is the one we use today.

A calendar year is exactly 365 days, 5 hours, 48 minutes, 46 seconds, so an extra day was

The exception to the leap-year rule is that there is a leap year in a centenary year only if it is divisible by 400. So 1900 had no February 29, but 2000 did.

added every fourth year to account for those extra hours. That's when we get a leap year, when the year is exactly divisible by 4. The date February 29 is added to make up the total number of days that are required over 4 years.

250.

Why is Newfoundland time half an hour earlier than the Maritimes? How do time zones work?

People playing Trivial Pursuit often argue about the number of time zones Canada has. (Mostly because people can't figure out if it is six or seven.) Trivial Pursuit is a Canadian invention, and so are time zones. Sir Sandford Fleming is widely credited with creating them, but why did he need to come up with a system at all?

For thousands of years time was purely a local concern because people didn't travel much and they certainly couldn't get anywhere fast. Sunrise and sunset marked the boundaries of the day, and the church bell might indicate other significant hours. As the pace of life picked up, so did the use of clocks and watches, but time was still a local thing.

Then the steam-powered ship came along, as well as the train. The world was shrinking and all of the uncoordinated times started to be both annoying and terribly confusing. The timetables were crazy.

When the United States finished its cross-continental railway in 1869 the confusion got worse. And in Canada there were five local times between Halifax and Toronto, rather than a single one-hour shift, as there is today. At the same time there was a revolution in communication. Telephones didn't exist yet, but there was a telegraph system. People needed some sort of solution, an east–west "measurement" around the world.

Although the equator, the longest line of latitude, which divides the globe into northern and southern hemispheres, was an obvious choice as the prime parallel for latitude, no one meridian for longitude was uniquely qualified as prime. Until a single prime meridian could be agreed upon, each nation was free to choose its own, with the result that nineteenth-century maps of the world lacked a standardized grid.

All sorts of people offered ideas. The navigators and astronomers and meteorologists had been complaining for years about inconsistencies with time in different locations, but now company presidents and politicians were in on it. Time was beginning to mean money.

An American, Charles Ferdinand Dowd, was trying to get the American railways to recognize uniform zones in the U.S., but it was Fleming, a Canadian, who pushed for the international view. He suggested dividing the world into twenty-four time zones of fifteen degrees each, starting it from a prime meridian drawn through the Pacific Ocean at some point that avoided land. This process took a while, but finally in 1884 the International Prime Meridian Conference decided to go with the Greenwich line as the prime meridian. It passes through London's Greenwich Observatory, where a metallic marker indicates its exact location. (The prime time zone actually extends

7.5 degrees to each side of the prime meridian.)

Each degree of latitude and longitude is divided into sixty minutes, and each minute is divided into sixty seconds, making it possible to assign a precise numerical location to any place on earth.

There are twenty-four standard time zones, each consisting of a one-hour segment. The day begins at midnight GMT or Greenwich Mean Time. Now it is called UT or Universal Time.

So what about Canada? If you look at a map, for each fifteen degrees of longitude there is one time zone, more or less. (Times zones tend to follow political boundaries, so that a whole province or country can share the same time zone.) Starting from the west we have Pacific, Mountain, Central, Eastern, Atlantic and Newfoundland time zones. But that's only six. There used to be a seventh. Until 1973 the Yukon shared a time zone with Alaska; now it is part of Pacific. (Trivial Pursuit has it wrong.)

And what about Newfoundland? The half-hour difference was decided upon in 1884 when Newfoundland was not part of Canada. Local mean time at St. John's was three hours and thirty minutes west of Greenwich, England, (as opposed to Halifax being four hours from Greenwich) so that's why it is always half an hour earlier in Newfoundland than in the Maritimes.

Is the Red Sea really red?
and Other Weird but USEFUL INFORMATION

251.

Was the moon landing just a big hoax?

The moon has no atmosphere, and therefore no wind, but in footage of the moon landing, the flag is able to flap. How could the flag fly without any wind?

There are many reasons to be skeptical about a lot of things in this world. It is always smart to examine the facts and make your own decision. Here are some of the facts about the Apollo 11 moon landing:

◎ The whole thing was seen worldwide on live television.

◎ The flag: On July 20, 1969, the first U.S. flag was planted on the moon by Neil Armstrong and Edwin "Buzz" Aldrin. It's still there. And it was no ordinary flag; it was a lunar flag. NASA says: "The design was based on a number of engineering constraints. For example, to compensate for the lack of an atmosphere on the lunar surface, the flag assembly included a horizontal crossbar to give the illusion of a flag flying in the breeze." The assembly was sophisticated, but the flag itself was a regular nylon 1x1.5-metre version from a government supply catalogue. It cost $5.50.

It turns out that Armstrong and Aldrin had a few difficulties getting the flag up. They couldn't get the horizontal crossbar rod to pull out all the way. NASA says, "This gave the flag a bit of a ripple effect," and later crews intentionally left the rod partially retracted. The Apollo 11 astronauts also noted that they could drive the lower portion of the pole only about 15 to 23 cm into the lunar surface. It is uncertain if the flag remained standing or was blown over by the engine blast when the ascent module took off.

In conclusion, you don't want to believe everything the media tells you, just on face value. But the flag flying *was* an illusion that NASA says they planned. We expect to see a flag flutter, so they made it happen.

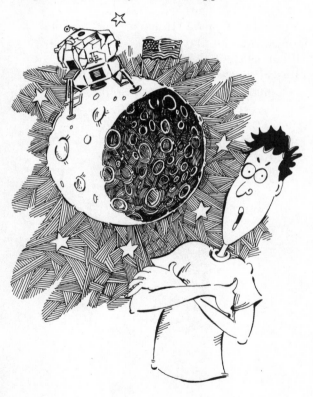

252.

Why isn't there a Q on the phone keypad?

There is no Q because when phone companies used words or letters for the beginning of phone numbers, they would be limited by the fact that U has to follow Q *in a real word.* So — no Q. (You've probably noticed that Z isn't there either.)

To play "Happy Birthday to You" on some phones, you can dial the area code first, and then press the following numbers to hear the "musical notes." (Some phones don't have notes associated with the numbers, so it doesn't work.)

112, 163
112, 196
110, 8521
008, 121

253.

Can you be electrocuted while on the phone in the bathtub?

This is not a recommended activity, but if you happen to drop your telephone into the tub, don't panic. You might get a bit of a shock, but you won't be electrocuted. That's because a phone doesn't carry a full electrical charge, like something that is plugged into an electrical outlet. A phone runs on a very small current, about 1/1000 of what would be needed to stop your heart. But it's best to be on the safe side — no chatting while you're soaking. Cellphones? Water is not suggested. Not much should happen to you, but you will definitely wreck the phone, and cellphones can be expensive. Make your bathtime a peaceful, talk-free time, and save yourself the aggravation.

254.

What was the first email?

Let's go back a bit first. The original idea of an Internet was to link university and government researchers together to make it easier and less expensive for scientists to collaborate on projects, to share data and to access one another's computers from afar. That's what Internet means: interconnecting computer networks. The U.S. Department of Defense did the first development in the 1960s. Originally it connected Stanford Research Institute, the University of California at Los Angeles and at Santa Barbara, and the

University of Utah, through something called ARPANET, which stands for Advanced Research Projects Agency Network. The key to this collaboration was the ability to send mail electronically — email.

In 1971 Ray Tomlinson, a computer engineer, sent the first email message — to himself, on another machine in the room. If that isn't anticlimactic enough, he can't remember what it was he said! He figures it was QWERTYUIOP or something like that. (That's the nonsense word you get when you type across the top row of a keyboard). At the time, Tomlinson was working for a company that had been hired by the U.S. Department of Defense to build ARPANET. He was tinkering with the idea of an electronic messaging program — so primitive at that point that it could only send and receive messages between people who were using the same machine. So it was a really big deal to send a message to *another* machine using ARPANET . . . even if it was in the same room. Tomlinson also came up with the @ symbol to tell a computer where to send a message.

For most kids nowadays, looking something up on the Internet or sending someone an email is an automatic part of life. But this technology completely changed the way people communicate with one another. Historians rank the birth of the Internet right up there with these three huge discoveries:

1. 1844: Samuel Morse sends the first telegram: "What hath God wrought!"

2. 1876: Alexander Graham Bell's first phone call: "Mr. Watson, come here. I want you."

3. 1895: Guglielmo Marconi's first wireless transmission: "We speak across time and space. . . . May the new power promote peace between all nations."

"QWERTYUIOP" wasn't much of a way to start the email revolution, but there has been no turning back since that very first message.

- Queen Elizabeth II sent the first royal email message on March 26, 1976, announcing that the Royal Signals and Radar Establishment in Malvern was available on the ARPANET system.
- Approximately 247 billion emails are sent per day, worldwide. 200 billion are spam.
- 90 trillion emails were sent in 2009. 81% were spam.
- In September 2009 there were 1.73 billion Internet users, 18% more than the year before.
- The number of email users is expected to approach 2 billion by 2013.
- Facebook had 350 million users by late 2009. 30 billion photos were uploaded to it that year.
- The number of videos YouTube served in one day was close to 1 million in 2009.

255.

Is there a real Sasquatch? Is there really such a thing as the Loch Ness Monster (Nessie)?

We don't know for sure. This is a great topic because people are so passionate in their convictions, either as believers about these amazing creatures or as naysayers about the whole phenomenon. This area of study is called "cryptozoology," a delicious sounding word that means finding out about unknown, hidden or not yet classified animals.

There may indeed be such a thing as a Sasquatch or the Loch Ness monster. Over the course of history other rumours or tall tales of odd animals have turned out to be true. For instance, the duckbilled platypus was considered a hoax when it was first discovered in 1797, and scientists thought the lowland gorilla was a myth until one was discovered in 1847. No one in the West believed there were giant pandas until 1913, when one was captured. And a coelacanth, a giant fish that scientists assumed had been extinct for 60 million years, was found in the net of a South African fishing boat in 1938.

It's always possible that Sasquatches and the Loch Ness monster are hoaxes, though. But there has been talk of a "Big Foot" or giant "wild man of the woods" since before Europeans first came to North America. Most of the 450 or so sightings of the estimated 2.5-metre-high Sasquatch are from the 1920s and the late Sixties and early Seventies in the Pacific Northwest (Washington and British Columbia). That includes some famous but controversial 1967 film footage, and ongoing sightings, of some large furred beast, casts of its footprints and reports of its strong odour.

Sightings of the Loch Ness monster in the extremely deep and murky lake (loch) in northern Scotland have been reported for even longer — 1500 years! Those who believe in Nessie tend to think she is somehow related to the plesiosaurs, giant sea reptiles from the time of the dinosaurs, some 60 million years ago. In the past 150 years "she" has been reported to be salamander-like, have a neck like a horse, have a giant humped back, have a long tapering tail and an eel-like head, and be a "horrible great beastie." One report even had Nessie looking like a giant log that upturned a boat.

Maybe the Sasquatch and the Loch Ness monster really do exist — nobody has proven that they do or don't . . . yet.

256.

Why is red considered Stop, green considered Go, and yellow Slow Down? Why isn't blue Stop, purple Slow and orange Go?

Why not indeed? It seems random, but stoplights were purpose-built — designed with a purpose in mind. At the end of the horse-and-carriage era when cars came into the picture, traffic was a big mess with people stopping and going wherever and whenever they wanted. To bring some order to the roads, planners used the best idea they could come up with: copy what the trains were doing.

Railroads used red for Stop because in western cultures red has been a signal for danger, death and blood for thousands of years. Red seemed to be the obvious choice for Stop, but green and amber were just luck of the draw. Way back in the 1830s and 1840s when railroads had just gotten started, the colour for Caution was green, and Go was clear white. You can probably imagine the problems. If Go was white or clear, then occasionally when you saw any old white light, like a street lamp, you might think it was a Go signal. One time a red glass lens fell out of a Stop sign, leaving the white light bulb. The train engineer, seeing the white light, saw Go when it should have been Stop, and his mistake resulted in a horrible crash.

Railroads came up with their current signal system — no white lights, just red, green and amber — none too soon. That way, any time they saw a white light they would know that something was wrong. Traffic engineers saw that the railway people had worked out the bugs in the system, and borrowed it for cars. The first traffic light was installed near the Houses of Parliament in London, England, in 1868.

The first electric traffic signals were installed in Cleveland, Ohio, in 1914. Planners thought they could get away with just red and green, but added the yellow for Caution a few years later because they needed to warn people that Stop was coming soon. Detroit, the home of automobiles, had the first modern four-way sign signals.

- How do colour-blind people distinguish red and green lights? They recognize the brightness, and know by rote that in vertical stoplights, red is on the top and green is on the bottom.
- If you're facing forward on a boat, the port or left side is marked with a red light, and the starboard or right side is green — you need to know the sides of the boat to follow the rules of navigating. (An easy way to remember which side is which is: *port* has four letters and so does *left*.)

257.

What was the first website?

As we learned in the answer to question #254, ARPANET was the predecessor of the Internet. The best-used part of ARPANET was email, which grew in popularity and spawned many other technologies. That was, until Tim Berners-Lee, an English particle physicist and computer scientist, working at the European Organization for Nuclear Research, or CERN, in Geneva, Switzerland, finally figured out a way to share more information between teams of researchers. (CERN is the world's largest particle physics centre. It's where physicists look into what matter is made of and what forces hold it together.)

Tim Berners-Lee posted the first webpage at 2:56:20 p.m. on August 6, 1991. Unfortunately this site is no longer accessible, but CERN has a huge history of the World Wide Web on their own website, since they consider the work of Berners-Lee and his colleagues one of their greatest achievements.

Berners-Lee proposed the idea of the World Wide Web in 1989, and it came together within two years. His contributions are many, but the four critical things he developed are:

◉ the very first Web browser
◉ HTML, the coding system for documents
◉ HTTP, the way computers communicate with websites
◉ URL, the way we address things on the Web

Paul Kunz, a research scientist at the Stanford Linear Accelerator Center (SLAC) near Palo Alto, California, posted the first North American Website on December 12, 1991. It consisted of three lines of text and two hyperlinks — not much to show off. But others caught on to the idea fast. After 1993, when the first browser, Mosaic, was introduced at the University of Illinois, the Web spread more quickly than anyone could ever have dreamed. By 2009 there were more than 234 million unique Websites.

A group called Foundation Technologies has figured that the time it took various technologies to reach 50 million people was:

Telephone	75 years
Television	13 years
The Web	4 years

258.

Why are there no letters to go with the numbers 1 or 0 on a phone?

Phone designers kept the numbers *1* and *0* for what are called "flag" functions. The *1* is reserved for long-distance, and *0* is for dialling the operator. That's why area codes don't begin wiht 0 or 1.

259.

How do they get the lines and logos underneath the ice at hockey games or skating shows?

If you have ever tried to flood your backyard to make a skating rink, you know that making a smooth, flawless surface is harder than it looks. Inside the concrete floor of an ice rink is a maze of pipes full of a liquid coolant. Its job is to make the concrete freezing cold, so that a good ice surface can be laid on top of it. The key to making good ice is keeping the temperature and humidity constant while you lay down the twelve or so layers of ice.

Take a hockey arena, for example. That ice is not naturally white. After the first layer of ice is laid down, the entire floor is painted using water-based white paint. Then the workers add another layer of ice, and the face-off circles and lines and sponsors' logos are painted on with stencils or by hand. (One trick is to freeze string into the ice to get the lines straight.) The

third layer seals the paint, and then layer after layer the workers build up the ice until it is the desired thickness and hardness. The total amount of water used to build a regulation-sized rink is around 45,500 L.

It turns out that hockey needs a cooler rink than figure skating — you weren't just imagining it if you have watched a live hockey game and shivered. Hockey players like harder ice (about -4ºC) than the figure skaters need (-2ºC). There are many reasons for this, but how the skate blade's edges react, and not having the ice shatter, are the most important.

Maintaining the ice is the next challenge. The ice-resurfacing machines (which are often called Zambonis after inventor Frank Zamboni) shave off the surface, bathe it with a spray of warm water and let the ice re-freeze into a clean, clear surface. Being the first to skate on clean ice is terrific.

260.

Vampires are corpses that come back to life — not ghosts — so why is it they don't have a reflection?

Whoa. First of all let's get the vampire story straight, as there are vampire myths from all over the world. Generally, a vampire is thought to be some sort of creature returning from the dead to make life for the living more of a challenge. There are actually said to be hundreds of kinds of vampires, with all sorts of powers, like changing shape, controlling the weather or controlling others' minds.

According to legend, there are dozens of reasons why someone might become a vampire. Here are a few:

- How you acted when you were alive: for example, if you were a very bitter person or if you practised witchcraft.

- How you looked: It could be the shape of your teeth, the colour of your hair or eyes, or whether or not you had a weird growth on the "tail" of your backbone. In the Balkan countries, redheads were thought to be vampires, and in early Greece blue-eyed people were suspected of ending up vampires too.

- Where you lived.

- How you died: Murder raises your odds of becoming a vampire, as does suicide. In Romania or Bulgaria, corpses who had a stake driven through their chests were almost certain to become vampires.

- If you were born out of wedlock.

- If a cat leaped over your grave.

You might think that all vampires wear long black capes, have sharp fangs and drink blood. If so, you likely got that image from the most famous vampire, Dracula, who showed up in a book written by Bram Stoker and published in 1897.

Heard of Vlad the Impaler? It sounds like a good name for an action figure, but in fact he was a fifteenth-century Transylvanian prince. His father was called Vlad of the

Devil. The son was *Vlad Dracula*, or the Devil's son. This Prince Dracula, also called Vlad the Impaler, got his name from his nasty habit of impaling and mounting his enemies on stakes. Stoker was inspired to model his own fictional vampire on Prince Dracula.

And now to your question about a vampire's reflection. It was Stoker who started the idea that vampires have no reflection. Why? Here are a few things we know about Stoker himself:

- He knew about the age-old superstition claiming that mirrors capture a bit of your soul. Mirrors were also considered to be a way into the spirit world.

- We know that Stoker had had a dinner conversation with playwright Oscar Wilde about the difficulty of capturing the essence of a person's character and soul in a portrait. (Oscar Wilde went on to write about this in his novel, *The Picture of Dorian Gray*.) Stoker apparently resolved this difficult question by making his character, Dracula, have no reflection and therefore no soul.

261.

How would you make a disco ball?

Disco dancing isn't dead. You can have your own dance party with one of those wacky mirrored orbs that reflect the light in a million different directions. Traditionally they are made of cut-up mirrors, but you can make one more safely, plus do it any size you want, for cheap! cheap! cheap! This is a great recycling project for all those old CDs your parents have lying around.

Gather up the following:

- an adult to help
- a stack of unwanted CDs
- a big styrofoam ball
- tacky glue
- glitter
- white glue
- a small brush
- scissors
- masking tape
- a fishing swivel
- some fishing line

1. (Here's where you need that adult:) Cut up the CDs into random-sized pieces using scissors. There is no "right" way – just do what works for you. Or you could wrap a CD in a towel and smash it with a hammer.

2. Put a piece of fishing line around the ball and make a loop at the top. Use masking tape to hold the fishing line in place.

3. Using the tacky glue, place the CD bits as close together as you can, starting from the top of the ball.

4. When it is all finished, paint a light coat of white glue in the spaces between the CD bits and sprinkle the glitter onto the wet glue. When it is dry, shake the ball to get rid of the loose glitter.

5. Put the fishing swivel onto the loop and hang the disco ball at the desired height.

6. Dance the night away!

262.

Why are carpenter pencils rectangular in shape instead of round or hexagonal like writing pencils?

They are shaped like that so they won't roll away from where a carpenter is working. This flattened octagonal shape is so well-designed that it won't even roll off a slanted surface such as a roof. The other smart thing about this simple tool is that the wide lead can be sharpened to a chisel point that will last longer than the point on a round pencil.

Carpenters rarely use up their pencils, because they are made so well they can last a very long time. The lead is extra strong for making heavy marks and for surviving the work site. Believe it or not, there are people who collect partially used or brand-new carpenter's pencils. That's because there's usually a logo of a lumber supplier or tool company on the pencils, which makes the various pencils popular with carpenters, collectors . . . and carpenters who are collectors.

263.

What does the Queen carry in her purse?

This is a much-asked question. For a long while there was only speculation for an answer. It was always assumed that Her Majesty didn't need identification or taxi fare. *Majesty* magazine, an amazing periodical packed with all things Royal, suggested that she carries: a comb, a handkerchief, a small gold compact, a tube of lipstick . . . and on some Sundays, folded bills to put into the collection plate at church.

As part of the Silver Jubilee celebrations in 1977, Buckingham Palace answered a series of Frequently Asked Questions, and this was one of them. They said: "The Queen uses spectacles to read her speeches, and carries her glasses in her handbag. The Queen doesn't need to carry any money. The Keeper of the Privy Purse is the official manager of the Queen's money. He carries the Privy Purse, a heavily embroidered wallet, at the Coronation."

There you go, dull but true. But one can only suppose that Buckingham Palace wouldn't mention if the Queen also carried a paperback novel, or a list of the ninety-six two-letter words accepted in Scrabble.

264.

How do most ships and planes sink in the Bermuda Triangle?

Most ships and planes *don't* sink in the Bermuda Triangle, which is the area formed by connecting Puerto Rico, Miami and Bermuda. But back in 1964 a writer named Vincent H. Gaddis wrote an article saying that an unusual number of planes and ships had gone missing in this area. He came up with the name The Bermuda Triangle. Gaddis's work was fiction, but there had been reports of strange goings-on in the area for hundreds of years. Some people believe that a super-race living under the sea or possibly in space is responsible for these disappearances. Giving the area a name caught the public's imagination and added fuel to the fire.

Here are a few claims about the Triangle:

- Christopher Columbus had weird experiences travelling through this area in 1492. His compass went wonky and the sailors saw odd lights in the sky.
- The earliest ship to disappear was the *Rosalie* in 1840.
- The first U.S. navy vessel to disappear was the USS *Cyclops* in March, 1945.
- The last known ship to disappear was the *Connemora IV* in 1956.
- Five Avenger fighter airplanes disappeared during a regular two-hour patrol flight from Fort Lauderdale, Florida, on December 5, 1945. This was right after they reported that things were looking strange and that their instruments were going crazy. Another plane tried to rescue them, having reported seeing an orange flash in the sky. It then disappeared too.

The Bermuda Triangle does have some scientifically proven oddities. There are only two places in the world where a magnetic compass will point to true north: the Bermuda Triangle and the "Devil's Sea" off the east coast of Japan (another area where weird disappearances are said to occur). And there are small, bizarre yet intense storms over the Gulf Stream that can brew, completely devastate the adjacent landscape, then clear up within minutes.

However, when investigators actually dug into the facts about all the accidents and the ships disappearing, they found no more occurrences in the Bermuda Triangle than in other places, and often the disappearances happened during big storms. Lloyd's of London, a huge international insurance company, determined that the area wasn't any more dangerous than other parts of the ocean.

265.

Why does the telephone keypad have 1-2-3 at the top and the calculator have 7-8-9?

First there was the rotary phone, which started with *1* at about the "two o'clock" position, and worked counter-clockwise to *0*. And there was the calculator and cash register.

Have you ever watched someone like a bookkeeper run a calculator or adding machine without looking at the keys? Their fingers fly so fast you can't believe they're keeping track of the numbers. Calculators, the keypad on your computer keyboard and the cash register keypad all have a grid of numbers, with *0* at the bottom left and *9* on the top right.

So why make touch tone phones essentially the opposite, with *1* at the top left and *9* at the bottom right? When Bell Labs started designing touch tone phones they tried to find out why keypads had been designed in the order they were. It turned out that no one had done any research — it was pure luck that the keypad layout of the existing calculators and computer keyboards worked out so well for fingers. Bell figured that three rows and three columns of numbers was still the way to go, but made a significant change: starting with *1* at the top left. It was logical (that's how we read), it's the easiest to figure out, and there were fewer mistakes in "dialling" this way. Also, if you look at your phone keypad, you will notice that there is an alphabet associated with the ten numbers (2=ABC, 3=DEF, etc.). This is because phone numbers used to include words. For instance, if you lived in Amherst, your number might have been Amherst 53, and you would dial it like this: AM 53 — or 2653.

Rarely are these different keypad designs a problem . . . unless you happen to be one of those people with flying fingers. Bookkeepers must get very frustrated when they "dial" a telephone. Machines such as automated tellers have used the phone keypad, perhaps just to keep folks on their toes.

266.

What's the difference between a second cousin and a cousin once removed?

When you figure this out, you'll be on the road to becoming an anthropologist. That's because anthropologists study kinship, and your cousins are your kin or relatives. I recommend making yourself a chart while you read this.

Let's start with some basics. In our culture, cousins are the children of your parents' brothers or sisters. The children of your aunt or uncle are your first cousins. I'll give you an example. I have a cousin called Kimo Meikle. He is the son of my father's brother, so he is my first cousin. (He lives in Hawaii, hence the name.)

What does "once removed" mean? It has to do with the generations. Removed always involves the children of your cousins. Once removed is one generation "away." Twice removed is the next generation down. Kimo, my first cousin, has a son called Ethan, so Ethan is my first cousin once removed. If Ethan has a child (Kimo's grandchild), that child will be my first cousin twice removed.

To understand second cousins, let's go back to the term "removed," which always means a relationship with another generation. Second cousins, third cousins and so on are parallel to each other, so my son Mac and my cousin Kimo's son Ethan are second cousins to each other. If our children have children they will be third cousins to each other.

For the ultimate test, try combining the two. If your second cousin (your parent's cousin's kid) has a child, that child is called your second cousin once removed. The next generation after that child would be twice removed. Confused? Ask your parents.

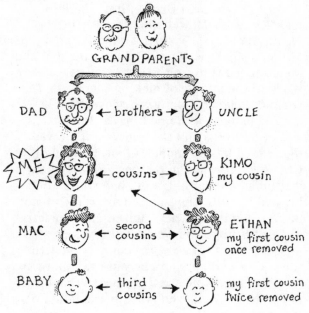

GRANDPARENTS

DAD ← brothers → UNCLE

ME ← cousins → KIMO my cousin

MAC ← second cousins → ETHAN my first cousin once removed

BABY ← third cousins → my first cousin twice removed

267.

Many people say that Disney's Pluto was named after the planet Pluto. Is this REALLY true, or has that been made up?

Yes, it is true, and it makes sense when you know that the planet was discovered in 1930 — the same year that the animated dog first appeared. In the first Pluto film, *The*

Chain Gang, Mickey Mouse was in prison and two unnamed bloodhound-like dogs were part of the posse that tracked him down when he escaped. This was very early in the Disney world. *Steamboat Willie*, the first Mickey Mouse film, was made just two years earlier, in 1928.

In 1930 the next Disney film, *The Picnic*, had "Rover" as Minnie's dog. Finally in *The Moose Hunt* (1931), Pluto got a name and a job as Mickey's sidekick. It takes a long time to make an animated film, so the Disney folks were likely in the middle of making *The Moose Hunt* when the planet Pluto was discovered.

The planet was named for the Roman god of darkness and the underworld. It was discovered by astronomer Clyde Tombaugh, who was following up on the work that another astronomer, Percival Lowell, had started before he died in 1916. The suggestion for the planet's name came from Venetia Burney, a schoolgirl in Great Britain who won a naming contest. She picked Pluto because of the connection with the god of darkness and because the first two letters of the name are the same as the initials of Percival Lowell, who is really the father of this discovery.

There is a Lowell Observatory in Flagstaff, Arizona, named for Percival Lowell. It was founded in 1894 to look into whether life on Mars could exist. Scientists at the observatory discovered the rings of Uranus and numerous asteroids, and ultimately the "planet" farthest from our Sun, Pluto. (Pluto was downgraded to a dwarf planet in 2006.)

What does a cow's tail have to do with rain?

and Other Weird and WACKY INFORMATION

268.

Does a cow's tail facing east mean rain?

This ties in with other "predicting weather" ideas: that crickets chirp faster in warmer weather . . . that a cow's tail facing west means clear weather . . . that turtles crossing the road means a dry spell is on the way . . . and that *broad* brown stripes on a caterpillar mean that the winter will be mild, but that *narrow* brown stripes mean it will be a terribly cold winter.

Any of these *might* be true. And then again, they might not be. Much of this can be considered superstition, and much has been debunked by scientists. But you can't knock the fact that for centuries and centuries farmers and shepherds and herdsmen — basically, people who hang out with animals and insects and birds — realized that these beasts often know when a change is coming. It also makes sense that animals would be equipped with sensors, since they need to know if a coming storm could rob them of their next meal or wipe out their nest. Generally, it has been observed that animals become unusually restless before dangerous weather, and that they tend to eat more too.

Naturalists are out there collecting all sorts of information on the behaviour of animals. How animals act when the weather changes is one of the things naturalists watch for. Here are some observations from a book called *Weather Lore: a Collection of Proverbs, Sayings and Rules Concerning the Weather* by Richard Inwards, first published in 1893.

And one more thing. Cricket chirping is not

a prediction of what the weather *will be*, but it is a reading of what the temperature *is*. The formula is this: Count the number of chirps in one minute; divide the number of chirps by 4, then add 40. That number will be the temperature (in degrees Fahrenheit), or pretty close to it.

◎ If animals crowd together, rain will follow.

◎ When a cat sneezes, it is a sign of rain.

◎ If horses stretch out their necks and sniff the air, rain will ensue.

◎ Hark! I hear the Asses bray;
we shall have some rain today.

◎ It will rain if bats cry much or fly into the house.

◎ Turkeys perched on trees and refusing to descend indicate snow.

◎ Magpies flying three or four together and uttering harsh cries predict windy weather.

◎ Porpoises in the harbour indicate a coming storm.

◎ Air bubbles over the clam beds indicate rain.

◎ When the glow-worm glows, dry,
hot weather follows.

◎ The louder the frog, the more the rain.

◎ Wasps building nests in exposed places indicate a dry season.

◎ Spiders work hard and spin their webs a little before a wind, as if desiring to anticipate it, for they cannot spin when the wind begins to blow.

◎ A fly on your nose, you slap, and it goes.
If it comes back again, it will bring a good rain.

269.

Can you really tell what spring will be like from whether or not a groundhog can see its shadow?

Well, that's how the story goes, but let's see if it is true. We call February 2 Groundhog Day, but it was originally called Candlemas, a Roman Catholic celebration day for the Virgin Mary. Even then, there was a weather connection:

> *If Candlemas Day be fair and bright,*
> *winter will have another flight.*
> *But if it be dark with clouds and rain,*
> *winter is gone and will not come again.*

Or,

> *If Candlemas Day be bright and warm*
> *Ye may mend yer auld mittens*
> *and look for a storm.*

In terms of astronomy, February 2 is called a "cross-quarter" day. It is halfway between the winter solstice in December and the vernal equinox in March. So perhaps Candlemas was like the balancing point of a see-saw — the weather could go either way. What isn't clear is why good weather on that day means bad weather to come, and vice versa.

And what about the groundhog connection? Well, in parts of Europe people also watched the local hibernating animal (hedgehog or bear or badger) to see when it emerged from its winter sleep. If the weather was clear and sunny on Candlemas, people would say that seeing its shadow had "scared" the animal back into its den. German immigrants brought this custom with them to North America and — since we are relatively hedgehog-free — they connected it to woodchucks (also known as groundhogs), which are well-known hibernators. These are the animals that you hear about on Groundhog Day.

Canada's official groundhog is Wiarton Willie. Willie's U.S. counterpart is Punxsutawney Phil. On Groundhog Day in the towns where Willie and Phil reside, there are huge parties, and the animals' "predictions" are broadcast across their respective countries.

But how accurate are they? A study in Canada over a number of decades in a number of cities gave the groundhog only a 37% correct score. And in the U.S., Phil's record isn't so hot either. Records from the National Climatic Data Center in Asheville, N.C., show that since 1887 Phil has only been right about 39% of the time. At the Oklahoma City Zoo the task of predicting the weather has gone to a pair of pot-bellied pigs, Bea and Kay. So far Bea and Kay are 0–4 in weather prediction. It's enough to make you think that you'd get a better prediction if you took Willie's and Phil's predictions and reversed them.

Despite the continually poor results, Groundhog Day continues, and folks across North America might be heard reciting one of these poems:

> *If Groundhog Day is bright and clear*
> *There'll be two winters in the year.*
> *Or if no shadow do ye see*
> *An early spring is what there'll be.*
> *Groundhogs, if your aim be true*
> *Then loving fame awaits for you.*
> *But guess ye wrong, and lickety-split:*
> *A groundhog carcass on a stick.*

270.

If a red sky at night is "a sailor's delight," then what is a red sky in the morning?

The old saying goes: "Red skies in morning, sailor take warning; red skies at night, sailor's delight." This particular bit of folk wisdom goes back a long way. In the Bible (Matthew 16:2–3), Jesus tells some fishermen that, "When it is evening ye say, it will be fair weather: for the sky is red. And in the morning it will be foul weather today: for the sky is red and lowering."

It would be easy to dismiss this bit of weather folklore but, as it turns out, it actually has a basis in scientific fact. At dusk a red sky indicates that dry weather is on the way. The high-pressure weather system that brings low humidity pushes before it a lot of dust particles, which filter sunlight and make it look red at the horizon. If the evening sky is grey, this means that there are many water droplets in the atmosphere, and they are likely to fall the next day.

Dust at sunrise also causes a red sky in the morning. In this case, however, the dust is being pushed *out* by an approaching low-pressure system bringing in moisture. But don't confuse a red sky in the morning with a red *sun* in the morning. If the sun itself is red and the sky is a normal colour, the day will be fair.

Morning! Some red sky up there today!

271.

Exactly what is El Niño?

It's a warm ocean current, and boy can it mess up the world's weather. El Niño is Spanish for Christ Child. Fishermen along the coasts of Peru and Equador came up with the name because often the current starts around Christmas time. El Niños show up every two to seven years and will last twelve to eighteen months. They aren't a new thing — they have been documented for about three centuries, and likely happened for centuries before that. But it was only about forty years ago that scientists started figuring out that El Niño might be responsible for some of the awful things happening all over the world: severe droughts, huge floods, hurricanes, forest fires, typhoons, torrential rains and freak snowstorms (in usually warm places).

Scientists watch the currents with satellites, and by putting out floating buoys which measure temperature, currents and winds around the equator. The data is transmitted electronically from the buoys to researchers and forecasters around the world. Scientists are now looking back over the world's history and trying to figure out El Niño's place in it. They are even thinking that the crop failures of 1787-1788 in France, possibly caused by El Niño, might have contributed to the flour shortage that ignited the French Revolution.

What's a stool pigeon?

and Origins of Other WEIRD WORDS AND PHRASES

272.

How do you say "the" in Pig Latin?

Here's ow-hay. Let's learn with this phrase:

Remember, boys, you must not squelch, must not repress the urge to belch.

Pig Latin is a specific language with definite rules. Pig Latin works easily for most words. Just take off the first consonant, move it to the end of the word and add *ay*. For a word like "the," with two consonants at the beginning, move them both to the end. "The" becomes *e-thay*. "Urge" becomes *urge-ay* because it doesn't begin with a consonant. It sounds like gibberish, but it is gibberish with a pattern.

Emember-ray, oys-bay, ou-yay ust-may ot-nay elch-squay, ust-may ot-nay epress-ray e-thay urge-ay oo-tay elch-bay.

Pig Latin has been used since before World War I, primarily with school children. In 1933 Ginger Rogers recorded the song "We're in the Money" in Pig Latin, and that made it even more popular.

Secret languages are pretty terrific. (Ecret-say anguages-lay are-yay etty-pray errific-tay.) In back slang you just turn words backwards. The trick with back slang is putting the *name* of the first letter instead of the *sound*, to throw people off: T-ndluow T-aht K-conk R-uoy S-kcos F-fo.

Ay-ay Ig-pay Oem-pay:

E-thay itsy-yay itsy-bay ider-spay ent-way up-yay
  e-thay ater-way out-spay,

Own-day ame-cay e-thay ain-ray and-yay ashed-way
  e-thay ider-spay out-yay;

Out-yay ame-cay e-thay un-say and-yay ashed-way
away-yay e-thay ain-ray,

And-yay e-thay itsy-yay itsy-bay ider-spay ent-way
up-yay e-thay out-spay again-yay.

Can you make it out? It's the nursery rhyme,
The Itsy Bitsy Spider, in Pig Latin.

Get it? Good. Now try your name, your
friends' names, your grandparents', your little
brothers' and sisters', your teachers' — anyone
you can think of! But beware, it's addictive, and
you'll find you keep thinking of everything in
Pig Latin! Eally-ray!

273.

What does it mean to be dead as a doornail?

It means to be really dead. This is one of
those wacky sayings that, when you really think
about it, makes very little sense.

Why a doornail? What is a doornail? In
earlier times, not iron nails but hardwood pegs
called treenails were used in building houses
and ships. Iron nails used to be made by hand,
a laborious and therefore expensive process,
so they were used only where they had to be —
doors, for example, because they got so much
use being opened and shut. People would drive
a nail in really hard, then bang down the head.
Because of this the nail could never be used
again, so these were "dead" doornails.

274.

What's a stool pigeon?

Someone who squeals, tattles, spies, informs on or betrays another is called a stool pigeon. But why?

Pigeon meat was a real treat for the British, but shooting pigeons did so much damage, the birds wouldn't be edible. The solution: Pigeons were lured into a trap by using another bird as a decoy.

The decoy bird sometimes had its eyes sewn shut, and was tied to the small stool that trappers sat on while they waited. The distressed bird would cry out to the others, who would come and get caught in the trap. So a "stool pigeon," now sometimes called a "stoolie," is something that lures its companions into being caught, betraying its own species.

275.

How are you supposed to "sleep tight"?

This expression comes from the eighteenth and nineteenth centuries. Mattresses used to have rope supports rather than the box springs or wire bases of today. A feather mattress would sit on a rope base, with the rope woven in and out of holes in the bed frame. The ropes would sometimes have to be tightened so the mattresses wouldn't sag. People would say "sleep tight," referring to the ropes — that is, hoping that they would be tied tightly so that the sleeper would have a good night's rest.

276.

What does it mean to be "one brick short of a load"?

No one is sure how or even when this expression originated, but it has come to be very popular. We all know that it is not polite to call someone stupid. So we sometimes use a "euphemism," a nicer expression that actually says something not so nice. One brick short of a load means that someone is not terribly bright. Not all there. Incomplete, like a load of bricks less one.

Some other expressions use similes or metaphors to say more or less the same thing:

◎ has a photographic memory, but the lens cap is on

◎ the elevator doesn't quite make it to the top floor

◎ a few clowns short of a circus

◎ not the brightest bulb on the tree

◎ as smart as bait

◎ not the sharpest knife in the drawer

◎ sharp as a marble

◎ bright as Alaska in December

◎ a few noodles short of a casserole

◎ the lights are on, but nobody's home

◎ you can look in one ear and see out of the other

277.

Why is someone called "mad as a hatter"?

This is mad as in crazy, not mad as in angry. So what's a crazy hatter? A hatter is someone who makes hats. When they were made of wool or beaver pelts, they were felted (to make the fibres matted and dense) with a chemical called nitrate of mercury. Inhaling this nasty stuff could give a hat-maker brain damage, and make him seem quite mad.

In Lewis Carroll's *Alice's Adventures in Wonderland* there is a Mad Hatter who wears a top hat, and acts really odd. It isn't known if the character was meant to be someone who had actually incurred brain damage, or if Carroll had modelled the character on a particular person who wore a top hat and acted eccentric. But Carroll's book certainly popularized the term "mad hatter."

278.

Why is it called an earwig?

Get ready, because this is pretty gross. Way back in the seventeenth and eighteenth centuries, anyone who was fashionable in France and England wore wigs. Some of those wigs were big — up to a metre high — and they could get awfully warm after a day of being worn. At night the owners would put these enormous sweaty wigs onto a stand, and moisture-loving bugs would climb in for a good time. When the fashion victims put on their wigs the next day, the bugs would fall out.

It looked like the bugs were coming out of people's ears, and that's how they got their name: earwig.

Okay, admittedly that's not the only explanation. Earwig is possibly just a poor pronunciation of *earwing*, which refers to the little ear-shaped hind wings of the insect, the ones that look like pincers. This probably explains why some people think earwigs can crawl into your ear, burrow into your brain and kill you. But that theory just isn't true.

279.

Why do we say, "There's a frog/toad in my throat"?

Is it because of that raspy, throaty sound of your voice? Back in the Middle Ages, if you had an infected throat, doctors might put a live frog into your mouth, head first. When the frog inhaled, it was supposed to get rid of *your* infection by taking it into *its* own body. We don't practise this odd procedure any more, thank goodness, but the saying is still used to mean hoarseness.

280.

What does "a murder of crows" mean, and who makes up these names?

These group terms are often called collective nouns or nouns of assemblage. James Lipton, in his excellent book, *An Exaltation of Larks,* prefers "terms of venery" — venery in this sense referring to hunting, because the originators of the phrases were word hunters, collectors of language subtleties and delights. Many of these collective nouns, like "a pride of lions," are centuries old, but more show up every day.

Who makes them up? Anyone. *You* could! Think about a group of things, and how they sound or look or act, where they live, or something special about them. You could be the originator of "a pocket of Pokemons" or "a slew of skateboarders."

Here are some favourite collective nouns:

a kindness of ravens

a rafter of turkeys

a skulk of foxes

a peep of chickens

a trip of goats

a paddling of ducks

a parliament of owls

an exaltation of larks

a congress of baboons

an army of caterpillars

a float of crocodiles

an ostentation of peacocks

a prickle of hedgehogs

a crash of rhinos

281.

What's the longest word in the English language?

According to *The Oxford English Dictionary* it is the 45-letter word for a lung disease: *pneumonoultramicroscopicsilicovolcanoconiosis.*

The only other word with as many letters is: *pneumonoultramicroscopicsilicovolcanoconioses* — which is just the plural form of the word!

In *Crazy English* Richard Lederer says the longest word has 1913 letters and stands for a chemical compound known in shorthand as Tryptophan Synthetase A Protein. (We'll pass on writing it out here.)

What other words are really long?

• At 28 letters, antidisestablishmentarianism, which means the doctrine against the dissolution of the establishment.

• At 29 letters, we have floccinaucinihilipilification, the categorizing of something as worthless or trivial.

• And at 30 letters, hippopotomonstrosesquipedalian, which — quite appropriately — means qualities pertaining to a long word.

282.

What do you call words you can read both backward and forward?

Words like *Bob, Mom, Hannah* and *madam*? They're called palindromes. Palindrome comes from a Greek word that means "running back again." The word was first used in English in 1629. A palindrome is a word, phrase, number, sentence or series of sentences that read the same backward and forward. Palindromes can be small words or large, from: *tot, peep, boob, kayak, radar* and *reviver*, right up to *tattarrattat, kinnikinnik, detartrated* and *redivider*. Palindromic prime numbers include 101, 131 and 313. Palindromes are not to be confused with something people do when they flip words backwards, like *stressed* for *desserts* or *drawer* for *reward*. Palindromes have to read the same both ways.

There is an old joke that Adam's first words to Eve were in the form of a palindrome, "Madam, I'm Adam." And it hasn't stopped since. Sotades supposedly discovered writing palindromically in the third century B.C. He wrote satiric verses . . . and met an untimely and bizarre end. Ptolemy II Philadelphus had Sotades sealed in a lead chest and dropped into the sea because Sotades had written a satire on him. Despite this cautionary tale, folks have been writing palindromically ever since.

Want to try your hand at this nutty obsession? You've got to look at everything backward and try it out, as in *live* becomes *evil*. Then try working up to a small phrase: *Live not on evil; Dennis sinned; A Toyota; Stop pots.* Unfortunately, these sentences make little sense. The goal is a real (although often stupid) sentence, such as *Was it Eliot's toilet I saw?* Bonus points go for really rare ones — names such as *Mr. Alarm*, or complete stories, like: *Doc, note. I dissent. A fast never prevents a fatness. I diet on cod.*

One of the most famous palindromes is: *Able was I ere I saw Elba.* The story goes that Napoleon may have said this about the island, Elba, where he was exiled. But he didn't write it. Pity.

You won't get rich (or probably even hired) with this talent, but it can be fun. Most articles and prepositions are excluded in palindromes, since they don't work. The characteristic style of a palindrome is phrases that read like odd commands or sensational newspaper headlines. Here are some good ones:

A Santa at NASA
Stack Cats
Stella Won No Wallets
Sit on a Potato Pan, Otis
Must Sell at Tallest Sum
Ma Is a Nun, As I Am
Rats at a Bar Grab at a Star

Some read a bit more like an actual sentence, like the spectacular:
Go hang a salami! I'm a lasagna hog!
Or:
A man, a plan, a canal: Panama.

283.

What do you call the plastic things on the end of shoelaces?

They are called aglets. The word comes from the Latin *acus*, which means an ornamental pin or needle. You get the idea that perhaps aglets were a lot more interesting in the fifteenth century than the snippets of plastic or metal we get on our shoelaces today. In fact, it is really an aglet if it is decorative; a more utilitarian tip is often called a tag.

The eyelet is the hole through which a lace is threaded (led by the aglet). Actually, the word *aglet* is also the term for any decorative pins or studs on your clothes, but we don't really use it for either, very often.

284.

Why do people say things are "baloney"?

People might say things are baloney, but what they mean is that things are just not true — they are nonsense. Spelling it boloney is a better hint at a plausible answer. This word has probably been around since the 1870s, when there was a popular music hall song, "I Ate the Boloney" (or the Bologna). Whatever the intention of the song was, eating Bologna means you eat a particular sort of smoked sausage made of a mix of leftover bits of all sorts of meats. Baloney (a slang version of Bologna) tends to be the staple for those who want to stretch their grocery dollars, and a favourite with children. It is inexpensive and tasty, but high in fat and made from lower-quality meats. (Which leads us to that other saying: "No matter how thin you slice it — it's still baloney.")

So what does all of this mean? It means that calling something "baloney" means it is mixed up, or pretending to be more than it really is. In other words, nonsense.

Some other great words for baloney (as in "what a load of baloney") are: hogwash, eyewash, hooey, malarkey, balderdash, foolishness, piffle, rot, humbug, jabberwocky, poppycock, bilge, folderol, gibberish, drivel, rubbish, bunk and babble.

285.

Supercalifragilisticexpialidocious — what does it mean?

All thirty-four letters of this word were made up for the movie *Mary Poppins*, by a writing team of two brothers, Bob and Dick Sherman. Their most famous song is "It's a Small World," which they wrote for the World's Fair in New York in 1964. You can hear it on the ride of the same name at Disneyland. The Shermans wrote all the songs for *Mary Poppins*, including "A Spoonful of Sugar," "Feed the Birds" and "Chim Chim Cheree." *Supercalifragilisticexpialidocious* means nothing, really. It is a very long nonsense word that is made up to sound like you are terribly smart and "you'll always sound precocious." Now we use it to mean that something is fantastic or super-fabulous.

286.

Where did "mind your own beeswax" come from?

Well, it does sound like "mind your own business," and it does mean that you should pay attention to your own issues, your own problems. But it came from a very surprising place — cosmetic history.

Some say the term comes from the days when smallpox was a common disease, and the resulting pockmarks (little irregular ugly holes) stayed on the face. Fine ladies would fill in the pockmarks with beeswax. The problem was that in warm weather, or if the lady got too close to the fire, the beeswax would melt. But it was considered rude to tell a lady that she needed to attend to her makeup — in the Victorian era wearing makeup wasn't considered proper, so the beeswax application was done in private and kept secret. If you mentioned it, you might get "mind your own beeswax" as a sharp response.

287.

Why do you call the Queen's 50th anniversary the "jubilee"?

We call the Queen's fiftieth anniversary the "jubilee" because jubilees are celebrations that happen every fifty years. The word comes from the Hebrew *yobel* (a ram's horn trumpet), which was blasted on Yom Kippur, the Day of Atonement, announcing the jubilee year. The Bible's Book of Leviticus lays it all out for the farmers of the time: farm for six years and take the seventh off for a sabbatical where you let the land rest (lie fallow), and after seven times this (forty-nine years) you take the fiftieth year for a jubilee, and don't work. Let the land go fallow, pay off your debts, free your slaves and generally forgive everyone. The trumpet heralds a year of grace.

For the last seven centuries the Roman Catholic Church made every twenty-fifth year a "jubilee year" for forgiving people and making things right in people's business and personal life. The last jubilee year was 2000.

The British Royals have had many occasions to celebrate jubilees. There have been a number of British monarchs who reigned at least half a century: Henry III, Edward III, James VII, George III, Queen Victoria and Queen Elizabeth II.

Queen Elizabeth II celebrated her reign with a Golden (fifty years) Jubilee in 2002, a Diamond (sixty years) Jubilee in 2012, and a Sapphire (sixty-five years) Jubilee in 2017. She became Queen in 1952, when she was twenty-seven.

288.

What is the most common word in the English language?

It is "the" by a big lead. "The," like many of the rest of the words in the following list, are articles, which are used with nouns to limit or define that noun. They are not much of a word on their own, but imagine how difficult it would be to write even one sentence without some of the following words. They're listed in order (starting with "the" and reading down), with the most common at the beginning:

the	his	when	them	time	way
of	they	we	then	could	find
and	at	there	she	no	use
a	be	can	many	make	may
to	this	an	some	than	water
in	from	your	so	first	long
is	I	which	these	been	little
you	have	their	would	its	very
that	or	said	other	who	after
it	by	if	into	now	words
he	one	do	has	people	called
for	had	will	more	my	just
was	not	each	her	made	where
on	but	about	two	over	most
are	what	how	like	did	know
as	all	up	him	down	
with	were	out	see	only	

In 1939 Ernest Vincent Wright wrote a book called *Gadsby: A Story of over 50,000 Words Without Using the Letter E.* (Seems he wasn't claiming that there was no *e* in the title.) He tied down the *e* key on his typewriter and went for it. Here is the first paragraph of his book:

*If youth, throughout all history, had had
a champion to stand up for it; to show a
doubting world that a child can think; and,
possibly, do it practically; you wouldn't
constantly run across folks today who claim
that "a child don't know anything." A child's
brain starts functioning at birth; and has,
amongst its many infant convolutions,
thousands of dormant atoms, into which God
has put a mystic possibility for noticing an
adult's act, and figuring out its purport.*

Eeeeeek!

289.

Why do we say something is out of whack? What is "whack"?

"Whack" can mean many, many things. It is sometimes a verb, sometimes a noun. Here are some of its meanings (including the one you're asking about):

Meanings for "whack"

◉ a blow or the sound of a blow. It's a sharp powerful hit with the hand or fist. A famous use is the rhyme associated with a horrible 1892 crime:

Lizzie Borden took an ax
And gave her mother forty whacks;
And when she saw what she had done
She gave her father forty-one.

◉ a portion or a share, as in: "He inherited a whack of cash."

◉ a state or condition; people in Great Britain might say, "I'm whacked," meaning exhausted.

◉ a chance to try something, as in: "take a whack at it."

◉ a single occasion: "all at one whack."

◉ out of shape or out of order, as in: "My back is out of whack," or "Today I'm feeling out of whack."

◉ Slang for large or tremendous, as in: "Isn't the English language a whacking great marvel?"

290.

What do you call it when you turn ten on the tenth?

You could certainly call it special, but there are some names designated specifically for the day your age matches the day of your birth, like seven years old on the seventh or twenty-nine on the twenty-ninth. The most common term for it seems to be "golden birthday," but "champagne birthday" and even "royal birthday" are used too. Whatever you call it, it is only going to happen once in your lifetime, so take advantage of this unique situation to have a particularly great party.

What did the birthday balloon say to the pin? "Hi, Buster."

291.

What does the expression "raining cats and dogs" mean?

"Raining cats and dogs" means it's raining extremely hard — so hard, in fact, that with the rain and wind it might even sound like a cat and dog fight.

The phrase has been around since 1708. Apparently humorists and cartoonists back then drew cats and dogs falling from the sky and added pitchforks and shovels. And there are other expressions that conjure up the same sort of vivid images: raining blue blazes, raining cat poles, raining blue thunderbolts, raining bullfrogs or raining heifer yearlings.

Different theories on this rather peculiar saying have been tossed about. Here's one: A few hundred years ago, few cities had garbage collection. Instead, all kinds of junk, including corpses of dogs and cats, were simply thrown into the streets, where they would pile up in the gutter. That pile up was called a kennel. A really violent rain would dislodge the dead cats and dogs from the kennel and sweep them along the street, thus "raining cats and dogs." Very yucky . . . but very interesting.

What's the worst weather for rats and mice? When it's raining cats and dogs.

If you don't buy that theory, another has to do with Nordic mythology. Cats, who are often said to have unusual powers (witness witches and their black cats), were also thought to have great influence on the weather.

Also, the dog and the wolf are both symbols of wind. The rumble of dog growls can sound like rain and thunder. In old pictures, wind was sometimes depicted as the head of a dog or wolf, out of whose mouth came blasts of wind. Both animals were attendants of Odin, the Norse storm god.

So back to the phrase, "raining cats and dogs." The cat could be taken as a symbol of the downpouring rain, and the dog of the strong wind that comes with a rainstorm. Even today when English sailors see an unusually frisky cat, they say, "The cat has a gale of wind in her sail."

It can't *really* rain cats and dogs, but over the past two hundred years there *have* been recorded cases of raining frogs, fish, stones, grain, seeds, salamanders, worms, straw, lizards, mussels, hazelnuts, leaves and green slime. While such occurrences have often stumped scientists, they figure that rainstorms, waterspouts or small windstorms called whirlwinds have swept up these items and poured them back down again on unsuspecting, umbrella-toting people.

292.

Why do we say "An elephant never forgets"?

We say it because we think elephants remember their keepers or their trainers. But it was actually the Greeks who first said it a different way: "A camel never forgets."

About a century ago elephants somehow got in on the act. Elephants have a fifty- or sixty-year life span, plus they have a long memory and are well known for recognizing people and other animals. In 1910 the popular author Saki coined a phrase about elephants he'd seen while growing up in Burma: "Women and elephants never forget an injury." It quickly became truncated to "Elephants never forget," and became part of popular language. There is even a song from 1934 called "The Elephant Never Forgets."

> How do you make an elephant float?
> Ginger ale, ice cream and one elephant.

293.

Where did the term "OK" come from?

This has to be one of the simplest but most widely used expressions. Too bad its history isn't as easy.

OK is definitely American, and it is not short for *Okay*. OK was a jokey way of abbreviating "oll korrect," which is itself a jokey way of saying "all correct." (This was probably a funnier joke if you had been there around 1839. Spelling things wrong in a goofy way was a fad then.) *OK* was a common sort of shorthand at the time, because people also used abbreviations like *PDQ* for "pretty darned quick" — the way we use *LOL* for "laugh out loud," *BTW* for "by the way" and *FYI* for "for your information" today. Most of the silly acronyms are long gone, but *OK* stuck, and it still means all correct.

294.

Where did the saying "hold your horses" come from?

Not surprisingly, this came from the equestrian world. When you want to keep your horses from getting too excited, you hold them still. If people want *you* to slow down they might say "Hold your horses," and they've been doing that since the 1840s. It's basically the equivalent of saying "Wait a minute!"

"Never look a gift horse in the mouth" is another horse expression that is "as old as the hills." Well, at least it is as old as the fourth

century. Again horses figure here, since you
check a horse's teeth to find out how old it is.
Even if it looks like a perky young filly, looking
at the teeth will tell an expert the truth.

You are showing horribly bad manners if
you receive a gift and make insulting comments
about it — just say thank you. St. Jerome, who
came up with the saying "Never look a gift
horse in the mouth," was reacting to people
who were critical of some writing he had done
for free. He was ticked off at their attitude, and
was telling them not to make slighting remarks
about something they'd been given.

295.

What's the meaning of "mind your p's and q's"?

Today it means that you need to behave
yourself, and to act smartly for the situation.
But that's a long way from where the saying
started. Back in the seventeenth and eighteenth
centuries, the barmaids and bartenders in
English alehouses were told to mind their *p*'s
and *q*'s, which was short for pints and quarts
(British units of measurement). In other words,
be careful with how you pour that beer . . . or
there will be no profits! Then, when it got rowdy,
the bartender would tell customers to mind
their own pints and quarts and settle down.

Typesetters who would set type by
hand (long before the time of computerized
typesetting) were also told to mind their *p*'s
and *q*'s, since it was easy to mix up the two
letters by reversing them. Check it out: *p* and
q are mirror images.

296.

Why is the last car of a train called a caboose?

Not because it rhymes with *vamoose*, which would be such a lovely explanation. Like many word origins, this one is a bit unclear, but there are some good theories. One is that it comes from two Dutch words: *kaban huis* (for ship's galley or cabin house or shelters to protect the crew's fireplaces), which eventually got mixed into one word: *kabuis*. But Texans claim the word originated there. They say that *caboose* is an Americanization of *calabozo*, a Spanish word meaning *jailhouse*, which is another small enclosed space. How that translates into the wooden shanty at the back of a long freight train, from which a conductor oversees the train's operation (and cooks his meals), seems to be lost . . . although the trips were long and the conductor or trainmen might have felt like they were in jail.

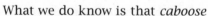

What we do know is that *caboose* began to be used in the western part of North America around 1859. It was similar to the sort of space for the crew that you'd find on a ship. In the east, that car was called a way car, cabin car, crew car, crummy, shanty, brakeman's cab, train car, accommodation car or conductor's van. *Caboose* is used in the West today, and *way car* is still often used in the East.

297.

What do you call these commonly found symbols?

¥ yen

¢ cent (You knew that, right?)

$ dollar (But you didn't know that the $ was used long before the U.S. dollar, did you? It's likely from the figure 8 for Spanish "pieces of eight.")

€ euro

What do these currency symbols have in common? They are all letters with one or two strokes through them.

Here are more symbols:

© copyright

\# octothorpe, referring to the eight points. It is sometimes called *pound* in North America, referring to telephone keypads, or a *hashtag* on social media. In musical notation it is a sharp.

@ at (originally a shortcut for the Latin *ad*, which was commonly used in price lists of goods)

/ forward slash, stroke, *solidus*, oblique dash or virgule

\ backslash

& ampersand, often used as the word *and* in signs or logos. It comes from the Latin *et* meaning *and*. "Scripty"-looking letters for the *e* and the *t* were combined, to make the new symbol &.

* asterisk, from the Greek word for a small star, *asterikos*. An asterisk is a five- or six-pointed star, indicating to the reader to look at the bottom of the page for a footnote or a short explanation. (When you are playing the piano, * points out where you should use the pedal.)

~ tilde has various meanings, but on a keyboard it is used for an accent in Spanish and Portuguese languages.

298.

What is a lb.? If you say "pounds," why is the abbreviation "lbs."?

Here's a secret — there's a good chance that answers to word origin questions are eventually going to go back to Latin roots, where much of the English language came from in the first place. And, bingo, that's the case here. *Pound* comes from the Latin word *pondo* or *pondus*, for weight. Dig a little further and you'll find out that the symbol £ and the *lb.* abbreviation are for *libra*, which is Latin for *pound*. So *libra pondo* means a pound in weight.

Now the tricky thing is why the British used the £ symbol for their currency. It was the symbol for the British pound sterling, and had been called that because the Roman pound (which was 340 grams or 12 ounces) of pure silver would make 240 silver pennies. The pound sterling was divided into 20 shillings or 240 pence (12 pence to the shilling).

When Great Britain shifted to the decimal system (using a base of 10 versus 12) in 1971, they just kept the name *pound*. It was hard enough for the people to give up their shillings, farthings, sixpence and half-pennies — giving up the pound would have created even greater strife. So now the £ is divided up like a dollar, with 100 pence = 1£. The coins are 1p, 2p, 5p, 10p, 20p, 50p, £1 and £2.

299.

Why do we say we are "pooped"?

We say we are pooped when we are exhausted, too tired to move or bone weary. And we've been saying it since about 1934. But *why* do we say *pooped*? Likely *pooped* comes from the nautical verb *poop*, which is when a sailing ship has taken in a lot of water over the stern, onto the poop deck (the partially raised deck at the stern or back of a ship). One term for a huge wave over the stern is a *pooper*.

And *poop* is the right word for that deck too, because long ago, sailors would rig a little structure aft of the deck so they could hang over the ocean and . . . relieve themselves.

But back to *pooped*. Whenever a big wave swamped the ship, at least temporarily stalling it, the ship was said to be pooped, meaning

something that is stopped, not moving anymore, exhausted. *Poop* is also used in the expression "to poop out" or to run out of steam. And of course a "party pooper" is someone who won't get into the big happy mood of a party — he or she has no energy and poops out. Oh, poop. There is also a famous Chuck Berry song worth having a listen to, called "Too Pooped to Pop."

Other words for extreme fatigue are: burnt out, keeled over, tuckered out, run ragged, bushed, knackered, on your last legs, out of it and zoned.

300.

What are the two-letter words you are allowed to use in Scrabble?

Memorize these, and Scrabble insiders say you can increase your score by 30 to 40 points a game:

The 96 Two-Letter Words Allowed in Scrabble

aa ab ad ae ag ah ai al am an ar as at aw ax ay
ba be bi bo by de do ed ef eh el em en er es et
ex fa go ha he hi hm ho id if in is it jo ka la li
lo ma me mi mm mo mu my na ne no nu od oe
of oh om on op or os ow ox oy pa pe pi re sh
si so ta ti to uh um un up us ut we wo xi xu ya
ye yo

Some of their definitions are quite scientific or exotic, but they *are* real words.

301.

Who came up with the question mark and the exclamation mark?

You can find both *?* and *!* used all over the world, even in China (since 1912) and Japan (1868). But in Spanish, both signs are inverted and placed at the beginning of a sentence, like this:

¿Qué pasa?   ¡Hola!

It wasn't really anyone in particular who invented the funny little squiggle over a dot to indicate a question.

Here's how it came about: *questio* in Latin meant "a seeking"; it eventually came to be used for an inquiry. It was put at the beginning of a sentence that asked a question. Seven letters is a lot to devote to that function, so after a while it was shortened to *Qo*, until the day that the scribes (remember, there were no typewriters or computers back then) made it even smaller by putting a *Q* over a tiny *o*. Over the years this then became a squiggle over a dot, and eventually worked its way to the end of the sentence too.

Questio ➞ Qo ➞ Q͓ ➞ ?

What about the exclamation mark? Same idea. The Latin *Io* was for an "interjection of joy," and the *I* came to be put over the *o* until the *I* was over a dot: !

Io   ➞   I͓   ➞   !

For a single mark, *!* has a lot of things going for it! It is terribly expressive! It can show all kinds of emotions and states of mind — surprise, wonder, contempt, disgust, regret and absurdity! But use it sparingly, because using *!* too often lessens the impact considerably!

302.

What do you call a number like 1691 that reads the same upside down?

Really cool, and really rare. It's not a palindrome. That's when something *reads* the same backward and forward, such as 2002 or "Madam, I'm Adam." This is more like an upside-down palindrome, but there isn't a unique term to describe it. Mathematicians describe it using the concept of "rotational symmetry."

Impress your friends with this: the number 1961 is actually a "rotational symmetry of order two." That means that if you rotate it about its centre two times (each time 180 degrees), it gets back to its original position.

The Mercedes symbol, the Woolmark symbol, the recyclable symbol or an evenly formed green pepper sliced in half illustrate an order-three rotational symmetry: it takes three turns of 120 degrees to get back to the beginning position.

A perfectly drawn plus sign (+) is an order four — four turns of 90 degrees get it back to its original position.

A snowflake has an order 6 rotational symmetry — using 6 turns of 60 degrees.

The order of rotational symmetry of a circle is infinity. If you look at hubcaps, you'll notice that most of the designs on them have rotational symmetry of some degree.

Try to think of what would be the next number after 1691 that's an example of order-two rotational symmetry. Give up? It works for 1881, 1961 — you figure out more. The numbers that work are *1, 6, 8, 9* and *0*, and the letters are capital *H, I, N, O, S, X* and *Z*.

Answer: 6090

303.

What is the dot over the letter i called?

Here's a short answer for a short question. It is a superscript dot, called a *tittle* or an *i-dot*. There are also those who call the dot a *jot*.

304.

What do the military say when they are using the alphabet?

The Alpha-Bravo-Charlie alphabet is one of the best-known codes in the world. The International Communication Alphabet (ICA) and the United Nations' International Civil Aviation Organization (ICAO) code use these set words in place of each letter of the alphabet. This practice started with the U.S. military around 1955, and is used around the world by airlines.

The idea is that using standard words (like Alpha, Bravo and Charlie) makes it easier for others to recognize which letter you are trying to say, rather than just saying A, B, C. This works especially well when it is noisy, or if you don't speak English. Try saying "C" and "T" in a loud room — it's hard to hear the difference. Now try "Charlie" and "Tango." Easier, isn't it?

Here's the ICA:

Alpha	Hotel	Oscar	Victor
Bravo	India	Papa	Whiskey
Charlie	Juliet	Quebec	X-ray
Delta	Kilo	Romeo	Yankee
Echo	Lima	Sierra	Zulu
Foxtrot	Mike	Tango	
Golf	November	Uniform	

Other organizations have developed their own alphabets. The New York City Police use:

Adam	Henry	Ocean	Victor
Boy	Ida	Peter	William
Charlie	John	Queen	X-ray
David	King	Robert	Young
Edward	Lincoln	Sam	Zebra
Frank	Mary	Tom	
George	Nora	Union	

305.

Why is a hoot or hiss called a catcall?

You know the sound — a whoop, or a high-pitched hoot or whistle that is made by an audience that doesn't like what it's watching. At least, that's the way it is in Britain. In North America, catcalls have come to mean an audience likes what it's watching. Go figure.

Why is it called a catcall? It started in British music halls, inspired by the cry of a cat in distress. Back in the 1600s people used an actual whistle to show that they weren't keen on what they were watching, or that they were bored with the show. Eventually this gave way to people sticking their thumb and forefinger in their mouth and whistling to imitate the sound of the actual whistle.

A hiss or catcall can be pretty rude, but it's not as bad as pelting a performer with rotten vegetables. That used to be a way of expressing disapproval in the days when William Shakespeare was writing and performing plays.

306.

What does the term "phantom pain" mean?

A phantom sensation or phantom pain happens to a person who has had a part of his or her body amputated, but can still feel where that body part used to be. It can be tingling, a feeling of warmth or cold, cramps, constriction, or mild to severe pain. Almost all amputees have experienced some kind of phantom sensations, but every person is different. A few may never have any phantom sensations, but some amputees have severe phantom pain for years. These are usually worst in the first year after amputation, but they can last for many years.

No one knows exactly what causes phantom pain. According to one theory, the thalamus — a part of the brain — is still sending messages through the nerves to the limb that is no longer there, causing a pain or sensation that feels as if the limb *is* still there. Some children born without a limb have said they can feel the body part, even though it has *never* been there.

307.

Why is it called chicken pox?

This is a great question, because the answer is absolutely not what you would expect.

It seems that when chicken pox was first noticed, the medical people of the time thought that the spots or blisters were stuck on the skin — when in fact the skin erupts into the rash. The stuck-on-the-skin school thought the spots looked like garbanzo beans attached all over the body. The Latin word for garbanzo beans is *cicer* — thus their more common English name, chick peas. And from that we get chick[en] pox. If the Spanish term, garbanzo beans, had been more popular, we might be using the term garbanzo pox today!

So likely the source of the term chicken pox is not about the animal — chicken — it's about the vegetable — chick peas.

Index

charm, 176, 321
cheerleading, 302
chewing gum, 166-167
chicken,
    flight of, 42
    lips, 9
chicken pox, 411
chicle, 166-167
chip, computer, 212
Chisholm, Dr. Hugh, 18, 21
chlorophyll, 56
chocolate, 123-124, 174
Christmas, 185
    card, 190
    gifts, 189
    gingerbread, 201
    holly, 185-186
    ivy, 186
    mistletoe, 202
    plum pudding, 176
    tree, 186-187
chromosome, 43-44, 257
    X and Y, 257
Church, Francis Pharcellus, 230
Churchill, Winston, 222
cilia, 221
circumference, world, 97
clinking glasses, 117-118
clotting, 55
Coca-Cola, 182
Coke, 182
cocaine, 182
coelacanth, 352
coffee, 182
coin, 234
    in cake, 176-177
collagen, 71
collective noun, 385
collie, border, 25
colour,
    axolotl, 17-18
    blindness, 2, 268-269
    favourite, Prince William's, 92
    red, See: red
    traffic light, 354-355
    Tyrian purple, 141
Columbus, Christopher, 365
combustion, spontaneous, 87
compass, magnetic, 366

concubine, 98
Conestoga wagon, 236
conjoined twins, 62-63, 319
constipation, 75
Coren, Dr. Stanley, 20
Coriolis force, 106
corncob, 228
corpse, 130
courting candle, 267
cousin, 368-369
    once removed, 368-369
    second, 368-369
    twice removed, 368-369
Crook, Dr. Janice, 46
crossbreed, 43
Crum, George, 171
crying, from onion, 150-151
cryptozoology, 352
crystal,
    liquid, 252
    meteorite, 284-285
    molecule, 281-282
    snow, 281-282
    triboluminescence, 273
cuckoo bird, 199
currency, 402, 403
    cent, 402
    dollar, 402
    euro, 402
    pence, 403
    pound, 403
    shilling, 403
    yen, 402
Curtis, John, 166
dachshund, 303
"dead as a doornail," 380
Dead Sea, 240, 283-284
deafness, 221
deaf, tone, 222-223
debit card, 234
decimal system, currency, 403
Delilah, 258-259
de Mestral, Georges, 208
Depression, 159
dermatitis, 73
dermis, 64
Diemers, Walter, 167
diet, 57, 174
digestion and elimination,